HUNTING DOGS

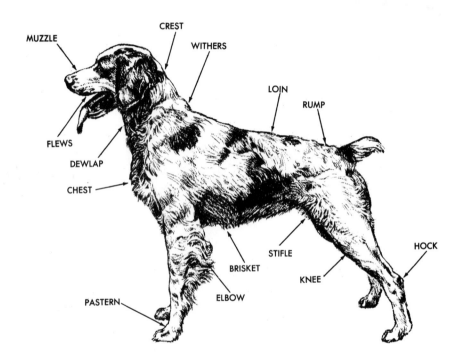

Parts of a Hunting Dog

HUNTING DOGS

F. Philip Rice
John I. Dahl

OUTDOOR LIFE · FUNK & WAGNALLS
New York

To
Ida S. Rice
and
Robert Hillstrom

Library of Congress Catalog Card Number: 67-14555
Funk & Wagnalls Hardcover Edition: 0-308-10324-6
Paperback Edition: 0-308-10325-4

First Edition: 1967
Second Edition, Revised and Updated, 1978

Third Printing, 1978

Manufactured in the United States of America

Contents

Introduction

THE TIME was 10 A.M., one hour after the opening of the pheasant season in North Dakota. One of the authors was hunting with his teenage son and several friends. The group had already shot three birds and now was preparing to tramp through a large uncut soil bank field. Three Labrador Retrievers were being used as flushing dogs. By the time the party arrived at the end of the field, three more pheasants and one mallard hen had been collected. But only a single shot had been fired!

"How," you may ask, "could three pheasants and one duck be brought to bag with only one shot?" The answer is simple: two of the pheasants and the one mallard were found wounded in the field. The Labradors smelled the wounded birds, trailed them down, and brought them to hand. Apparently another party of hunters had tramped the field ahead, had shot the birds, but had not been able to find them, and left them to die.

The above story illustrates the most convincing argument for owning a hunting dog. Dogs save game. What a pity that thousands of fine game birds are shot every year never to be brought to hand—all because of the lack of a good dog!

There is no doubt also that hunting is more efficient when dogs are employed. It is most difficult to find and walk up a covey of quail, a cock pheasant, or some woodcock without the aid of a dog. It is even harder to walk through the mud and slime of a shallow slough to retrieve a downed duck. And it is very difficult to find and shoot a coon or fox without a good hound.

Certainly a good dog can add to the efficiency of hunting and also to the joy of it. A beautiful pointer or setter in a classic pose, an effervescent spaniel merrily bounding through the grass, a dynamic retriever leaping into the air and hitting the water with a loud splash, the mournful, excited bawl of a hound on a hot trail, are sights and sounds which add to the sheer pleasure and joy of hunting.

This book is written for those of you who like dogs and who want to know more about the various breeds, their uses, selection, care, breeding, training, hunting, and use in field trials. All of the most common breeds of hunting dogs are discussed here, and, for purposes of clarity, the breeds are grouped together into four major categories according to use and method of hunting. These categories are:

1. Pointing dogs
2. Retrievers
3. Flushing dogs (Spaniels)
4. Trailers and trackers (Hounds)

The authors have tried to make this a comprehensive work and to include more practical, helpful information on all of the principal breeds of hunting dogs than has ever before been put together in a single volume of this size. The information contained herein is based upon our own experience in raising, training, and hunting dozens of dogs of many breeds over a total period of over 70 man-years.

F. Philip Rice, Orono, Maine
John I. Dahl, Pinehurst, North Carolina

1

Pointing Dogs

THE POINTER

It is probable that the Pointer was widespread in Europe as early as the 14th or 15th century. Sporting scenes of the period show dogs that closely resemble the Pointer. The exact origin of these fine bird dogs is uncertain, but there were early developments in Spain, Portugal and France. However, England probably had more to do with setting the type that we know today than any other country. The nobility of England have always been avid sportsmen, and much of the development of many of our leading sporting breeds can be attributed to them. The Labrador, Golden Retriever, Flat-Coated Retriever, English Springer, English Cocker, English Setter, English Foxhound, the Pointer and others are the result of English breeding efforts. Among the early English Pointer breeders, such names as Moore, Whitehouse, Corbet and The Earl of Sefton stand out.

The Pointer in England was a large, slow, heavy-boned worker, suitable for hunting the slow, tight-setting grouse that were domestically raised and released in restricted hunting areas. After the Pointer was introduced into the United States, the breed underwent a metamorphosis. The game in the United States was almost always wild rather than pen-raised. It was widely scattered and required a wide-ranging, fast-moving dog to seek it out and pin it down. As a result, the Pointer was developed into the very fast, wide-ranging dog that is predominant in American field trials today.

Since the 1870's, the Pointer has enjoyed popularity in the United States, and has undergone constant improvement toward the "class bird dog" ideal of today. Such people as T. H. Scott, S. A. Hayes, Thomas Alford, R. R. Dickey Jr., U. R. Fishel and A. G. C. Sage, among others, figure prominently in the development of this breed in the United States.

The Pointer has become the leading dog of the pointing breeds, in field-trial performances, as well as in the hunting field. He has proven by his speed, stamina, nose and bird sense that he can more than hold his own in

1

any company. His range, coat, color, and his ability to stand long hours of work in hot weather, have distinguished him in the warmer parts of the United States where he holds sway as the leading quail dog. To a lesser extent, at least in numbers, he has proven himself on pheasants, one of the most difficult upland game birds for a pointing dog to handle.

The Pointer is a beautifully streamlined hunting dog, powerfully built for stamina and speed. Though he is an extremely fast mover, the Pointer should not be whippety or overly slender in build, as such dogs lack staying power. The chest should be moderately wide and muscular, with well defined musculature, the ribs well-sprung, giving ample lung space, and the hindquarters muscular and strong. The Pointer's legs should be straight, and of ample bone.

The Pointer's head is distinctive in its rather long, squared-off muzzle, its broad muscular dome, and fairly high-set, but finely textured ears. The expression of this breed is one of alertness, keenness and intelligence.

In color, the Pointer's coat can range from liver and white, the most common color, to black and white, lemon and white or solid white. Any of these colors offers the advantage of being readily visible in the hunting field. All of them are extremely attractive colors on the well-marked Pointer. In texture, the Pointer's coat is very short, flat and firm. This coat is a particular advantage in very hot weather, and affords some protection against the abrasion of briars and other rough cover as well as the cold. It is not so protective, in these respects, however, as the coat of the English Setter. Occasionally, the extremely active tail movement of the Pointer causes it to beat its tail raw against underbrush, producing a chronically bloody tail.

In size, the Pointer might be described as a medium to medium-large dog.

Pointer

Walter Chandoha

Some smaller specimens of the breed weigh as little as 35 to 40 pounds, especially in the bitches, while some of the larger males may run as heavy as 80 pounds, though this is comparatively rare. A good average Pointer will weigh from 50 to 60 pounds, in working condition, and measure from 24 to 25 inches at the shoulder.

Many advocates of other breeds complain that the Pointer has too much drive, and that he is not suited to the hunting conditions that prevail today, considering that most hunters hunt on foot. This complaint can be answered in two ways. First, almost any Pointer, as we will show in the chapter "Training and Hunting the Pointer," can be broken to range; that is, he can be taught to work at the distance from the guns you desire. Furthermore, it is much more difficult, often impossible, to encourage a lazy dog to hunt with sufficient activity so that he will locate birds consistently. The better Pointers do not have this fault. They are usually busy and aggressive workers. The old saying, "You can take it out of them, but you can't put it in them," really holds here.

Second, there are several strains of Pointers being developed today, such as the famous Elhew strain which has National Pheasant Championships to its credit, which are bred for medium to close range. The breeders of this type of Pointer have consistently tried to maintain a very active Pointer with lots of style, but with closer working qualities. The ability to work within reasonable range of the guns can be developed in tractable dogs through training, or can be developed in any strain of dogs by selective breeding.

Much of the pleasure in owning a shooting dog is to be found in the companionship enjoyed in addition to those hours spent in the field. Most of the best Pointers have good dispositions, but are not demonstrative. Some of them are aloof in their response to men. Whenever a breed of dog is bred for a special job, his whole being seems directed toward that job, often giving him an appearance of indifference toward people. This is a minor point, as one is more disposed toward liking a dog that is a good worker, even if he is not affectionate, than a hand-licker who is an indifferent worker. Actually, this rugged disposition is an asset when it comes to training. Most Pointers will tolerate quite a bit of force and still come back to do a good job. This is one of the chief reasons why they are handled so widely by professionals in field trials. The professional handler has neither the time nor the facilities to coddle dogs with timid dispositions.

There are two stud files in the United States that register Pointers: the Field Dog Stud Book of the American Field Publishing Company in Chicago, and the American Kennel Club in New York. Most of the top hunting strains of Pointers are registered with the Field Dog Stud Book, and the show type with the American Kennel Club. Some are registered with both. A pedigree from either one, however, does not guarantee that your pup will turn out to be any good either as a show or field dog. You must study the pedigree for dogs of known quality, and be sure that the sire and dam of your pup are the type that you would want to own.

THE ENGLISH SETTER

The English Setter, like most of the pointing breeds, is of ancient origin, and probably originated in Spain. Many authorities believe that the English Setter originally came from a cross of the Spanish Pointer with some sort of spaniel, perhaps with more than one variety. There seems to be little doubt that the Spanish Pointer was used, since the body conformation of the Setter is much like that of the modern Pointer. The only major difference is the coat. The English Setter's disposition, working range, retrieving instinct and water-going qualities would also suggest the presence of spaniel blood in his make-up.

There are concrete pictorial evidences of a pointing breed very closely resembling the English Setter existing as early as the 16th century, but the first major breeder of the English Setter was probably Edward Laverack, who, through a process of rigorous inbreeding for thirty-five years, set the type of this breed. During the latter part of the 19th century, Laverack sold a number of Setters to sportsmen in New Jersey. During this same period, about 1875, Purcell Llewellin was also importing a number of very fine Setters to North America. Llewellin's Setters were reputedly a cross between some of Laverack's strain, and some Setters from North England. At any rate, the Llewellin strain has enjoyed extreme popularity in this country as hunting and field-trial dogs. The Llewellin strain has enjoyed such popularity, in fact, that it has been recognized as a sub-breed of the English Setter by the Field Dog Stud Book in Chicago which registers these dogs as Llewellin Setters. Few Setters of today, however, are pure enough in Llewellin blood to warrant this appelation. One of the greatest competitors of the English Setter breed, a dog imported directly from Llewellin by Dave Sanborn of Michigan, was Count Noble. This Setter, in his youth, was apparently an incorrigible hard-head, and an inordinately wide ranger. It was not until his original owner died, and he passed into the hands of B. F. Wilson of Pennsylvania, that he came into his own as a field-trial competitor.

In recent years, due to the virtual monopoly of the field-trial scene by Pointers, the English Setter has not been a spectacular success in field trials. Nevertheless, there are some very good trial Setters around as was evidenced in 1965 by the fact that the National Bird Dog Futurity was won by an English Setter. Because the English Setter can, at his best, offer stiff competition for even the best Pointers, and because of his excellent coat, ruggedness and pleasant disposition, he will undoubtedly continue to flourish in popularity on the American sporting-dog scene.

The English Setter is the only breed among the pointing dogs that approaches the Pointer for drive, speed and class performance. Still, the Pointers so far outnumber the English Setters in field-trial wins that the Setters are almost out of sight. This is not to say that the English Setter is inferior to the Pointer, but that the Pointer has caught on as the standard field-trial competitor. This seems to happen in any category. The Labradors, among the retrievers; the English Springers, among the flushing breeds; the Walkers, among foxhounds; and the Treeing Walkers, among the coonhounds, all stand out in this manner. Despite this predominance of particular breeds, it must be admitted that there are outstanding performers in the other breeds.

There are many English Setters of excellent quality throughout the quail hunting areas of the South, and many of their owners profess a preference for them over the more common Pointer because they tend to range a little closer and still have plenty of energy and ambition in the field. Certainly, this is an argument of worth where the heaviness of the cover and restricted range indicate a closer-working dog. There is no argument that the English Setter is better equipped to cope with cold weather than is the Pointer, and some authorities say that the Setter's coat insulates against the hot rays of the sun as well as against the cold. Considering that dogs do relatively little perspiring through their skin, the majority of their excess body heat being dissipated through the mouth tissues and the pads of the feet, there may be some merit in this argument. In practice, however, we have seen English Setters tire more quickly in the hot field than Pointers. The English Setter will work more comfortably in the very cold climates of the northern states and Canada, however. During the upland seasons in those areas, temperatures down to zero are not uncommon, and the going is often wet and miserable for both man and dog. Moreover, in heavy cover, the Setter's body is protected from brambles and brush more effectively than the Pointer's. We have noticed chronic conditions of a bloody tail and underparts of the body, in the pointing breeds, particularly where the heavy saw-grass of the Midwestern sloughs is found in abundance. Pheasants are often found hiding out in that kind of cover during the middle of the day, and these areas are frequently the only ones where birds can be found. The heavy coat of the English Setter will go a long way toward averting these unpleasant and disabling conditions.

While the English Setter is especially beautiful to look at, a feature which is important to many dog owners, his long, silky feathering can prove to be a maintenance problem during the hunting season. Practically all good hunting areas are loaded with burrs during the bird season, and when these

English Setter

Leonard Lee Rue III

burrs become lodged and matted in the coat of the Setter, they take hours to remove, usually at the expense of large clumps of hair. This problem can be solved by trimming the feathering on the underparts and tail, and the long hair under the ear flaps. This will temporarily damage the appearance of your dog, but, in the long run, it will do his looks much less harm than if you have to pull handfuls of burr-fouled hair out by the roots, leaving numerous bare spots open to infection. The rest of the Setter's coat is not so long as to pose a problem when it comes to keeping it free from burrs. An occasional brushing, even during the hunting season, is all that is needed.

Most of the English Setters we have hunted over have been excellent dogs, particularly adapted to hunting pheasants. They have a strong sense of hunting for their master, more than do many of the harder-going Pointers. This quality causes them to constantly keep the gunners in mind and, when possible, to swing wide beyond the birds and work back in toward the guns, avoiding wild flushing of the game. This sounds like almost miraculous intelligence for a dog, but we have seen several English Setters, and one Irish Setter, work in this manner. Learning to hunt in this way requires age and experience. The pheasant is the most wily of the upland game birds, so the dog must learn to employ all of the tricks of the field.

Another admirable quality of the English Setter is his propensity for water work. In the areas of the South where quail hunting predominates, this may not be much of a consideration, but in the midwestern and northern states, where much of the hunting for pheasants is done around prairie potholes, this can be very important. A dog who is hesitant about entering the water is practically useless under such conditions, as most of the birds might be sitting on the dry hummocks and clumps of slough grass in the shallows. Part of the English Setter's aptitude for water work is a result of his protective coat, but much of this quality is a result of a fearless mental attitude. One of the boldest Setters we have known was a small bitch of top field-trial breeding. Rather than run around a slough, if she thought the cover looked promising on the other side, she would hit the water at a full run, swim to the other side, and work out that area. This is the kind of initiative it takes to make a really top performer.

Like the Pointer, the English Setter is gracefully built, and has the quick movements and alertness characteristic of the best of the pointing breeds. Generally, English Setters are not as strongly muscled, broad-chested or stout in the hindquarters as are Pointers. If they are from a good working strain they do have a good chest and well-sprung ribs, along with strong, straight legs and tight, well-knit feet. Almost all of the show-type English Setters, like the Irish Setters, are overly tall and thin, lacking in the physical ruggedness required of the top field performer.

The head of the English Setter is not quite as broad and square as that of the Pointer, but is similar in size and length. The dome is more inclined toward an oval shape; and the muzzle, particularly in the field-trial strains, is less squared-off. The eyes are dark and well-set in a defined stop. The expression of the English Setter is somewhat softer than that of the Pointer, but no less intelligent or alert.

The English Setter comes in a wide variety of colors, although the predominant hue is white with a mixture of black, tan, lemon and orange in various combinations. One of the most beautiful coats of the English Setter is white with black spots, black ticking and tan points over the eyes, on the feet, chest and at the stern. Other combinations are: black and white, blue belton, black, white and tan, lemon and white, lemon belton, orange and white, orange belton, liver and white, liver belton and solid white.

The average English Setter is about the same size as the Pointer, averaging about 50 to 55 pounds in weight, and measuring 24 to 25 inches at the shoulder. We have seen a number of very small Setters, in the 35-pound class, but fewer of the really large dogs, up to 75 pounds or so, than we have seen among the Pointers. This can be attributed to the heavier musculature of many Pointers.

IRISH SETTER

By the last quarter of the 19th century, the Irish Setter, an import from the British Isles, had established an enviable record as a hunting dog. In those days Irish Setters were regarded as exceedingly versatile, rugged performers, called upon not only for the usual upland game work, but employed as duck retrievers as well, particularly in the largely unsettled Midwest where millions of prairie chickens, ducks and geese could be found in the fall. As late as the 1870's, the Irish Setters were doing very well, winning several big trials in the early pointing-dog competitions, such as the Greenwood Stake of the Tennessee State Sportsman's Club. This trial was won in 1876 by an imported Irish Setter named Erin. A year later, an Irish Setter named Berkely won the puppy stake in a trial sponsored by the same club. These were the golden years for the Irish Setter.

Owing largely to the influence of show breeders, the Irish Setter has suffered steady decline in popularity as a hunting breed, but has gained in numbers as a pet and showdog. Many show breeders say that their methods of breeding, often for looks alone, and frequently for physical characteristics that are a handicap in the field, have no adverse effect on the working properties of a breed. Any breeder who has been working toward excellence in a hunting breed knows that this is not so. It has become increasingly evident that when you skip even one generation of proven performers you begin to decline in quality. It is difficult to maintain a high percentage of good hunting dogs even in the most carefully carried out breeding program. It has become obvious that if you remove a breed of dogs from the field, and breed primarily for nonfunctional characteristics, hunting abilities in the individuals of that breed will quickly diminish.

The Irish Setter was originally a dog of strong physique, with good bone and muscle, a rather heavy, flat and silky red coat, frequently spotted with white, particularly on the chest, feet and face, a good broad head and powerful quarter. The bench fancy has removed practically all of these attributes in favor of tall, slender, slim-hipped, weak-quartered, narrow-headed dogs with excessive weight in the muzzle, fine legs and exaggerated long, silky coats of solid dark mahogany which, while very beautiful, hardly justifies the loss of the working Irishman of old.

In physical type the Irish Setter is the red counterpart of the English Setter. The same general proportions, grace of movement and other physical

Irish Setter

characteristics are common to both breeds. The Irish Setter, though, perhaps due to a stronger influence of strictly show stock, tends to be a little bit taller, more slender and of lighter bone than the English Setter. Many individuals of this breed tend to be slab-sided—that is, they lack adequate roundness in the rib cage—and, as a result, are short on endurance. However, some of the more highly developed strains of hunting Irish Setters have got away from this fault.

The head of the Irish Setter is nearly identical to that of the English. The head is, perhaps, a bit longer and narrower, the ears may be set a shade lower and have longer, silkier hair on them, but in other essentials they are the same.

The correct color for the Irish Setter's coat is solid red of a deep mahogany hue. This color is extremely rich and beautiful, but offers the disadvantage of not being as easily seen in cover as either the coats of the Pointer or the English Setter, which are predominantly white. The coats of all setters are characterized by a silky texture, and long, luxuriant feathering. Many people regard this feature as the Setters' most attractive feature, although it can be an inconvenience in hunting when it comes to picking up burrs. A small amount of white on the chest of the Irish Setter is admissible, but by no means desirable. The early Irish Setters were predominantly light red with medium to large amounts of white on chest, toes, and face.

Irish Setters, again due to the influence of show breeding, tend to run somewhat taller than the English Setters, often standing from 25 to 26 inches high at the shoulder. The weights run about the same, however, with a good average specimen of normal height weighing about 55 pounds. We might make the generalization that an Irish Setter, because of its lighter build, will weigh slightly less than either a Pointer or an English Setter of comparable height.

We once knew an Irish Setter that carried a high percentage of some of the good hunting and field-trial dogs of the old type. He had tremendous speed, range and bird sense but had received no hunting training. Yet he took to working pheasants magnificently his first season, and within a year had progressed to a point where he could be released at the edge of any field, no matter how large, and he would work it out. When he struck a point, we could proceed to him at a leisurely pace, knowing that he would hold his point, and that there were birds under his nose. This dog was probably not exceptional for the breed of the old type.

In recent years we have hunted over few Irish Setters which were worth much. Few of them had any pointing instincts whatever, tending to flush their birds wild, and several of them were just incorrigible nincompoops. There are some breeders who are trying to get away from the show type of Irish Setter and back to a serviceable hunting strain. A few years ago, there was some publicity given to a man who was experimenting with breeding hunting Irish Setters to English Setters, then breeding the strain back to solid red, in an effort to combine some of the English Setter's superior working qualities with the Irish Setter's type. This is a very good idea, if the problems of getting them registered and breeding true to color can be resolved.

GORDON SETTER

Like the Irish Setter, the Gordon Setter has slipped from its previously esteemed position as a bird dog, a position which it held in the 19th century. There is little question that when many more birds were available, and when the birds were less wild, all of the pointing breeds were of heavier build and were slower workers. The Gordon was no doubt of this same type, but did not catch on with the field-trial enthusiasts as did the English Setter, Pointer and, to a lesser extent, the Irish Setter. In more recent times, these breeds were bred rigorously to handle situations of decreasing game populations, and to hunt the big, cut-over quail fields of the South, and the equally expansive terrain of the Midwest.

Perhaps one explanation for the failure of the Gordon to catch on with the big breeders and professional trainers is in his reputed tendency to be strictly a one-man dog. This characteristic is an asset, so far as his value as a watchdog and companion are concerned, but it works decidedly against him as a professionally trained competitor in field trials. Practically all of the best hunting dogs of any breed become so involved in their work that it is small matter to them by whom they are handled. Dogs of this disposition can be campaigned by one or more professional handlers during the trial season, and returned to the owner for use during the hunting season. The transition from handler to handler seems to pose no insurmountable problems. It is the nature of the so-called one-man dog not only to have difficulty adjusting to new handlers, but, if shifted from owner to owner, soon to become useless to anyone. The one-man tendency in a dog is basically a kind of shyness, a general lack of confidence in all men; you might even say that it constitutes wildness in a literal sense. Without question, if you plan to

Gordon Setter

own a dog coming from breeding with this as a known characteristic, you must be sure to get him as a very young puppy (five to eight weeks of age is best) and plan to keep him for his entire life.

There is no significant difference between the conformation of the Gordon Setter and either of the other two setters discussed here. The body type, symmetry and proportions are much the same. We can say, however, that the individuals we have seen have appeared somewhat heavier, and were built a little bit closer to the ground, than either the English or the Irish Setters. This effect may be a result of the color, or the somewhat longer, heavier coats we have observed on several individuals of this breed.

While the champions of the Gordon Setter breed have tried to breed for the same streamlined qualities of the other pointing breeds, on the average they are somewhat heavier of build and coarser in the head than the other setters. Rather than proving to be a disadvantage, this quality, along with their heavier coat, may prove to be a distinct advantage in the heavy grouse covers where they are reputed to excel.

The Gordon Setter, like its cousin the Irish, should be as free from white hair as possible. The color is jet black over the entire body, with the exception of tan points over the eyes, and on the chest, feet and at the stern. The black portion of the coat should be as free as possible from tan hair. The coat should be smooth, silky and well-feathered on the legs, underparts and tail, like those of the other setters.

The Gordon Setter is comparable in size to the English and Irish Setters. The weights may run slightly higher, owing to the heavier bone and muscle structure for the same height, but the Gordon should by no means be cumbersome or stockily built. A dog of from 24 to 25 inches in height, with a weight of about 55 pounds, is about right.

There are a few breeders in the United States still making efforts to develop Gordon Setters as gun dogs. Most of these dogs will not have the speed and drive of the other Setters and the Pointer, but if you want a close-working dog for ruffed grouse, woodcock or quail in heavy cover and small fields, a Gordon from proven working stock may serve your needs nicely.

It must be remembered that color in a dog is a superficial characteristic, and that working qualities can be developed in time in a dog of any color. At the same time, it must be admitted that finding a Gordon Setter puppy who is fairly sure to develop into an adult with speed, staunchness on point, and bird-finding ability is practically out of the question, at least at present.

GERMAN SHORTHAIR

Of the German pointing breeds, the Shorthair has been in the United States the longest; hence intensive effort has been made to adapt him to our game birds and terrain. Still, the purpose for which the German Shorthair was originally bred by the German nobility is evident in his working characteristics. No accurate accounting of the various breeds which were used to form this breed is available, but it is known that the Spanish pointer was used, probably in conjunction with the Braque, a French pointer similar to the German Shorthair. To this bird-dog stock, Bloodhound was added for scenting qualities, and Foxhound blood for speed, endurance and chasing instinct.

This mixture of breeds may seem strange when considered by the American hunter, but it was very practical in its own setting—the shooting preserves of Germany. Many different types of game were available on these preserves, and, like the English counterpart, much of this game was hand raised. Thus, the hunter might encounter several different species of game, both large and small, in a day's outing. Grouse, rabbits, fox and perhaps a deer or wild boar might be taken in a single day. To meet this need, the German gun-dog fancier has consistently tried to breed multiple-purpose dogs: nose and trailing ability for the furred game; pointing instinct and bird interest for upland birds; and size, strength and courage for the large game animals. In a typical German field trial for this breed, a dog may be called upon to point birds,

German Shorthair

Walter Chandoha

retrieve them from land and water, trail furred game, usually rabbit or fox, and retrieve them as well.

With this many demands being made on a dog, it is understandable that this breed lacks the class and efficiency of the specialist. The age of specialization has proven that it is extremely unlikely that you will get the best performances out of any but the dog bred and trained for a particular task.

While there are small, fast individuals in the German Shorthair breed, the tendency of this breed is toward greater height and weight than the other pointing breeds, with the exception of the Weimaraner. Nevertheless, a good specimen is not slow or cumbersome, but moves gracefully and with speed, although not as quickly as the faster pointers and setters. Owing to its greater height, the German Shorthair frequently possesses a longer stride than the other pointer breeds; as a result, he may give the impression of slower movement while covering comparable ground. Good specimens of this breed are beautiful dogs. They are tall and strong, slightly lower in the hips than the shoulders, have good straight legs and are powerfully built throughout. An advantage to this breed, with respect to type, is that there is not nearly so great a disparity between the field and the show type as there is in the other pointing breeds. In fact, dual champions—that is, dogs who are both bench and field champions—are quite common in this breed.

The head of the German Shorthair is similar in general design to that of the Pointer, although it is usually longer, proportionately narrower, less markedly squared off on the muzzle. The ears are set lower on the head and are a good deal longer, often displaying a distinctively hound-like quality.

The Shorthair's coat should be short, flat and firm, usually running to a somewhat heavier texture than that of the Pointer, offering better protection from cold water and heavy thickets. This breed is restricted to liver color or combinations of liver and white, sometimes spotted, sometimes ticked and frequently a combination of the two. The tail of the German Shorthair is docked to about one-third of its original length and is carried almost straight out behind him in a merry fashion.

In size, the German Shorthair is somewhat larger than the other pointing breeds, except for the Weimaraner. A dog of 25 to 26 inches at the shoulders is common, and weights often run to 75 pounds, although the breed standard calls for a maximum of 70 pounds. This discrepancy between the limits for weights set in the breed standards, and the actual weights of good working and show specimens, is frequently observed in the sporting breeds.

There has been notable movement in recent years, particularly among breeders and handlers of the Midwest and California, to develop the Shorthair into a class bird dog. The trials are being set up similarly to those for Pointers and Setters. The whole emphasis is on bird finding, and retrieving is not mandatory. If carried out in selective breeding for a number of years, this can have an immense effect on the performance of the breed. The German Shorthair will cease to be the all-round dog of the past who could be called upon to execute a wide variety of hunting chores but with only fair performance.

Even though there has been an emphasis among field-trial breeders toward the faster type, the dog is still far from possessing the speed and drive of the Pointer or Setter. We have had close contact with several of the better field-trial strains of this breed, including one famous stud who was a National Field Trial Champion. But he still threw a large percentage of the old, heavier-type, close-ranging dogs. This indicates that it takes many generations to completely remove a characteristic and develop a fairly homozygous strain. However, the slower-type dog that you are likely to get in a Shorthair may work out well enough as a grouse or woodcock dog or with quail or pheasant in heavy cover and small fields. We can hardly recommend the German Shorthair for pheasants in big, open country, or where the wider-ranging bird dog is indicated for quail or sharptailed grouse. Most Shorthairs do not have the speed, intensity, bird interest or range for that kind of work.

If much of your hunting consists of a combination of upland game in heavy cover, and an occasional shot at ducks which also calls for a retriever, one of these dogs may be what you need. They usually have superb noses, work out their game carefully, have a pronounced retrieving instinct, and are usually good in the water. We have known very few German Shorthairs who would not hit the water after a downed bird with great gusto despite the fact that their rather thin coat affords little protection from icy waters. Most of these dogs are of even disposition; some of them tend to be possessive and, as a result, make formidable watchdogs. This characteristic, known as "sharpness" to the Germans, is typical of most of the German breeds. Some dog owners consider this a desirable quality, while others consider it a drawback. We consider it a rather serious fault.

WEIMARANER

The Weimaraner had its beginning better than 135 years ago through the efforts of the nobles of the Court of Weimar. The idea in developing the breed was primarily to come up with a multipurpose dog, much on the lines of the German Shorthair, that would have a distinctive coloration, thereby conferring exclusiveness to the owners of the breed. The Weimaraner Club of Germany, as originally formed, intended never to let the dog get out of the hands of the German nobility, and to keep it always within German national boundaries. By this means, a noble could be identified by his dog, and it was actually a legal offense for a commoner to own one.

This exclusiveness was presented to the public as a selling point when the dog was introduced to the United States. For a while the buyers of this breed in America had to join the Weimaraner Club; affidavits were signed to the effect that no one would crossbreed a Weimaraner, and such nonsense as that. The ruse was designed to lend a note of aristocracy and snob appeal to the breed.

Probably no dog received as much publicity as did the Weimaraner for a few years after World War II. They were billed as the miracle dogs, supposedly better at everything than any of the specialists. Their sponsors claimed the dog could trail a man better than a Bloodhound, hunt coon better than any of the hound breeds, point upland game with the best pointers, and retrieve as well as any blue-blooded, field-trial Labrador. At times, the publicity enthusiasm ran so high as to suggest that many of the dogs were capable of such feats as answering the telephone, taking care of small children and other responsibilities usually requiring human intelligence and manual dexterity. All of these claims have been shown to be absolutely without foundation in fact, and the hoax has become public knowledge, especially to those who paid high prices for these dogs in the late 1940's and early 1950's, and were hoping for miracles.

The Weimaraner is built very much along the lines of the German Shorthaired pointer. The only distinctive feature they possess, perhaps, is greater size and weight. Their standard calls for a gracefully moving dog in keeping with the established pointer type, but this breed has a long way to go before it will achieve the speed and grace of the faster pointers and setters. On the other hand, the Weimaraner, with its great size and heavy musculature, is an imposing animal to look at. Like the German Shorthair, many individuals of this breed have made outstanding records both in the field and on the bench, and there is not a great diversity between the bench and the field type.

Except for size, the only really distinctive feature of this breed is its color, which is always some shade of gray, leaning toward silver, bright, dark, bluish or yellow. The breed is truly self-colored, that is, the coat, nose and eyes are all the same general hue. A small amount of white on the chest is permissible. In texture, the Weimaraner's coat is short, flat and dense, perhaps heavier in texture even than that of the German Shorthair. The tail is docked to one-third of its full length, about 1½ inches at birth, and 6 inches at maturity.

As has been suggested, these dogs frequently are quite large. The standard calls for heights at the shoulders from 24 to 26 inches, and weights from 65 to 85 pounds for males.

Fortunately, this breed has survived its rather rocky first twenty-five years in this country. There have been enough dedicated breeders who have stayed with the Weimaraner through its bad years; now the tide is changing. Probably the public will never again be fooled by advertisers as it was with this breed; it's unfortunate that this good sporting breed had to suffer as a result. Many Weimaraner owners and breeders have started to make serious efforts

Weimaraner

Leonard Lee Rue III

toward the development of the "gray ghost" as a working gun dog. In many cases the results have been gratifying, although, since the goals of the field trial men in this breed are similar to those of the Shorthair enthusiasts, they clearly have a long way to go.

The Weimaraner's style is similar to that of the Shorthair. It tends to work rather carefully and close to the gunners, but has good bird sense, is a fairly staunch pointer and has a well-developed retrieving instinct. Like the Shorthair, it seems to like the water and enters it with reckless abandon after downed game.

Accepting the Weimaraner as a close and rather slow worker, we have only one negative observation to make about its field work. Many individuals of this breed tend toward hard-mouth. This is somewhat of a problem in the Shorthair too, but not nearly so prevalent as in the Weimaraner. Perhaps this is due to the fact that the Shorthair has been in this country much longer, thus giving the breeders more time to reduce hard-mouth. This hard-mouth tendency in both of these breeds may be the result of the large amount of hound blood in their backgrounds. The nature of a hound is to tear his game to ribbons when he catches it. This is a desirable characteristic in a hound, making them better fighters, but it is very bad in a bird dog.

We have always been struck by the beauty of the Weimaraner breed. There seems to be a closer adherence to type in this breed than almost any other sporting breed, and many of them are magnificent animals: majestic in size, beautifully muscled and proportioned, and of striking silver-gray coloration. We can see no reason not to consider seriously one of these dogs if you want a fairly slow, close worker, a dog that will retrieve from land or water, and that may do a fair job on other small game such as rabbits, if properly trained for it. Weimaraners also make excellent family pets, are good watch dogs, and, like most hunting breeds, are reasonably intelligent.

BRITTANY SPANIEL

The name of the Brittany Spaniel might be considered a misnomer. Although called a "spaniel," the dog is more of a pointing breed as evidenced by its range, style and other working characteristics. The Brittany's small size and softer disposition is generally reflected in its somewhat restricted range and lack of great stamina when compared to that of the Pointers and Setters.

Like the other pointing breeds, the Brittany's ancestry goes back to medieval Spain where, despite the absence of firearms, they were used in the field to point upland game. One may wonder how a pointing dog was of much value when it was not possible to shoot the birds once they were flushed. The answer is that hawks and falcons were used to fly down and kill the game birds after they were pointed and flushed.

Probably the ancestors of the Brittany came to France with the Irish invaders of the 5th century A.D. No such single source can be cited as absolute, of course, since a great deal of traffic in dogs has occurred among the nobilities of Europe for centuries. Nevertheless, it is clear that the development of pointing breeds in France had their beginnings better than 1,000 years ago.

The setting of type in the Brittany Spaniel occurred in the beginning of the 20th century within the cautious and scientific breeding program of Arthur Enaud, a Frenchman. Along with establishing the true type of Brittany as we know it today, M. Enaud introduced the blood of Spanish pointers and the French Braque in order to intensify hunting and pointing instincts.

Although Louis A. Thebaud imported two Brittany Spaniels to America as early as 1912, and many others were sent later by J. Pugibet, a Frenchman, it was not until 1934 that intensive efforts began to establish the breed in the United States, with Thebaud a leader in the movement. The Brittany has since taken a strong foothold among its fanciers and has never had the misfortune, as has the Weimaraner, of being overpublicized. As a result, the breed runs very true to type and has proven to be consistently a valuable, if close ranging, pointing dog.

The Brittany is the smallest of the pointing breeds, but his small size is compensated for by an active and brisk hunting style. This breed is unusual for its comparatively short, almost cobby body, and its proportionately long legs. Thus it has the attributes of an ample heart and lung capacity in the short, well-rounded body and the speed of long legs—an unusual combination. Another unusual feature in this breed is the short tail, which it is often born with, but which must be acquired in some individuals by docking.

The head of the Brittany is a good deal like that of the English Setter, only it is shorter, proportionately wider across the dome, shorter and higher set in the ears, and lighter in the muzzle. The expression is one of extreme, almost terrier-like alertness, friendliness and tractability. The eyes of this breed are generally amber in color, unlike most of the pointing breeds, which have dark-brown eyes.

Brittany Spaniel

Leonard Lee Rue III

The Brittany's coat is somewhat like that of the Setter's only heavier in weight and tending slightly to waviness. The coat of this breed should not be so heavily feathered nor silky in texture as those of the setters. The color of the Brittany runs from orange and white to liver spots on a white background. Generally the white predominates in this breed as it does in the English Setter and Pointer, making them easy to keep track of in the field.

The Brittany standard calls for heights ranging from 17 inches to a maximum of 19¾ inches. The weights of these dogs generally run from 35 to 45 pounds. Most of the Brittanies we have seen have fallen within the middle range of the sizes listed here. Rarely do they run over or under size.

These dogs do not have as much speed or range as the Pointers and Setters, but they are as a rule extremely birdy and intense on point. Tractability is one of their chief characteristics. As a result, most individuals of this breed work well within sight of the gunners. This is a distinct advantage in heavy cover.

The Brittany's coat offers excellent protection against brambles and other cover which could injure a less well-protected dog, and his stub tail never becomes bloody and sore after he has been run for hours in cutting and abrasive grasses. One characteristic the Brittany inherits from his Spaniel ancestors is the retrieving instinct. Most individuals of this breed are very easily trained to retrieve from land and water, and as a rule handle their game carefully, without damaging it.

Some Brittany fanciers have been campaigning their dogs in recent years in open pointing-dog competition. The results have been gratifying to those participants, by and large, and there is no reason to think that this breed will not make its mark in formal competition, especially in the shooting-dog stakes.

The Brittanies must be classed then as pointing specialists, and they seem to be as adaptable to a variety of game birds as any of the pointing breeds. However, they are at their best in wooded terrain and heavy cover where their restricted range is an advantage. One of the chief advantages of these dogs is their compact size. They are very convenient to maintain and transport, and make exceptionally fine companions and family pets.

2

Retrievers

LABRADOR RETRIEVER

The Labrador Retriever gets his name from his place of origin. The first dogs were imported to England by fishermen and were seen by the 2nd Earl of Malmesbury, who arranged to have some transported to England early in the 19th century. These dogs were probably crossed with Flat-Coated and Curley-Coated Retrievers. The 3rd Earl of Malmesbury, writing in 1887, mentioned that he called his dogs Labradors and tried to keep his breed as pure as possible. It was due to his efforts that the Lab name originated and that certain characteristics predominated in the breed.

The pedigrees of modern Labs can be traced back as far as 1878 to two English dogs: M.A.C. Butler's Peter of Faskally and Major Portal's Flapper. It was not until 1903 that the breed was recognized by the English Kennel Club. In 1906 the first Lab was entered in field-trial competition in England.

However, it was not until the late 20's and 30's that many Labs appeared in the United States. The first licensed Labrador trial was held in this country in 1931. The first all-breed trial was in 1934 and Labradors placed first, second and third. Because of this and subsequent outstanding success in field-trial competition, the Lab has since outdistanced all other retriever breeds in popularity. In 1931, there were only forty Labradors registered by the AKC. By 1961 there had been a total of 73,054. At the present time Labs comprise about 65 percent of all retriever registrations, which makes them more than twice as popular as the remaining five retriever breeds combined.

There are many good reasons for the Lab's popularity. From 1934-1961 Labs comprised 60 percent of all retrievers registered with the AKC, but they won 87 percent of all the placings in open championships. In 1964, out of 179 Retrievers placing in Open, Limited and Special All-Age stakes, 164 were Labs (156 black and 8 yellow), 10 were Golden Retrievers and 7 were Chesapeakes. In all fairness, however, it must be pointed out that among the top retrievers of 1964 (those entered in Open stakes), the Chesapeakes had the highest percentage of placements. The following figures give a comparison of the breeds for 1976.

Breed	Open Placements
Chesapeakes	13
Labradors	485
Goldens	34

Among the three available retriever breeds, the Labrador is by far the most numerous. As a result, the prospective puppy or grown dog buyer has more from which to choose in this breed. This numerical advantage is perhaps the strongest point in favor of the Labs. First, when picking a puppy, you have more litters and varieties of blood lines to choose from. So you can pick a pup from parentage that suits you perfectly. Secondly, when it comes to breeding, with the great variety of studs and brood bitches available, you can more easily select for complementary traits, line breeding, or out crossing.

Figures have been compiled in recent years to show that, percentage wise, Chesapeakes scored more consistently in field trials than Labs or Goldens, or that Goldens ran a greater percentage of series in the National Trials than Labs, and so forth. However, the fact remains that by far most trials are won by Labs, the high-point open dogs for the year are virtually always Labs, and that all of the great retrievers with 100 or more points in the open all age stake are Labs. Maybe the other two breeds would do as well if they enjoyed the popularity of the Lab, but this is pure speculation and may or may not be true. Certainly, we cannot give them credit for accomplishments they have not achieved. If you select a good Lab, he has these advantages:

1. Pleasant, likeable, friendly disposition.

2. Versatile—probably the best all-round retriever for both land and water work, for both flushing and retrieving. Takes naturally to water yet easily trained to quarter in flushing upland game. Makes an excellent pet as well as a hunter.

3. Very fast and stylish, appeals to field-trial handlers.

4. Short, sleek coat is easy to care for, sheds water easily, is resistant to burrs.

Labrador Retriever

5. Rugged, stockily built, can stand extremes of temperature, a good ice-water dog, but not as rugged as the Chesapeake.

6. Intelligent, easily trained.

7. Excellent sense of smell.

8. Most can stand correction and discipline without quitting.

9. Numerous good Labs from which to choose or breed.

It must be remembered, however, that dogs are as different as people. Not all Labs are tractable; not all are good water dogs; not all are fast and stylish. The above characteristics apply to good Labs.

Among the disadvantages of the Labrador are the following:

1. Coat color—usually black since that is the dominant color. Beautiful but noticeable in boat or blind. This disadvantage can be overcome by keeping him out of sight while shooting over decoys or by buying a chocolate or dark yellow color. A white spot on the chest only is permitted by the standards for the breed.

2. Sometimes too rough, aggressive to make the ideal pet, especially for children. Never mean, but will knock small children down or break your best china while growing up in the house. Puppies may chew furniture and rugs. The best hunting Labs with the most aggressiveness make the poorest house pets since they are too active.

The Lab is at his best as a retriever, either on land or in the water. Retrieving is his specialty and the job for which he was bred. He is best trained to lie quietly in boat or blind, or to walk at heel on land until ordered to retrieve. He can be used to retrieve any type of bird: geese, ducks, pheasants, grouse, quail, partridge, woodcock, snipe, or doves.

Even though flushing is not his specialty, he takes naturally to quartering, so can be easily taught to flush upland game. He is fast and aggressive and especially useful on running birds like pheasants.

He is not a tracker, trailer or pointer, so don't expect him to be a rabbit, coon or bobcat dog, although he will trail wounded birds—pheasants, for example—for a distance.

He has done well in bench shows, obedience trials and as a guide dog for the blind. His outstanding record in field trials makes him a wise choice for this purpose.

GOLDEN RETRIEVER

In the year 1860, Sir Dudley Majoribanks of England was so impressed with a visiting troupe of Russian performing dogs, which he saw in a circus, that he purchased the entire troupe of eight. These dogs, then called Russian Trackers, were bred by Sir Dudley for ten years without outcrossing. The dogs often weighed as much as 100 pounds and were considered too large and cumbersome for sportsmen, so Sir Dudley outcrossed them with the Bloodhound in 1870. This outcross reduced the breed in size, increased its scenting powers and developed a darker, more refined texture of coat. By 1911 a Golden Retriever Club had been formed in England and the English Kennel Club recognized the dogs as a separate breed.

The first Goldens in North America were brought to Vancouver Island and British Columbia in 1900 by British army officers. The breed spread rapidly up and down the West Coast, and through the efforts of Bart Armstrong of Winnipeg, Manitoba, many Goldens were bred. The Golden was recognized by the Canadian Kennel Club in 1927 and by the AKC in 1932. Between 1932 and 1961 a total of 33,850 Goldens were registered by the AKC.

The first Golden to win his field-trial championship was Rip, owned by Paul Bakewell III of St. Louis, Missouri. Rip won his championship in 1939 and the Field and Stream Trophy for the outstanding dog of the year in 1939 and 1940. The first Golden Retriever bitch to win her field-trial championship was Banty of Woodend; the first Dual Champion was Rip's Pride. Other Goldens won the honor of Best in Show at bench trials across the land, so the dog became well established as both a field-trial and bench dog and continues as the second most popular retriever today.

It is a mistake to say that all Goldens have certain characteristics. They are as individual and as different as the dogs of any breed, but they are known particularly for the following:

1. Beautiful, golden coat of thick, wavy hair with a dense, water-repellent undercoat.

2. Exceptional nose and ability to scent game.

3. Superior intelligence and tractability, the latter trait equalled only in the Lab.

4. Tender-mouthed.

5. Loveable, friendly, affectionate disposition.

For these reasons, Goldens make the best pets of any of the retriever breeds. They have excelled in bench shows because of their beauty and in obedience trials because of their tractability. They will stand a moderate amount of corporal punishment and usually love their work and try hard to please.

Golden Retriever

Walter Chandoha

The Golden, at his best, is an excellent dog on land and water. Some of our best cold water dogs have been Goldens. It must be said, however, that water-going qualities vary greatly with this breed and this should be taken into account when selecting an individual. The Golden's coat is extremely thick and heavy, often having a bushy appearance. When emerging from the water the coat seems to retain a great deal of moisture. Usually, one good shake will get them quite dry, however. The Golden is an excellent upland game dog and stands the heat better than the other retriever breeds. His longer coat presents problems in picking up burrs, however. The Golden's superior scenting ability enables him to find downed game under the toughest conditions.

While Goldens are frequently not quite as fast as the fastest Labs, they often have excellent style and make fine field trial dogs. Often they are superb markers and are tractable enough so that they can be trained to do good blind retrieves.

If you want a good, all-around hunting and field trial retriever, plus a fine pet that is relatively easy to train, the Golden is a good choice. If you select your breeding carefully, you may come up with a dog that can stay with the Labs and Chesapeakes in cold water, too.

CHESAPEAKE BAY RETRIEVER

It is generally agreed that the Chesapeake is at least partially descended from the Newfoundland dog of 150 years ago, possibly from the same stock as the Labrador. In 1807, an English brig was wrecked off the coast of Maryland with two Newfoundland puppies aboard: a dingy, red dog and a black bitch. Stories disagree as to the subsequent ownership and breeding of these dogs. One account suggests they were crossed with coonhounds, another that they were crossed with English water poodles. All stories agree that the Chesapeakes were superior duck dogs, able to plunge into the roughest surf or strongest current, shedding water easily, and staying warm under the most adverse cold-weather conditions.

By 1885 a definite type was developed; during World War I the dead-grass color was developed. Colors today range from a light dead-grass color to chocolate brown. The first successful club of national scope was the American Chesapeake Club, founded in 1918.

By this time the dog had gained a national reputation as a waterfowl dog. He was used in the rough surf of Chesapeake Bay and along the Atlantic seaboard, in sloughs and lakes of Manitoba, Minnesota and in the Mississippi Flyway. From that time until the present, the dog has been promoted by the Chesapeake Club as a peerless dog in zero weather and heavy seas. From 1931 to 1961, a total of 14,757 Chesapeakes were registered with the AKC.

The Chesapeake has four qualities which make him an ideal dog for adverse conditions:

1. Water-going aptitude. He has an astounding love for the water, leaping, not pussy-footing, into the coldest water with enthusiasm. He will frequently submerge after a bird.

2. Thick, woolly, oily, wavy, heavy coat with a dense undercoat. This coat enables the dog to swim without getting wet or cold.

3. Endurance. He has great strength, aggressiveness and stamina and has been known to retrieve 200 or more ducks a day under punishing conditions, or to swim for over a mile after a single duck.

4. Memory. He has an extraordinary memory and may learn to mark down three or more ducks at a time.

One definite disadvantage of the Chesapeake is that he is inclined to fight in the kennel. He does not take to strangers the way Labs or Goldens do, often remaining aloof. Some people would call this latter characteristic an advantage, but it is harder to make the dog a pet.

Most Chesapeakes are rugged individualists; when severely punished, some will run off and refuse to hunt, but the Chesapeake is overrated as a tough, unpliable dog. Many are as sensitive as any dog. His enthusiasm makes him difficult at times to train, but the serious trainer would call this drive and aggressiveness a distinct advantage. It is definitely a mistake to label all Chesapeakes as hard-boiled. Like any breed, they respond best to patience with firmness.

An occasional Chesapeake will be inclined to be hard-mouthed. Gripping the bird firmly with his massive jaws, he seldom drops it, but may clamp down too hard unless cautioned by the trainer. But hard-mouth can be prevented by any trainer; if a dog develops it, it is the result of poor handling and training.

As has been suggested, the Chesapeake is a specialist in waterfowl retrieving. He will work on land and seems to have good resistance to heat, thus making him an adequate upland flusher.

Chesapeake Bay Retriever

The best Chesapeakes do superior work in field trials, but many owners complain that trials, particularly on water, are not tough enough to bring out the dog's true abilities. The dog is not popular in some places, probably because he is not as handsome a dog as either the Golden or Lab, and because of his tendency to get into kennel fights. In spite of these considerations, the prospective trainer who knows how to train aggressive dogs, wants a good field-trial prospect, plus a retriever for cold climates, ought seriously to consider a Chesapeake of proven field trial or hunting breeding.

FLAT-COATED RETRIEVER

The Flat-Coated Retriever traces its ancestry back to two breeds used in the original cross: the St. John's Newfoundland and the Labrador Retriever. As time went on it is likely that the Gordon Setter, Irish Setter and Russian Tracker (from which came the Golden Retriever) were used to advantage also. But the earliest known specimen, a dog exhibited at the Birmingham show in England in 1860 by R. Braisford, looked very much like a black Lab except it had a much heavier, longer-haired coat and was slightly larger than a Lab.

The dog caught the eye of sportsmen immediately. He was a natural water dog, an excellent and stylish marker and retriever, and worked well also on upland game such as pheasants. By April, 1864 a separate class was established for the breed at the regular shows.

Leading breeders began to set their ideas of the type permitted. Dr. Bond Moore of Wolverhampton believed the dog should resemble the Lab in color and conformation. It was largely due to Moore's influence that the breed type was stabilized.

Flat-Coated Retriever

Walter Chandoha

The dog is officially recognized by the AKC, but has never become popular in the United States. From 1931 to 1961 only 120 Flat-Coated Retrievers were registered with the AKC. None has become a field-trial champion, owing principally to the scarcity of the breed and the consequent difficulty of finding outstanding dogs to which to breed.

This dog combines the qualities of the Lab and the Golden Retriever without having been bred enough (at least in the U.S.) to develop as outstanding specimens as either. He is of pleasant disposition, intelligent, tractable and a fine retriever, especially on upland game. Because of the flat, long coat, he has the same disadvantages in icy water as does the Golden. The dogs in the United States have never measured up to the Chesapeake, Lab or Golden in field trials, so they are seldom seen in trials. None won any points in field trials during 1964. Between 1931 and 1961, only one dog placed in a field trial, winning fourth.

The real disadvantage is the scarcity of dogs in the United States, allowing only a limited number from which to select, or to which to breed. Either black or liver color is permissible. A white spot on the chest is occasionally found but not desirable.

CURLY-COATED RETRIEVER

The exact origin of the Curly-Coated Retriever is unknown, although it seems likely that it is a cross of several breeds. Some people believe the dog to be descended from the English Water Spaniel, others from the Irish Water Spaniel, which was then crossed with the St. John's Newfoundland. In the early 1880's, it is said to have been crossed again with the Poodle (the one-time retriever of France) which gave it the coat with a tight curl. Whatever the exact origin, the dog is the oldest of all the breeds now called retrievers.

The dog was first shown on the bench in England in 1859 and was given a separate classification in the international shows in 1864. The Curly-Coated Retriever Club was formed in England in 1896, but died out after a number of years, so the Curly Retriever Club was formed in 1933. It was this club which set the standards of the breed. The dog appeared in the first trials for retrievers in 1859.

Curlies were exported widely to New Zealand in 1889, where they are still a favorite breed. They have been popular in Australia and in England, and were exported to the United States in 1907, but have never become a popular breed here.

The Curly-Coated Retriever is a good example of a dog of unquestioned ability and good looks which has never been popular in the United States. The dog is said to be easier to train than many varieties of gun dogs. He is very affectionate and has a sweet disposition.

The chief advantages of the dog are his fine water ability and phenomenal staying power. He loves the water, will swim for hours in the iciest temperatures and heaviest cover and will dive for crippled ducks. He is a good, but not outstanding, land dog also and will trail wounded birds. In New Zealand he is used exclusively for both water-fowl and California quail.

The dog has never become popular in American Field Trials, as he is considered too slow by some handlers. From 1931 to 1961 only 109 dogs were registered with the AKC, but those entering field trials placed four times during this period. None has ever become a field-trial champion in the United States. Either black or liver color is permitted. A few white hairs on the chest is allowed, but a definite white spot is not.

IRISH WATER SPANIEL

The Irish Water Spaniel, like other spaniels, originated in the dim past in Spain. But its modern history can be traced back only to the year 1850 when Justin McCarthy of Ireland was actively breeding the spaniel as we know it today. Before McCarthy began his breeding program, two distinct breeds were found in Ireland. One, from the North, was small, parti-colored, with a wavy coat, similar to the English Water Spaniel. The second, from the South, was larger with a curly coat. It is this larger dog which McCarthy bred and which is the ancestor of the modern dog.

The dog was bred to hunt the heavy cover and icy waters of Irish marshlands and soon became popular in America. He was used in this country in the 1860's, but the first official registrations in a stud book were in 1878. In that year, twenty-three were registered; the only other retrievers were two Chesapeakes. There were no Labradors or Goldens, so this spaniel is one of the first retrievers to be imported to this country. The breed was used extensively by market hunters in the Midwest, retrieving thousands of ducks and geese to be shipped to markets all over the country. The breed's popularity spread to the East, to Long Island and Cape Cod, and then to the West

Irish Water Spaniels

Walter Chandoha

Coast. In the Field Dog Stud Book of 1922, the Irish Water Spaniel outregistered the other popular retriever breeds.

In the 1930's, however, the registration of the dogs dropped as the popularity of other retriever breeds increased. One reason for the decline was that this breed just did not measure up to the other retrievers in field-trial competition.

The Irish Water Spaniel is the largest of the Spaniels, weighing 45 to 65 pounds. A solid liver color with tight, crisp ringlets of hair, the coat enables the dog to stand extremes of temperature and to shed water easily. Long legs enable him to hunt heavy rushes, sedge and marshlands easily and to wade through the thickest mud. He is a strong swimmer and loves the water, his favorite element.

Some of these spaniels have a peculiar temperament. They are loyal to those they know but suspicious of strangers. They are willing workers, however, and were the first sporting dogs in this country to win an obedience trial. The dog will not stand abuse, but thrives on companionship and affection. He develops physically slowly, sometimes not reaching full physical growth until two years old.

The dog is best used as a retriever of waterfowl or to flush shore birds such as the sora rail. He can be walked at heel and sent to retrieve upland game. Ordinarily the dog is just an average field or hunting dog, and lacks the drive and style that is needed in field-trial champions. These dogs are fairly scarce, although far more numerous than the Flat-Coated or Curly-Coated Retriever. Total registration with the AKC was 2,233 between 1931 and 1961. Considering the number of registrations, they fared very poorly in field-trial work.

3

Flushing Dogs

ENGLISH SPRINGER SPANIEL

The term "spaniel" comes from the Roman term for Spain—Hispania. Dr. Caius, an English dog authority who wrote about 1570, divided the spaniels into land spaniels and water spaniels. Gradually the land spaniels came to be divided into two groups: Springers, which were used to flush game, and Setting Spaniels, which pointed birds and became our setters.

The Spaniel is of very ancient origin. The Metropolitan Museum has a figure of a dog resembling a spaniel which dates back to 3,000 B.C. Laws in Ireland mention the spaniel as early as 17 A.D. Gaston de Foix, a French Nobleman, writing in 1387, mentions spaniels which "quarter about in front of their masters." The North American Indians had spaniels when the white man landed. In 1637, Aldrovandus, an English sporting authority, gives a description of a "Spaniel dog with floppy ears, the chest, belly, and feet white, picked out with black, the rest of the body black."

From about 1800 on, spaniels were divided into Lap Spaniels (under 14 pounds), Cocker Spaniels (14 to 28 pounds and used for woodcock hunting), and Springers, English Spaniels or Field Spaniels (over 28 pounds). Bloodlines were not kept separate in the beginning; the dogs were named according to size and looks. About 1812, however, the Boughey family of Shropshire, England, began to keep a pure line of Springer Spaniels. Finally, in 1895, the sporting Spaniel Club held its first field trial. At succeeding trials, the larger, faster dogs began to beat the Clumbers, Cockers and Field Spaniels, so agitation grew for a separate classification. This came in 1903 when Springers were first exhibited at English bench shows. Sportsmen then began to comb the British Isles for dogs which looked like Springers, some of which won bench and field championships.

Purebred Springers came to America as early as 1907, but did not catch on until Eudore Chevrier of Winnipeg, Manitoba, began to import and train them in huge numbers in 1921. These dogs were sold, trained or partly

English Springer Spaniel

trained, all over North America. In the United States, Freeman Lloyd interested a group of New England sportsmen in the breed. The English Springer Field Trial Association was formed in 1924 and held its first trial at Fishers Island that year. A standard for the breed was approved, then revised and adopted in 1932 and approved by the American Kennel Club. The new standard helped to make the breed more uniform, so the Springer Spaniels have become much more standardized on the bench and in field trials.

The Springer Spaniel weighs between 45 and 50 pounds for males and 42 to 47 pounds for females. He should have a flat, wavy (not curly) coat of medium length, with sufficient density to be waterproof, weatherproof and thornproof. A variety of colors are allowed: liver and white, black and white, liver and tan, black and tan, tan and white, black and white and tan, liver, black, roan or anything except red and white or lemon and white. The dog has long ears, a docked tail, is heavy boned and has webbed feet for swimming or for work in soft mud.

The dog has a natural tendency to quarter within shooting range of his master, so is easily taught to flush birds. Many of these dogs inherit an aptitude for retrieving and can learn to mark fallen birds easily. They are superb workers in briars, swamps and thick land cover.

29

The breed is a warm, friendly companion, gentle with children, and possesses the disposition to cope with them.

The Springer Spaniel's rise to popularity came as the pheasant became the chief game bird of the northern part of the country. Since the pheasant loves to run ahead of hunter and dog, a good pointer has to break his point and give chase, a practice which destroys his staunchness and steadiness. The spaniel, however, can run the pheasant down and force it to flush, a practice which fits into his natural hunting procedure. For this reason, the Springer Spaniel is a much better pheasant dog, in our opinion, and one of the best breeds for this purpose that one can buy.

Obviously, the Springer can also be used on other upland game birds, particularly those that have a natural tendency to run, such as some of the desert quail. The dog is less desirable than the pointing breeds for birds which lie tight.

Although the Springer Spaniel should be taught to mark and retrieve any and all downed birds, it does not do as fine a job as the retriever breeds, being slower and less capable. He will also retrieve waterfowl, but is not as good a cold-water dog as retrievers. Many Springers will retrieve as many ducks as the average hunter can shoot, but, still, retrieving is his second, rather than his first job and inclination.

Well-trained Springers are taught to drop at flush or shot and to remain put until ordered to retrieve. It is not easy to train any high-spirited spaniel to do this, but it is standard procedure in field-trial work and certainly adds to the dog's usefulness. The Springer is the most popular of all the hunting spaniels; many thousands of fine dogs are registered, so it is not hard to find a good one to hunt or to which to breed if the buyer is willing to pay the price.

Our advice is if you want to hunt mostly upland birds, especially pheasants, with some waterfowl shooting thrown in, then certainly consider the Springer. But if you want the best all-round retriever on both waterfowl and upland birds, with some flushing of upland game thrown in, then get a Labrador Retriever. A good Labrador will make an English Springer look like a novice when it comes to retrieving difficult falls in water. However, the Springer is easier to handle as a flushing dog because he has a more natural tendency to quarter and flush within range. The retriever breeds tend to range out too far, unless kept under perfect control.

COCKER SPANIELS

The early history of the spaniel family is outlined in the section on English Springer Spaniels. Note that spaniels were first divided into Land Spaniels and Water Spaniels, then later divided according to size: Lap Spaniels (under 14 pounds), Cocker Spaniels (14 to 28 pounds), and Springers, English Spaniels or Field Spaniels (over 28 pounds).

The history of Cocker Spaniels as a separate breed begins with the birth of Obo, belonging to Mr. Farrow of England, in 1879. Obo was 10 inches tall, weighing 22 pounds. Four years after Obo's birth, Cockers were granted a separate classification in British dog shows, and given separate registration in the English Stud book in 1893. The first field trial was in 1899.

Many of Obo's descendants were sent to America, and a separate strain of American Cocker Spaniels was developed. A spaniel named Braeside Bob is considered the father of the Amercan Cocker.

The American Cocker became very popular as a pet and a bench dog, but breeding for these purposes destroyed much of his. value as a hunting dog. The Cocker declined in favor as a hunting dog between 1850 and 1900, but after the organization of the American Spaniel Club in 1881, some efforts were made, largely unsuccessful, to restore the dog's favor as a hunter.

The first championship field trial held in the United States was sponsored by the Cocker Spaniel Field Trial Club of America in 1924. Cocker trials began to prosper and many dual champions were developed. A number of English Cockers were imported just before World War II, and many became field-trial champions or produced them.

World War II almost mortally injured Cocker trials. Few trials were held; old dogs died and it became increasingly difficult to buy good hunting and field-trial strains. Trials that have been held since have proved of tremendous value in maintaining performance standards and identifying blood lines which will produce top field dogs.

The modern Cocker Spaniel was divided into two main types by the ken-

Walter Chandoha

English Cocker Spaniel

nel clubs in 1935: the English Cocker and the American. The English Cocker is the larger of the two, resembling somewhat a small Springer. Males run from 28 to 34 pounds; females from 26 to 32 pounds. The dog is leggier and the muzzle is slightly longer than that of the American dog; there is not the excess of hair of the American black type. Colors may vary; self colors include all black, liver and red, but a self-colored dog with a white shirt frill or white feet is undesirable. Parti-colored dogs must have broken coloring on the body, evenly distributed. No large portion of any one color should exist and white should be shown on the saddle. Roans come in various colors: blue, liver, red, orange and lemon. Black and tans should have a black coat, tan spots over the eyes, tan on the side of the muzzle, on the throat and chest, on the forelegs from the knees to the toes, on the inside of the hind legs, and on the stifle extending from the hock to the toes.

The American Cocker is divided into three color varieties: black; any other solid color, but including black and tan; and parti-colors. Blacks generally have a more profuse coat and more feathering than the others. Blacks should be jet black without shading of brown or liver (although shading does not disqualify). Other solid colors should be of sound shade. A small amount of white on chest and throat of solid colors is penalized. White elsewhere does disqualify. Parti-colors should have at least two definite colors appearing in clearly defined markings distinctly distributed over the body. Dogs (except black and tans) which have 90 percent or more of one solid color and limited markings of another color are disqualified, since they are neither solids nor parti-colors. Roans may follow any typical roaning shade or pattern and are

American Cocker Spaniels

Walter Chandoha

classed as parti-colors. Black and tans are shown under the variety classification of "solid color other than black." Black should be jet and the tan rich in shade. Tan solely under the stern or on the underside of the ears does disqualify. White markings on black and tans penalize the same as on solid colors. The American Cocker Spaniel should weigh not under 22 nor over 28 pounds.

Twenty years ago the Cocker Spaniel was the world's most popular dog. Five times more Cockers were registered with the AKC than were any other breed. Yet, this popularity of the Cocker as a pet and a bench-show dog resulted in too-close inbreeding, the loss of hunting ability, and the development of undesirable traits. Cockers should have a merry, effervescent disposition, but many in recent years tend to shyness and even to hysteria. Many are very high-strung, nervous animals, with a tendency to piddle on the floor when excited, or to snap at household visitors on slight provocation. The British require their Cockers to display their skill in a field trial before being eligible to qualify as a bench (or breed) champion. This requirement has partially kept the English Cocker from the kind of breed deterioration which has plagued the American Cocker, although many English Cockers are also high strung and snippy.

Present-day Cockers vary widely in their hunting ability. The best dogs should search the air currents for body scents of birds, and have some ability also to follow trail scents. Those dogs who hunt by body scent are at an advantage when working into the wind or when the birds are setting. Those dogs who have some trailing instinct and good noses are effective only when the game is moving and the dog can pick up a trail. The best dogs have body-scenting noses which enable them to find more birds, but can occasionally pick up and follow a scent trail of a wounded bird that runs away.

Spaniels differ widely in other necessary hunting aptitudes. Some are good water dogs; others refuse to enter the water. Some are natural retrievers; others must be force trained. Some will smash into briars at top speed; others are shy and timid about entering cover. Some are tractable, attentive and will take correction; others are stubborn, inattentive and fold up or quit when corrected. Some are good at fence crashing—they will unhesitatingly go over, under or through; others never seem to learn how best to overcome such obstacles.

Cocker Spaniels cannot all be characterized in certain ways, however. They are as individual as people. But, in general, good hunting Spaniels should possess the following characteristics:

1. Disposition—Effervescent, happy disposition, free of excessive nervousness, hysteria, shyness or tendency to bite. Should possess courage, well-developed bird instinct, willingness to work and be tractable and easy to train.

2. Water ability—Like the water and be willing to dive in even when slightly rough or cold.

3. Retrieving instinct—Have some natural instinct for picking up and carrying birds, or be able to be trained to do so. Proper carry of the bird and soft-mouth can be taught to any dog with good retrieving instinct.

4. Boldness and hunting instinct—Since these traits cannot be taught, it is essential that they be inherited, otherwise the trainer has little to work with.

A tendency to hunt by body scent is an advantage over a tendency to follow trail scents. Some strains of Cockers exhibit the unfortunate trait of following foot scent in a houndlike manner. The dog should like birds, hunting and be willing to work the cover with enthusiasm and speed to find and flush game.

The Cocker Spaniel has no real advantage over the English Springer Spaniel. The Cocker is the smallest of the spaniels, so is not as effective in heavy cover, or in rush and cattails while working in the water. Most Cockers get completely fouled up in the heavy rushes in which Labradors, Chesapeakes or other retrievers are expected to work. The Cocker is not as fast as the Springer and generally not as effective in flushing upland game. The Cocker is much faster than the Clumber or Sussex Spaniels, however, so is preferred over these. The English Cocker Spaniel is slightly larger and more long-legged than the American Cocker so is usually a better choice for hunting. Also, you are more likely to find good hunting strains among the English Cockers than among the American Cockers.

The real disadvantage of the Cocker lies in the fact that it is hard to find good hunting strains, in spite of the heroic efforts of the field-trial club to find, promote and preserve hunting stock. Too many individuals have lost their hunting ability. This, plus the fact that so many present-day dogs are nervous, shy or with a tendency to hysteria, decreases the chances of finding a good hunter. The Cocker Spaniel is a good example of a hunting dog that has been ruined by popularity and indiscriminate breeding. However, if you select your individual dog with care, and prefer a smaller, yet quick-moving dog as a flusher and retriever for upland game, then you might consider a Cocker.

Never think of buying a Cocker to use primarily on waterfowl. He just does not have the physical size, stamina and ability to do first-class retriever work under demanding conditions. Some Cockers, however, will work well as retrievers of waterfowl, particularly warm, quiet-water conditions.

Cockers are particularly prone to ear cankers (sores in the ears), and may develop a tendency to bite persons who touch their sensitive ears. Like other spaniels, the coat easily picks up burrs and clinging seeds, so there is some disadvantage in using them in this type of cover.

The best advice to the prospective buyer is to do some pedigree research to make sure there is good hunting and field-trial stock in the first several generations. Also, scrutinize the parents and pups for nervous traits and general disposition, and test the parents on water, briars, fences, curiosity and courage, and for hunting and retrieving instinct. If the parents are supposed to be good hunters, it is best to see them working before buying the pup.

AMERICAN WATER SPANIEL

Very little is known of the origin of the American Water Spaniel, but the breed existed in its present form before the beginning of the 20th century. It has been used in New England for decades, but its development has been primarily in the Middle West in the heart of the pheasant belt. The dog was formally recognized as a distinct breed by the AKC in 1940.

The American Water Spaniel is a likeable, friendly dog with even disposition and a liking for companionship and children. He is a medium-size dog, weighing from 25 to 45 pounds. The coat is closely curled, but not kinked, and should be dense to afford protection in water and in heavy cover. Liver color or dark chocolate with a little white on the toes or chest is permitted. He is very intelligent and, when well bred, has a good nose and a natural instinct for hunting, showing enthusiasm for flushing and for retrieving. He should love the water and be able to stand a fair amount of cold.

This dog is occasionally classified as one of the retrieving breeds, but is not allowed to participate in Retriever trials, so ought to be listed as a flushing dog. Actually, the dog ought to be able to flush and retrieve both, although he is not as rugged or stylish, or as good in icy water, as some of the purebred Retrievers.

Like the other flushing spaniels, the American Water Spaniel can be taught to quarter in front of the hunter, to scent and flush out upland game, to drop to shot and then to retrieve on command. For these reasons it is used primarily with birds that tend to run rather than hold tight to a dog. The dog is well adapted, therefore, to hunt pheasants, and some of the species of Western quail that run.

This spaniel is a more rugged water dog than any of the other spaniels, but still inferior to the retriever breeds for retrieving waterfowl. However, if the hunter wants a smaller dog to use in a small skiff, and hunts under only moderately cold weather conditions, the American Water Spaniel will do nicely. Like all dogs who are trained and used for several purposes, this dog will both flush and retrieve, but is certainly not as good a retriever as the Labrador, Chesapeake or Golden, and does not have as good a reputation for flushing as the Springer. But if a hunter wants a flusher and retriever for upland game, plus a retriever to do a fair amount of waterfowl work, then this spaniel is a good buy.

American Water Spaniel

Walter Chandoha

Welsh Springer Spaniels

Walter Chandoha

WELSH SPRINGER SPANIEL

Like the English Springer, the Welsh Springer Spaniel is of ancient origin. The exact date of his appearance is unknown. The color has always been red and white, in contrast to Cockers and Springers, who may be many different colors. The Welsh Springer Spaniel was found principally in Wales, but has now found its way to Scotland and England. From England it was imported to America, India, Australia, Siam and other countries. The standards for the breed were established by the Welsh Springer Spaniel Club of England. These standards were adopted by the American Kennel Club.

The red and white coat of the Welsh Springer is flat and thick, of silky texture, with a soft undercoat which prevents the skin from injury, water or thorns. The dog is able to stand extremes of temperature, especially on land, but cannot take as icy water conditions as can some of the retrievers. He is able to hunt upland game under warm weather conditions, something which the retrievers are not able to do so well.

The dog is smaller than the English Springer, but much larger than the Cocker, and is able to do more demanding work. He has a very keen nose, is a keen and willing worker, but is a little slower than the Springer. He makes a faithful, delightful companion, is gentle and kind with children and has a very pleasant disposition. It is fairly easy to keep him free of skin diseases, to which many long-haired dogs are prone.

The dog requires good obedience training to work his best; if untrained he tends to wander off and hunt by himself. Training procedures are the same as for the English Springer.

CLUMBER SPANIEL

The first story of the origin of the Clumber Spaniel in England appeared in the British *Sporting Magazine* in 1807. This article referred to the gift of some Spaniels to Henry Clinton, Duke of Newcastle, from the Duke of Noailles of France. Since the Duke of Noailles died about 1766, it is supposed that the dogs may have been given to the Duke of Newcastle about 1760. An engraved portrait accompanied the article and showed a picture of William Mansell, gamekeeper to the Duke of Newcastle, surrounded by a group of spaniels, obviously Clumbers. The Clumber gets his name from Clumber Park, the estate of the Duke of Newcastle.

Some early writers say that the Clumber owes his long, low, heavy body to crosses with Basset hounds and his heavy head to St. Bernard crosses, but such crosses are open to question. One writer in 1860 describes the Clumber as follows: "This Spaniel is red and white, is larger than the usual Spaniel, strong made, an intelligent countenance, dark eyes, and the ears not very long." The writer goes on to say: "These dogs have excellent noses and display great spirit in beating strong covert . . . They are naturally ill tempered, and rarely form any attachment but to their master or game keeper." One dog of this period is described as being 2 feet 10 inches long from the tip of the nose to the root of the tail, with an 11-inch tail, and standing 17 inches tall.

The American dog authority James Watson, writing in 1906, wrote somewhat disparagingly of Clumbers in the field. "One dog was of little use, so slow are they in their movements, and it called for a team of several braces . . . to be of use for a shooting party. This entailed special training, and looking after by a man who could handle them, for they would not work for every person, or any person."

Reference has already been made to the first spaniel trials held in 1899. At this time, all of the spaniel breeds competed together. A Cocker Spaniel won both the Puppy and Open stakes in this first trial, but in the second trial, the same year, Clumbers won both stakes. In these days, the pedigrees of all of the spaniel breeds were mixed up. Thus, Beachgrove Teal, a Clumber,

Clumber Spaniel

Courtesy Mary Meyer

was the dam of Longbranch Teal, one of the first Springers to be shown in Canada.

While the Clumbers began to take field trial honors, however, pressure was applied to separate the spaniel breeds. This was done, but the Cockers and Springer became faster and gained in favor as all-round dogs. The Clumbers never had any specialty or parent club to back them in America and thus never became as popular here as in England.

The Clumber is to the spaniel family what the Basset is to the hounds: a slow-moving, short-legged, large-bodied dog. It does not, however, give tongue when on a hot scent as does the Basset Hound and the Sussex Spaniel. The modern Clumber Spaniel is 17 to 18 inches tall at the shoulder and weighs 55 to 65 pounds; thus it is somewhat larger than the Springer. Breed standards limit the ideal bitch from 35 to 50 pounds and the ideal dog from 55 to 65 pounds. The head is large and massive; the dog has the appearance of great power with a long, thick, powerful neck and strong, muscular shoulders. The back of the dog should be long, broad and straight, free from droop or bow. The legs should be short and heavy-boned, with large feet. The coat should be silky and straight, not too long, but very dense, with long, abundant feather.

Coat color varies between lemon and white and orange and white, but with the white predominating. The fewer the markings on the body, the better. Ears should be solid lemon or solid orange, with head and eyes evenly marked, and muzzle and legs ticked.

The only real advantage of the Clumber is that he is one of the most easily trained of the spaniels. He is not headstrong, remembers his lessons well, and does not have to be retrained. Because of his light coat, he is said to be the finest of all hot-weather hunting dogs, although this may be disputed.

The Clumber was bred for the small, well-populated game preserves of England where a slow-moving, methodical, short-range worker was a distinct advantage. Hunting conditions in America, however, demand a faster-moving, bustling spaniel, so the Clumber is not ideally suited for hunting in the United States. However, he will do nicely for game-farm shooting where game is plentiful on a small area. The Clumber is a sure finder of game, and will retrieve nicely when trained. Therefore, while useful as a flushing dog and retriever for upland game in small, thick patches of cover, he is not best suited to more open-range hunting. He is seldom, if ever, used as a retriever of waterfowl. The dog is so scarce in America as to make finding good dogs for breeding or buying difficult.

SUSSEX SPANIEL

The Sussex Spaniel was developed primarily in England, where the first and foremost kennel belonged to a Mr. Fuller of Brightling. It was Fuller who developed the rich, golden, liver-colored coat which is distinctive with this breed. The breed has never been imported heavily to this country, lacking the speed of the Cocker and Springer. It was, however, allowed support in a separate class at the Crystal Palace Show in 1862, and is recognized as a separate breed by the AKC.

Like the Clumber, the Sussex Spaniel is a heavy-set, massive, muscular, short-legged, heavy-boned, slow-moving dog. The muzzle is about 3 inches long, and square. Ears are thick, fairly large and carried close to the head with soft, wavy hair. The neck is short, strong and only slightly curled; the chest is deep, round and wide. The back and loin should be long, straight and muscular. The tail, as on all spaniels, is docked. The coat should be thick, flat or slightly waved without curl, and always of the rich, golden liver color. A coat color which is too light or too dark (dark liver) is penalized. White on the chest is not permitted. Weight should be between 35 to 45 pounds. The dog is only slightly smaller than the English Springer.

The unique feature of the Sussex is that he is inclined to give tongue when on scent, a trait for which he would be penalized in a field trial. Otherwise, this spaniel behaves and works much like the Clumber. He is methodical, slow-moving and is easily trained, especially in working upland game in thick cover in small areas. He can be taught to retrieve very nicely.

FIELD SPANIEL

This spaniel breed was also developed in England and passed through many exaggerations of type before evolving into the useful and handsome breed known today. One exaggerated type was developed by Phineas Bullock of England, who repeated crosses of the Sussex and Cocker Spaniels until a dog was developed which was extremely long and low to the ground. This dog, with its long back bone and short legs, was a grotesque caricature of a spaniel.

Considerable difficulty was encountered in the United States in trying to eliminate these exaggerated proportions and in establishing a modern Field Spaniel. Considerable credit must be given to Mortimer Smith who made great strides in developing a type which spaniel lovers could admire. This spaniel is usually black in color, is sound and straight in the front legs, has good balance of height for length, and unquestionably ranks with the handsomest of his cousins.

The Field Spaniel should be of moderate length with a straight or slightly arched back. The neck should be long, strong and muscular; shoulders should be long and sloping, set well back; the chest should be deep and well developed, but not too round and wide. The head should have a well-developed skull; the muzzle should be long and lean, never snipey or squarely cut. Ears are moderately long and wide, set low, and with setter-like feather. Hind quarters should be strong and muscular, with the stern slightly below the level of the back, if possible. Forelegs are of good length, with straight, clean, flat bone, and nicely feathered. Immense bone is no longer desirable; feet should not be too small, with short hair between the toes and good, strong pads.

The coat should be dense, not too short, silky in texture, glossy and refined, and flat or slightly waved, never curled. A self-colored dog is preferred, especially black, but also liver, golden liver, mahogany, red, roan or any one of the colors with tan over the eyes, on the cheek, feet and pasterns. Other colors such as black and white, liver and white, red or orange and white, while not disqualifying a dog, are less desirable, since the spaniel clubs seek to distinguish the Field Spaniels from the Springer Spaniels.

The dog is about 18 inches to the shoulder and generally weighs from 35 to 50 pounds. He is built for endurance, speed and agility, has great perse-verance, and is very level-headed and intelligent. He has an excellent nose, is easily trained as a flusher and retriever, and runs a close second to the Springer Spaniel as an excellent hunting dog. The chief disadvantage is there are fewer specimens to choose from or to breed to, since the dog was interbred to Cocker and Springers for so many years to eliminate its unde-sirable physical characteristics. This dog will give a good day's shooting for any hunter, and ought to be seriously considered if a flushing dog and retriever is needed.

4

Hounds

BEAGLE

The Beagle is one of the few little dogs who possesses the characteristics of big dogs to a high degree. It often happens in reducing a full-sized breed that working qualities, disposition or other essentials are sacrificed. A careful look at the history of this breed would explain why this has not been true of the Beagle. In the first place, the Beagle is not a foxhound bred down to small size as many think. He is, in fact, the predecessor of the foxhound. In medieval England, where most of the development of this breed occurred, foxhounds, as a distinct breed, were not known. The prized game in those times was either big (deer, boar, etc.) or small (rabbits or hares). There were generally two types of hounds in use: the very large and strong, used for big game; and the smaller Beagles, which were used for trailing rabbits. Later, when foxhunting became popular, a larger type of Beagle was bred for that purpose. The Beagle, then, has not been plagued with the usual small-dog disposition, primarily because he is not the product of accelerated size-decreasing selection which has, in many breeds, precluded selection for any other desirable qualities.

The Beagle was introduced in numbers to this country in the last quarter of the 19th century. Such men as Eugene Reynal, James W. Appleton, George Post, Harry Peters and H. C. Phipps are notable for their efforts in the early days of the American development of this breed. All of these men were residents of the East Coast. Without question, a large percentage of the Beagle blood in the United States today stems back to the dogs of these early pioneers of the breed.

In appearance, as in performance, the Beagle exemplifies the ideal hound type on small scale. Its movement, tail carriage and mannerisms are similar to those of the larger hound breeds. The body of the Beagle should be well proportioned and strong, with a wide chest and well-sprung ribs. The

Beagle

legs should be straight, of good bone, and have compact feet which will stand a lot of running over rough terrain. The tail is carried high and straight, not curling too far over the back, and should be as much an indication of the Beagle's having struck a rabbit's trail as the opening of his bell or bugle voice. The Beagle is built fairly closely to the ground, but a dog should not be heavy, cumbersome or slack in the back. Powerful, quick, easy, rhythmic movements characterize this breed in action.

The Beagle possesses the typical hound head. The dome is rounded and fairly broad, the muzzle is substantial, but free of superfluous flesh, and the ears are fairly long and set moderately low in the head, without much erectile power. The eyes should be dark, large, with a pleasing, kindly hound expression.

The Beagle can be of any true hound color, but we have always preferred those with the black saddle with tan head, tan markings and white background. This coloration is also the most prevalent in the Beagle breed, so one needn't sacrifice other qualities to find an individual of this coloration.

The Beagle is one of the smallest of the sporting breeds, running, as a rule, somewhere between 11 and 15 inches in height at the shoulder. His small size can only be viewed as a convenience, however, since, as previously explained, he possesses the stamina, working qualities and courage of the larger hounds, although he may lack their speed.

Activity in the Beagle breed has been vigorous in this country since the turn of the century. Field trials are held frequently, generally along the lines of a foxhound trial, only the quarry is rabbit.

There is competition for individual competitors and for matched packs of various sizes. Beagles have also done exceptionally well in bench shows. This is one of the few breeds, along with Labradors, Chesapeakes, the German pointing breeds and the other trailing hounds, which has been bred to keep the show type very close to the field type of dog. As a result, many

Beagles have achieved the status of dual champion, indicating that they excel both in the hunting field and on the bench. This is an admirable trait of the breed. You can have a superb-looking animal and an excellent worker in the same dog. It seems ridiculous to keep two dogs; one for looks and one for hunting; nevertheless, this is done by many sportsmen who are dedicated to a breed in which there is no universal type, and who want to participate both in bench shows and field trials.

While the Beagle is a wonderful pet, faithful companion and will occasionally turn in a fair day's work on pheasants or other upland game, he needs no other excuse for his existence than as a rabbit hound. He is the rabbit hound par excellence. He is neither too fast, forcing the game to hole quickly, or is he so slow that the chase lacks the element of excitement. He works hard for hours on end, is extremely game and possesses one of the most melodious voices in the hound family. He generally surpasses the foxhound for voice. His voice is pitched a little higher than the larger hound's, but is generally clearer, either with a ringing, bell-like quality, or a beautiful drawn-out bawl.

It is wonderful sport to follow a pack of Beagles, but there is no reason to assume that a single hound cannot be followed with good results. It seems to make no difference to this breed how, where or in what company he is hunted, just as long as you put him down where there are rabbits he can chase. He is very easily trained, taking to his work almost instinctively the first time he sees a rabbit. In this respect he is ideal for the hunter who does not have the time for elaborate training procedures, or cannot afford the high cost of a professional trainer. Partly due to his small size, but also to the restricted range of the cottontail rabbit, you can usually turn him loose with the assurance that he will stay within hearing range, and can be fairly easily caught when you want to go in. He is unlike many other hounds in this respect.

Occasionally, however, a Beagle will range. We owned an excellent 11-inch Beagle bitch a few years ago that one would have thought would always be within range. Generally she was close when working cottontails. But occasionally she would hit the fresh track of a jackrabbit, and she would be gone. When this happened, we would often have to spend the next couple of hours trying to find her. She would not give up on a jackrabbit track. Still, she did not have the speed to make one take a hole, so the only way we could get her back was to head her off and catch her on the track.

We heartily recommend the Beagle to anyone loving a good hound and the music of a chase. The real beauty of Beagling is found not only in the quality of the dog work, but in the fact that you are not threatened with bankruptcy because of your sport. A good Beagle can earn his keep with meat on the table in almost any area of the United States.

BASSET HOUND

The Basset hound, despite his exterior measurements, gives the impression of a large dog. This breed has an illustrious history extending back to medieval times. They were kept by the French aristocracy as trailing hounds, as they moved slowly enough to be followed on foot. Legend has it that the

Basset Hound

French aristocracy, at the time of the development of this breed, was so debauched and out of shape that they could follow only a very slowly moving hound. The very short legs of this breed and his slow, bloodhound-like trailing characteristics prevent him from moving at anything but a leisurely pace.

The ancestry of the Basset goes back to the old French bloodhound and the St. Hubert's Hound, now extinct. Some sources say that the Basset is the closest direct link to this extinct St. Huberts Hound. This may be so, but it would seem that the Gascony Bluetick and the bloodhounds might claim this distinction, especially since they are proportioned far more like that ancient breed than the Basset. The Basset's very short legs come from rigidly selective breeding. Actually, a process of reducing leg length does not take so long as one might think. When a mutation occurs, expressing itself in very short legs, for example, the animal is paired off with another animal exhibiting the same characteristics. Since dwarfism in the legs is a recessive trait, the breed can soon be made nearly homozygous (genetically pure) with respect to that physical trait. When this is achieved, it takes a mutation to move back to the previous physical form.

With his short legs, long, heavy body and very long ears, the Basset presents an incongruous spectacle, but the dog has a good deal of charm and humor about him and one learns quickly to love his peculiar appearance.

There are two predominant types of Bassets, both of French origin: the Comte Le Contealx and the Mons Lane de Francquevilli. The Lane Basset is broad-headed and has a prominent eye, while the Contealx Basset has a narrower bloodhound-like head, with heavy folds of skin around the face, very long ears and deep-set eyes. The Contealx type is far more numerous in the United States than the Lane.

The body of this breed is generally quite heavy and long, giving the impression of great distance between the front and hind legs. Usually, Bassets are powerfully built, have well-rounded rib cages, broad, powerful chests, muscular hindquarters and very heavy bones. The legs should be straight, but often they are very crooked—a result of their unnatural shortness.

The head should resemble the bloodhound's as closely as possible. The ears are very long, the lips, flews and flesh around the head is heavy and pendulous, and the dome high and rounded. The eyes should be deeply sunken, of very sad expression, and should be deep brown in color.

The coat should be similar to that of the Beagle: fairly short, dense and of medium texture. The color should be of any good hound color, but generally will be some version of the tri-color (black, tan and white) combination of the Beagles and Foxhounds. The black saddle with the tan trim, tan head, and white background is perhaps the predominant color in this breed as it is in the Beagle, although the Basset's coat frequently shows more ticking than the Beagle's.

Basset hounds will usually stand no higher than 15 inches but are much heavier than the Beagles. We have known several of this breed to tip the scales at 75 to 80 pounds. These weights are extreme, however, and a more average figure would be about 50 pounds. Even that weight is extremely heavy for a dog of such short height.

Many Bassets today are bred strictly for show competition, and have been for a number of generations. On the other hand, several breeders throughout the United States have given close attention to the hunting properties of this breed, and have kept a strong hunting strain. These are the dogs you should be looking for if you want a hunter, while the showbred Bassets are only good for family pets. We have seen several examples of the strictly show-type stock in the field, and they seemed to lack all instinct for the chase. On several occasions, rabbits were jumped right under the noses of these hounds, and no effort to chase them was made.

The Basset's voice runs as deep and rich as that of any hound. However, most of them do not bark as freely on trail as the Beagle. Some handlers prefer a hound that is not a free tonguer, arguing that a dog who barks all the time is a babbler: that is, he gives tongue when not actually moving a track. We have not seen many Beagles who can be accused of this fault. Many of them have so much energy that they cover more of the track than a slower hound, consequently they have more opportunities to open. Champions of the Basset breed say that their slow pace is an advantage in hunting rabbits because they do not push their quarry hard enough to cause it to take a hole, nor do they run it so closely that they cause it to leave the area. The reasoning here is that the rabbit is not particularly worried about being chased by a dog so slow as the Basset, and will take a leisurely course, describing a comparatively tight circle and offering the hunters more frequent opportunities for a shot. Theoretically, this sounds plausible, but we have yet to see the Basset that can produce as many bagged rabbits as a good Beagle. Of course, a gamebag full of meat is not the only reason, nor the most important, for hunting. Sport is the important thing for most of us today, and if you get more fun out of hunting with the slower, deeper-voiced Basset, then there is no reason not to choose one over his faster cousin, the Beagle.

Like the Beagle, the Basset can be hunted singly or in a pack. Any hound with hunting and trailing instinct does not rely on others to do his hunting for him. Dogs who hunt in that manner are known as "hitch-hikers," and are disdained by all serious houndsmen. The chief advantage in running a pack is that losses may often be picked up more quickly, and the track moved with more speed and excitement.

Most Bassets can be faulted with respect to their range. A good Beagle will range out well away from the gunners in order to pick up a trail, whereas the more cumbersome Basset will often hang very close to the gunners until he strikes a track close by. This is looked on by some as an advantage, since the dog will generally be close and under control, but you get fewer cases with a dog of this type, and less game. Contrary to the old term "dumb-bunny," cottontails are not stupid. After they have been run a few times they become very shy, leaving the area quickly or "holing up" the minute they hear hunter and hounds coming. If your hound will not range out, take the initiative, and work for that hot track; the chances are that by the time you get to where the rabbits were, all of the tracks will be old, cold and, for the most part, unworkable.

AMERICAN FOXHOUND

The development of the American Foxhound has been going on since the days of the English colonists, who brought them from England for sport and food procurement. The setting of a true type of Foxhound has occurred within the past 150 years, and has been achieved through the efforts of certain southern families. From these families, the various strains of American Foxhounds have got their names. Such names as Walker, Trigg, Bird-

Walter Chandoha

American Foxhound

song, Hudspeth, Goodman, Robinson and Tucker stand out for their efforts in perfecting the Foxhound. All of these families bred for speed, endurance, tracking ability and voice, and a "sorry" hound was not tolerated in their hunting packs or breeding programs. If the same care were exercised in the breeding of sporting dogs today, we would not have the large number of rejects that we do. Some strains of early Foxhounds, such as the old, long-eared Black and Tan and the Redbone, have disappeared from the scene as fox hunters, and have been taken up by the tree-dog enthusiasts and developed for that purpose. The unpopularity of the Redbone and Black and Tan among the leading breeders of the Foxhound during the 19th century was undoubtedly due to their tendency to be cold, slow trailers. The only hounds of this type that are used for fox-hunting today are in the northern states where foxes are run in the winter during the daytime, and a slower, cold-nosed dog will run the fox in a circle so the hunters may get a shot at it. The pattern of hunting here very closely resembles rabbit hunting, only on a larger scale. In most sections of the South, where the fox is reserved strictly for running, and is rarely killed, shooting one is a serious offense.

Although the leading strains of Foxhounds were developed largely within such families as Walker and Trigg, there was a great deal of interplay between these breeders, and they no doubt knew each other, hunted together and exchanged studs and brood matrons from time to time. Since these breeders were working toward the same kind of dog, in terms of both working characteristics and conformation, it is understandable why the National Foxhunter's Association permits registration of hounds crossbred from these strains. The amount of blood of each lineage is kept on record in their pedigree, however, and the hounds are registered as a mixture—for example, one-quarter Walker and three-quarters Trigg. These distinctions are made until the blood in the minority reaches one-eighth; then the hound is referred to as purebred in his dominant strain. In this way, the breed, not only within its various strains, but within the entire breed, has avoided a strong differentiation between the families. As a result, the bench shows sponsored by the National Foxhunter's Association judge all Foxhounds by the same standard. There is no separate class for Walkers, Triggs, Julys, etc.

Certainly, for gameness, speed, tenacity, endurance and courage, no breed of hounds surpasses the American Foxhound. This breed is both faster and lighter than its ancestor, the English Foxhound. It is also possessed of greater range and game-getting ability. The English Foxhound, as a result of the American Foxhound's superior qualities as a hunter, has practically dropped out of the picture as a hunter, and has been relegated to the show ring. Like the coonhounds, the American Foxhounds are mostly registered in their own stud book instead of the AKC. Their registration files are kept by the Chase Publishing Company under the name "International Foxhunters Association, Inc." The Chase Publishing Company prints the magazine *Chase*, which has the largest circulation in the foxhound world.

The American Foxhound must be built for the utmost combination of endurance and speed. These hounds are sturdily made throughout, with strong, straight legs, good cat feet, powerful hindquarters, muscular chest and well-sprung ribs. They should not be built so heavily, however, as to slow them down, or cause them to fatigue rapidly in a long chase. Generally, their build is very symmetrical, with body length proportionate to height, and no excess or exaggeration in any part of their makeup. The foxhound should give the impression of being able to hold a rhythmic and tireless gait for great lengths of time.

The Foxhound's head should be in proportion to the rest of his body; not too large or small, cleanly formed, and without the heavy facial skin of the Basset. The ears should be set rather low on the head, and of medium length, reaching almost to the tip of the nose when stretched out. The eyes should have a soft, pleading expression, and be dark brown in color.

The coat of this breed should be close lying, hard textured and of medium hound length. The hound's coat, in general, while it lies flatly against the body, is somewhat longer than the coats of either the Pointer or the German Shorthair. Generally these hounds are similar in coloration to the Beagle and the Basset. There is a considerable number of Foxhounds in other colors, though—solid red, saddle-back black and tan, black and tan, orange and white, and so on down the list of hound colors.

There is considerable variation in the size of Foxhounds, as there is in most sporting breeds. They should not exceed 25 inches in height, however, nor be shorter than 22 inches. This is for males, bitches may run an inch less on the average. The weights of Foxhounds will usually fall somewhere between 50 and 65 pounds. Extremely heavy Foxhounds usually carry too much excess flesh to be of much service in hunting foxes.

While the American Foxhound is clearly a specialist in the field of fox-hunting, it would be a gross injustice to the breed not to mention some of its other considerable achievements. The Foxhound has been adapted to hunting practically every kind of game, large or small, found on the North American continent. In the South he (as well as crosses with the Pointer and ordinary curs) is to this day used extensively as a deer hound, driving deer from the heavy, impenetrable swamps into view of the hunter's stand for a shot. Often Foxhounds which have been incorrigible deer chasers have been made use of in this manner. The Foxhound has also been widely used by big-game hunters in the West and Southwest for bear, boar and mountain lion. Although the Treehound breeds dominate here, the fact that Fox-hounds have excellent noses, loud carrying voices, and indomitable fighting hearts has made them valuable for this purpose.

Less spectacularly, but of no less importance to those who use them this way, the Foxhound has been widely employed as a rabbit dog. An objection to his use on rabbits could be legitimately raised, however, in that the Fox-hound is too fast and will push the rabbit to hole quickly. Finally, it should be noted that the Foxhound has had a very important role in the development of the Treehound breeds. The Treeing Walker, for example, is a direct descendant of the Walker strain of Foxhounds, and has been the leading contender in formal coonhound competition for the past several years. This says a great deal for the Walker breed in light of the fact that it is by far the dominant strain in Foxhound competition today.

TREE HOUNDS

The early American settlers quickly recognized the value of tree hounds for producing food and clothing. Because of the kind of game present in Europe, a trailing hound with a strong treeing instinct had not been developed. In

Black and Tan Coonhound

North America, however, there was a general prevalence of game that would climb a tree if pursued closely by a pack of hounds. Such game included bear, cougar, bobcat, gray fox, opossum, raccoon and mink. For many years pure Foxhounds, mixtures of Foxhounds and Shepherds, hound-terrier crosses and dogs of unknown ancestry were used as tree dogs. In the mountains of the Eastern states a little hound-like dog with a natural stub tail, dewclaws, and a brindle, brown or black coat, often with white, was developed as a tree dog and for his keenness and treeing instinct. These little dogs were widely used and bred by mountain men and became known as the mountain cur. Some of these dogs are still in existence in fairly pure breeding, and several dedicated sportsmen are doing what they can to continue this old breed and make further improvements on it.

The breeding records of the early development of the true open trailing tree hound, of which there are six breeds recognized by the United Kennel Club, are extremely vague, and any attempt to make absolute assertions concerning their origins must go beyond the realm of fact. We do have enough information, however, about their development to indulge in some considered guesswork. All of the standards for the coonhound breeds are taken from the official UKC standards. The AKC recognizes only one breed of coonhound: the Black and Tan. This is of no concern to coonhunters, however, as even in the Black and Tan breed, the vast majority of the working hounds are UKC registered.

Black and Tan

The oldest of the coonhound breeds is the Black and Tan. He is often thought of as the "grand old breed" of the coonhound world, and he seems to have set the standard for what a coonhound should be in looks and performance as well as voice. There is little question that the Black and Tan originated from the early Black and Tan foxhounds of the last century, such as the Ferguson Virginia Black and Tans. Some strains of these Black and Tan foxhounds were long-eared and were slower trailers than the Walkers,

Triggs, Julys and others; as a result, they became widely used as tree dogs. The type of Black and Tan most well known during the early part of the 20th century was heavy of body, stout-legged, heavy-headed and had very long ears. These hounds were wonderful cold-trailing dogs with excellent voices, if a little slow on trail, and their characteristics can be seen in many individuals of the breed today.

The late Hans Wagner from Signal Mt., Tennessee, and a few others in the early years of this century, were not satisfied with the old heavy type of Black and Tan, and bred for lighter, shorter-eared, faster hounds. The hound resulting from these efforts is still very houndy, retains the cold nose, good voice, head and ears, but in a modified form. The demand for a faster hound by those interested in formal competition, and by hunters, is met more satisfactorily by this newer Black and Tan.

The Black and Tan, at his best, is hard to fault as a coon or big-game tree dog. He is fast on trail, one of the most open of all hounds, possessed of a superb voice, and has a strong treeing instinct. We regard it as a mark in favor of this breed that most hunters, regardless of the breed they hunt, hold great respect for the Black and Tan, and will usually comment that some of the best hounds they have known have been Black and Tans.

The modern hunting Black and Tan is built for speed, while it retains a good measure of its previous extremely houndy appearance. Like the foxhounds, the Black and Tan should have a strong, rather short body, with muscular hindquarters and a broad, powerful chest. Also, the legs should be straight and strong, and the feet catlike, well-knuckled and heavily padded. The importance of foot and leg structure in hounds cannot be overstressed. In movement, the Black and Tan should be graceful and quick, giving the impression of exceptional mobility, never of clumsiness. On the other hand, while these hounds should give a speedy appearance, they should not be so slender as to appear weedy or skinny. Adequate bone and muscle is required in any hound expected to endure a long, hard chase.

Black and Tans have among the most beautiful heads of the tree hounds. The head should be broad, and rounded across the dome, the muzzle square and deep, the eyes clean, large and of dark-brown color, and the ears long, of fine texture, and set low on the head, without erectile power. The length of the ear spread should measure about the same as the height of the hound at the shoulders, or they should come just past the tip of the hound's nose.

The coat of the Black and Tan is usually somewhat finer and shorter than the other hound breeds. This often gives them a glossy, race horse finish that is very beautiful. Some hunters say that this coat works to the detriment of the breed when hunting in cold-water areas and heavy briars. This might be so, but we have not been able to observe this as a fault in the slick-coated Black and Tans we have owned and known. The color should be solid jet black, except for tan points over the eyes, and tan on the chest, feet and stern. Some white on the chest is permissible, but not desirable.

The Black and Tan is a medium-sized hound, running from 23 to 25 inches in the males, and an inch less in the bitches. The weight should in all cases be proportionate to the height and bone structure, rarely exceeding 60 pounds in the males and not less than 40 pounds in the bitches. Extremely large Black and Tans are a disadvantage in that they generally lack the energy, speed and drive of a smaller hound.

Bluetick Coonhound

Bluetick

The Bluetick, as a distinct breed, is of comparatively recent origin. It was included in the English breed since the first years of the 20th century, and was granted separate registration by the UKC in the mid-1940's. The Bluetick origin, however, like that of most hound breeds, goes back to a set type at a much earlier date than the American developments in this breed would suggest. Many authorities, most of them champions of the old-time heavy-headed, long-eared Blue, insist that the French Gascony Bluetick is the progenitor of the modern Bluetick breed. This Gascony hound does come very close in type, voice quality and general conformation to the heavier type of Bluetick of today. The Gascony hounds were used widely as stag and boar hounds in both France and England as early as 1200 A.D., and were noted for their voice, impressive appearance and working qualities. O. O. Grant, one of the leading breeders of the old-type Bluetick, quotes in his fine little book, *History of the Bluetick Hounds,* a passage from Shakespeare that alludes to these wonderful hunting hounds:

> My hounds are bred out of the Spartan kind,
> So flew'd, so sanded; and their heads are hung
> With ears that sweep away the morning dew;
> Crook-kneed and dew-lap'd like Thessalian bulls;
> Slow in pursuit, but match'd in mouth like bells,
> Each under each. A cry more tuneable
> Was never holla'd to, nor cheer'd with horn,
> In Crete, in Sparta, nor in Thessaly:

In recent years, however, the Bluetick breed has split into two camps: those promoting the old, heavier type; and those trying to achieve a lighter, faster type of hound. While many of the older breeders have stuck by their guns in breeding the heavier type of hound, some of the breeders, such as Warren Haslouer of the famous Smokey River Kennels, who used to breed the old-type Bluetick, have gone to a lighter modification of the breed. The

51

Bluetick breed is similar to the Black and Tan in that even the lighter specimens are still very houndy, have good noses and are possessed of excellent bawl voices. We would class the Bluetick with the Black and Tan as being a superb, cold-trailing, open-voiced hound, and as we suggest in the chapter on breed selection, some strains of this breed seem to have treeing instincts beyond any of the other tree-hound breeds.

The Bluetick is one of the most impressive and houndy of the tree-hound breeds. Many of them are extremely large, heavily muscled, massive in the head—possessing the appearance of great strength and ruggedness. There has been a tendency, among modern breeders, however, to breed for a lighter, faster type. The bodies of these hounds are substantial and well-muscled in every way. Often the body in the Bluetick is a bit longer in relation to its height than that of the Black and Tan or the other tree-hound breeds. The shoulders and chest are broad and well muscled, and the hindquarters are powerful as well. The legs should be substantially boned, straight, and must have good, well-padded hound feet. Still, despite this extra weight and muscle, the Bluetick should appear to move easily with grace and rhythm. A good one can clear a 5-foot fence in a single bound, almost without losing stride.

The head of the Bluetick is very much like that of the Black and Tan, and, depending upon the individual, may be either slightly heavier in the head and longer in the ears than the average Black and Tan, or the reverse. It should be noted, however, that the hounds with the longest ears and the heaviest heads are Black and Tans, owing to the influence of the old long-eared strain. However, if a Bluetick's head gets to the point where it is saggy and bloodhound-like, like that of the Basset, it is considered to be a fault.

The Bluetick's coat is really its most distinctive feature. In texture and quality it is no different from the Black and Tan's coat, with the exception of a tendency to be a little bit heavier, but the coloration is unique. These hounds are usually almost solidly ticked with black, which, when mixed in close proximity with the white, gives them their characteristic "blue" effect. Usually, the Bluetick has a black head, some black body spots and tan trim. This combination of colors along with the distinctive ticking, makes the Bluetick one of the most colorful and attractive dogs in the sporting field.

The Blueticks, at the extremes, run to larger sizes than any of the other tree-hound breeds. We have known several specimens, even bitches, to be in the 90- to 100-pound class, and several of the famous old mountain-lion and bear-hunting strains characteristically ran to these heavy weights. The modern Bluetick, however, is generally a little smaller, with the heights running from a minimum of 21 inches for bitches to maximum of 26 inches for males. A 26-inch dog in any breed is large, and in a heavily built hound such as a Bluetick he is likely to weigh in the vicinity of 100 pounds. The official standard calls for weights in this breed anywhere from 45 to 80 pounds. Obviously, they can run considerably above that upper limit in weight.

English Coonhound

The English Coonhound, because of his diversity, and his "melting-pot" character, is very difficult to typify. In short, there are so many different kinds of hounds representing this breed, besides the old Blueticks and Red-ticks, which are actually the same except for color, that you must list the types of hounds admitted to the registry of this breed. This breed had its beginning as a formally registered hound in 1900, and at that time was com-posed mainly of the old-time heavy Blue and Redticked hounds. In recent years, however, more and more single registered hounds (hounds that have no record of breeding) have been admitted.

The English breed will now admit registered Treeing Walkers, Blueticks, grade dogs of these types and their own Redticks and Blueticks, of course, to their files. The advocates of this program argue for it on the basis that the English breeders are paying no attention to color, but want quality in their hounds, and will get it regardless of color. There is something to be said for this approach. Those who breed for color, at the expense of working quality, are bound to do serious damage to their breed. However, it is possible to keep type, color and breed characteristics intact, while steadily improving the working quality of the breed. If the problem of color is viewed scientifi-cally, and it is concluded that color is a purely superficial physical character-istic involving none of the hound's hunting ability, then strict selection for color should make no difference in the quality of the hounds you breed, *so long as stud dogs and brood matrons are selected both for working qualities and color.* To make this clearer, there is no more chance of eliminating the best hounds in a litter by keeping only the desired colored offspring, than by any other method of color selection.

The problem of type and color in hounds is primarily one of aesthetic pref-erence. In the thinking of many, the beauty of the hound is just as important as his working quality. Most houndsmen prefer a good-looking hound that is an excellent performer to one that is of indifferent type, but equally good in the woods.

Another point should be considered concerning the English breed. Since there are so many different hounds in this breed, it follows that there are as many different working characteristics among the individuals composing that breed. The English cannot be typified as cold, slow trailers, though there are those in the breed who work in this manner. Nor can it be said that they are consistently a wide-ranging, "drifting" type of hound. For this reason it is extremely important that you know what you want, and are thoroughly familiar with the individuals of the pedigree, and with the parents of the breed you may be considering.

Since the Bluetick is really nothing more than an offshoot of the English Coonhound, one would think that the standards for both breeds would be about the same. Actually, the type of many individuals within these two breeds is about the same, and the registrations, in fact, may be changed from one breed to the other. The English standard now calls for a lighter, smaller dog than the Bluetick standard, and by breeding down to a smaller type hound, along with introducing blood from the Walker breed, they have achieved an average size and weight slightly below that of the Bluetick. Since there are so many different types within the English breed, it is difficult to describe the general appearance of the breed. The ideal, however, is a medium-sized hound with typical hound proportions, built for speed and stamina, well-muscled, and with a good barrel rib cage and a broad chest.

The head, like the body, is of the average hound type, broad across the skull, square in the muzzle, ears set on low and of medium length, eyes large and widely set. The nostrils should be large and open, indicating good scenting abilities.

The texture and quality of the English Coonhound coat is identical to that of the Bluetick, but the color allows for a great deal more variation. Included among the colors in this breed are: bluetick, redtick, tan and white, black and white and any other good hound color. It should be remembered, however, that the predominant colors of this breed are bluetick and redtick, with redtick the more common of the two.

The English Coonhound stands from 21 to 25 inches, the lower figure being for the smallest bitches, and the higher figure for the tallest males. Weights run in proportion to heights, and a good average specimen in the 24-inch class would weigh about 60 pounds.

Plott Hound

The Plott Hound has one of the most interesting and well-authenticated histories of any of the hound breeds. The lineage of the modern Plott Hound goes back to the boar hounds that a German immigrant, Jonathan Plott, brought with him from Germany to the mountains of North Carolina in 1750. His pack was kept intact, and no outside blood was admitted until his son, who took over the pack in 1780, used the blood of some "spotted leopard" bear dogs from Georgia in that year. This combination of breeding has been kept fairly pure down through the years by the Plott family descendants, and by the local hunters of the Great Smoky Mountains in North Carolina and Tennessee. The Plott Hound was recognized by the UKC as a registered breed in 1946.

In looking at the representatives of the Plott breed today, one is led to think that, owing to the wide diversity of type, some breed other than the pure Plott has been used in developing some strains. In the distant past this

Courtesy Pioneer Kennels

Plott Hound

may have been true, but the modern breeders who breed the heavy, long-eared type of Plott, and have been accused of breeding to Bloodhounds, should be exonerated of this charge. If we look back into the history of the Plott Hound, it can be shown that Von Plott, who is still breeding Plotts today, was known for his longer-eared strain of hounds. From this strain came the famous stud dog and fountainhead of the long-eared Plott, Smith-deals Nigger. The shorter-eared type was bred by John Plott in recent years, and an intermediate type by Gola Ferguson, also of North Carolina.

If there was an infusion of the blood of another breed in the distant past of the Plott's history, it was probably the Black and Tan rather than the Bloodhound. The Black and Tan is far more numerous in good hunting country than the Bloodhound, has equal or better earage, a better voice and a gamier nature as well as more treeing instinct. In the face of this evidence, coupled with the fact that many Plotts of today are predominantly black, with brindle trim in the same pattern as the tan on a Black and Tan, it would seem obvious that this was the cross used to achieve a houndier type of Plott.

The Plott is really a game hound to the end, either in the short-eared or long-eared variety. The shorter-eared hounds are, however, possessed of greater speed, and are usually more efficient and evasive fighters on such dangerous game as wild boar and bear. For this reason, the shorter-eared variety is preferred by most hunters of those animals. The longer-eared type usually has better voice. Bad voice is characteristic of the short-eared type, which usually does not have excellent cold-trailing abilities, and is less open on trail. There are strains of Plotts which are midway between the two extremes discussed here, and they are not to be overlooked. It is entirely possible that this medium-type Plott may dominate finally over the other two, because more hunters seem to prefer this type of hound.

Because of their gameness, care should be exercised in kenneling the Plott Hound in order to keep several adult males from close contact. They have a tendency to fight in the pen, so if you have three or more males in one pen, you stand a chance of having two or three hounds gang up on one, often killing him. This can be particularly dangerous if there is a bitch in heat kenneled nearby. Actually, this is an aspect of dog care to be considered no matter what breed you keep.

In terms of length of ears, heaviness of head and other "houndy" characteristics, most Plott hounds are less well endowed, on the average, than any other of the treehound breeds. Instead, they give the appearance of wiriness and speed, which most of them have to spare. The bodies of these hounds are not so heavily muscled and boned, nor so inclined to be ponderous, as the Black and Tan or the Bluetick. On the other hand, few of them are fine boned or spindly, but are built rather like a well-built pointer. In movement, this breed is extremely agile, and is able to maneuver in the tightest spots with almost catlike grace.

The head of a Plott hound is generally not of the low-set, long-eared hound type, but rather with higher set, shorter ears, and clean in the flesh and skin around the face and neck. As might be expected, the higher-pitched chop voice of the Plott hound reflects its less houndy physical type.

We have found the Plotts to have among the heaviest, thickest and most protective coats of the tree-hound breeds. Two of them we have owned have had coats almost as heavy as that of a Labrador Retriever, with the same dense, woolly undercoat. In both cases, these hounds would take to the ice water while hunting, and stay in it for long periods of time without getting cold. We regard the color of a well-colored Plott to be about as beautiful as that of any hound. Most of them are solid brindle (a kind of mottled or striped effect) in various shades of brown, brown and black, or greyish brown. Some of them have a black saddle back with brindle, and others have solid black, like the Black and Tan, with brindle trim. All of these colors are permissible. A small amount of white on the chest or feet is not a disqualification.

While the standard calls for dogs of no more than 60 pounds, and bitches of no less than 40 pounds, this breed runs a bit smaller on the average than the other tree-hound breeds. This is by no means a binding rule, however. Some specimens of this breed are large, heavy dogs. One of the most famous is the late Brandenburger's Pioneer Drum, who was in the 90-pound class. In height, this breed runs the normal hound range from a minimum of 21 inches for bitches to 25 inches for males.

Redbone Coonhound

The Redbone Coonhound goes back, even in name, to the Redbone strain of Foxhounds of the last century. As was the case with the Black and Tan Foxhounds, most of the breeders of the late 19th century felt that the Redbones were too slow and deliberate on trail. For this reason, they disappeared almost entirely from the foxhunting scene, although the occurrence of all red hounds in the American Foxhound breed would indicate the presence of Redbone blood. The early Redbone was not solid red, as a rule, but often was marked with white on the chest and feet. Another feature common to this breed, but which has been practically removed by recent breeding efforts, was the black saddle. This trait still turns up occasionally in Redbone breeding.

During the first half of the 20th century, the Redbone was brought to the forefront among coonhounds, and was admitted to the UKC stud files with the Black and Tan and English in about 1900. Many breeders have contributed to the improvement of this breed, but most notable are the efforts of such old-timers as Brooks Magill, breeder of the famed Magill's Jungle Jim and Magill's Punjab; R. J. Blakesley and his great Northern Joe strain, which is very current in Redbone breeding today; and W. B. Frisbee and his noted line of Redbones. These three men have been with the breed practically since its inception as a registered breed, and have been very instrumental in bringing it to the position of prominence it enjoys today.

The typical Redbone characteristics include excellent loud voice—bawl in some strains and chop in others—good cold noses, tenaciousness, and well-developed treeing instinct. While there is some diversity of type and hunting characteristics in this breed, they run about as uniform as the Black and Tans and Blueticks. Some breeders have tried to stay away from the very cold-nosed Redbones, thinking that a medium-nosed hound would waste less time on a bad track. However, the Redbones we have hunted with have

Treeing Walker and Redbone Coonhound

been predominantly in the cold-nosed class, and had the virtue of being able to move the track speedily. Frequently, in the Bluetick and Black and Tan breeds, you will find individuals who will give lots of voice, even on a very bad track. Some houndsmen object to this on the ground that it constitutes babbling. The Redbones we have known have been notably lacking in this characteristic. Most of them will bark only occasionally, every 100 yards or so, on a cold feeding track, and will give tongue more frequently as the track becomes hotter. This makes it very easy to determine the freshness of the track your hound is working, although most hounds change their voices sufficiently according to the hotness of the trail. Redbones generally have a very marked change at the tree, usually going to a deep, hoarse chop. We often refer to this as a "bulldog" chop, since it so closely resembles the ordinary barking voice of that breed. So far as fighting quality is concerned, we would class the Redbone with the Plott Hound—very good. Often the other breeds, especially the Black and Tans and Blueticks, while excellent in other respects, are comparatively hesitant fighters. However, fighting instinct, at least in coonhounds, if not in cougar, bear or boar hounds, is the least important aspect of their make-up.

Redbones are among the most impressive looking hounds, according to many schools of thought, because of their solid red coat. At their best, these hounds are beautifully built, with large, powerful bodies, long, straight legs, powerful hindquarters, and a stylish tail carriage. They are very agile, as a rule, and, like the Walker and the Plott, have proven to be exceptionally good fence dogs because of their jumping ability.

The usual head type of the Redbone is not extremely houndy as it often is in the Black and Tan and the Bluetick. The ears are set somewhat higher, the muzzle and skull are a little lighter, and the lines of the face and neck are usually cleaner. Some Redbones have very long ears and heavy heads, however, particularly those of Roy Blakesley's "Northern Joe" strain.

The color of the Redbone, of course, is its most distinctive feature, usually coming in a solid, deep red. Most breeders prefer the deep red over the lighter tannish colors. This, of course, is purely a matter of taste, and has nothing whatever to do with the working qualities of the hound. In the early days of hound hunting and breeding, the Redbone often had a large amount of white on the chest and feet, and frequently some on the face. This has been largely removed by selective breeding, but small patches of white on the feet and chest still occur with some frequency.

The Redbone is of typical hound size and proportion, hanging from a minimum of 21 inches for females to a maximum of 26 inches for males. The weights usually run from 45 to 75 pounds, with a few individuals in the 80- to 90-pound class.

Treeing Walker

The Treeing Walker Coonhound came into being as a registered breed with the Plott Hound and the Bluetick in the mid 1940's. In order to understand the history of this breed, however, it would be necessary to go back to the history of the Walker Foxhound. The Treeing Walker comes predominantly from that breed, but no doubt includes the genes of many other strains of which there are no records. Spotted hounds have long been used as tree dogs, and the Walker breed is more or less a collection of the best of those hounds at the time of original registration, and of the single registered Treeing Walkers of recent years. It has been suggested that practically all of the early individuals of this breed were working Foxhounds who, because of age, lack of speed and treeing instinct, took to treeing coon.

With respect to formal competition, the Walker has made remarkable progress in the few years of its existence as a breed. Most of the national championships, and a disproportionate share of the placings in all registered night hunts, have been won by Walkers since the mid-fifties. It may well be that the range, speed and general aggressiveness they have inherited from the Foxhound have made them the hound most suited to competition. As we have explained, a very speedy hound with a medium nose will produce more game under ideal hunting conditions than the cold trailer, and the Walkers usually fit the previous description. Many Walker owners argue that their breed gets many first strikes in competition, that is, they open on track first, so they must be called cold-nosed hounds. The obvious answer to this is that they get their strikes as a result of their ambition and range, rather than as a result of an unusually cold nose. It is often possible that a hot-nosed hound, if he is sufficiently rangy, will get lots of strikes over a cold-nosed hound who works closely.

Among the Walker greats of the past twenty years have been such outstanding dogs as The Incredible Rock, Merchant's Bawlie, House's Bawlie, Merchant's Banjo, Stan's Sailor Boy, Merchant's Banjo II and Nelson's Butch. It is difficult to speak of Walker breeders, however, since many of the best Walkers have been single registered, and little is known of their background. One of the most famous of these, a hound who is a world champion and famous stud dog, is known to be half Walker and half Bluetick of the famous Elbert Vaughn's breeding. This hound, however, shows no ticking in his coat, and does not seem to throw much of that trait in his pups. There have been some outstanding breeders in the Walker breed, despite this preponderance of single registered hounds. Such names as Nance, Motley, Bixler, Baker and Stanfill stand out in this respect.

The hunting characteristics of the Treeing Walker are quite different, as a rule, from most of the other coonhound breeds. Where the Black and Tan, Blueticks and many of the English and Redbones can be typified as "track straddlers," the Walkers rarely possess this trait. Usually they are what is known as "drifters"—that is, when the track gets tough, rather than puzzle it out at close quarters, they range out to pick it up where it is hotter. Many hunters do not like this trait in a hound as it gives the effect of spottiness when listening to the hound work out a trail. The trail seems warm here, cold there and finally the hound trees. There is not much argument, however, that this method produces game, perhaps more game than any other method, except under the most adverse conditions where only the coldest-nosed hound can do the job. Most Walkers have excellent treeing instincts, and many of them "tree coming," which means they begin to bark treed almost before reaching the tree. On a cold tree, however, where there is a good chance of the coon's having jumped out, the cold trailer who checks out his tree very carefully may do better.

The Walker foxhound is the predominant ancestor of the Treeing Walker breed, and the breeds are very similar. Owing to the fact that several strains of the Treeing Walker carry Bluetick blood, as well as foxhound blood, many of them have heavier heads and longer ears than the general run of fox-hounds. In general, then, the Treeing Walker can be thought of as much like the Walker foxhound, of the American Foxhound breed, but a bit houndier in appearance. Of the other tree hound breeds, the one which comes closest to the Walker in type is the English, with the Redbone, perhaps, a close second. Both the Bluetick and the Black and Tan are more houndy, on the average, and the Plott hound is less houndy.

While a wide range of colors is permissible in the Walker breed, the color most favored is the white background with black spots and tan markings. Like the well-colored Beagle, many Walkers come in the black saddle back, with a red head and markings, on a white background. To our thinking, this is the most ideal color for the Treeing Walker, in purely esthetic terms. Like those bird dogs who have a large amount of white in their coats, they are more easily seen in the woods or fields. This can be a particular advantage late at night, or early in the morning, when you want to pick up your hounds and go home, especially if your hounds are no better trained to come when they are called than most.

The Treeing Walker is no exception to the standard size recommendations for most of the tree hounds. The minimum recommended height for females is 21 inches, and the maximum for males, 25 inches. Weights may run from 50 to 75 pounds in males, and 40 to 65 pounds in females.

5

Which Breed?

WHEN LOOKING into the breeds of dogs available, a sportsman usually is guided by the type of hunting he does. In each of the breed categories, one breed seems to stand out as the star performer, at least in organized competition; and the prospective dog buyer who wants the best may well choose an animal of that breed. This can, however, be a time-consuming and expensive mistake. One cannot conclude that because the Labrador Retriever holds sway in the domain of retriever trials, or because the Pointer, Walker Foxhound, Treeing Walker Coonhound or Beagle excel in their respective fields of competition, that any dog selected from these breeds is necessarily going to make a good hunter, or the kind of dog who will please you. If, by some stroke of luck, you stumble on a dog who could do well in formal competition with the right training and handling, he might be just the opposite of what you need in a hunting companion.

Many of us are not "hard hunters" and we need a dog who will adjust himself to our pace and the conditions of our hunting terrain. Of what use is an extremely wide-ranging Pointer or Setter in heavy thickets? Or of what use is a greased-lightning coonhound who covers a square mile before you can get out of the car, in mountainous country where a strike a half-mile away could mean a dog lost for a week?

We have often seen a dog just as unsuited to his owner as to a particular terrain. Some men, by their nature and disposition, cannot abide a nervous, highly charged, energetic dog who is always on the go. On the other hand, other men are irritated by a dog who is easy-going and perhaps a little lazy or slow. Pride in ownership is an important part of having a dog, but don't let it dictate a breed that may be totally unsuited to your hunting or personality.

Once you have decided on the game you will hunt, you are ready to give some thought to the various breeds available. There are excellent individuals in almost all of the hunting breeds. Some breeds have been bred for generations for purposes of show only, so you must be exceedingly careful, or be willing to put up with a less effective hunting dog, if you make your choice from one of the currently field-proven breeds. Among the pointing breeds, the Irish Setter, Gordon Setter and some strains of the English Setter are more notably show than field dogs. Among the other breeds, the Cocker Spaniel, the AKC registered Black and Tan coonhound and some strains of Golden Retrievers are more prominent as bench than as field dogs. It should be borne in mind that among all these breeds there are strains which are bred primarily for show; these should be avoided. None of this is intended to degrade the bench-show fanciers or their dogs; it would be just as ridiculous to present a wiry, small, snipe-nosed field champion English Setter at the Westminster Dog Show as it would be to throw away an entry fee on an English Setter Show dog in one of the big field trials of the South.

POINTING DOGS

In selecting a breed from the group of dogs who point their game, perhaps the most important aspect to consider is the kind of hunting terrain in your area. If you have good legs, or a horse, and live in the part of the South that offers excellent quail shooting on the big, open grasslands, then you cannot go wrong in picking a pup from wide-ranging field-trial dogs. Most of these dogs will be of the Pointer breed, but there are also a number of performers in this class of the English Setter breed. These dogs usually must be more highly trained than the close workers since they will range tremendously wide (from a few hundred yards to a half mile), yet must be under complete control of the handler's hand and whistle signals. If a dog of this type is not well controlled, he will constantly be going out of sight, getting lost, chasing deer and rabbits, and will be of no benefit to the hunt. It should be noted, however, that there are strains within these "big-going" breeds that are medium or even close rangers. If your heart is set on a Pointer or English Setter, you may be able to find one of the right type by doing a little careful research.

In much of the United States and Canada, the condition of natural cover and the lay of the land is such that a medium-ranging dog is required. This type of dog is generally a little slower than the "class" field-trial dogs, although they should be energetic and busy workers, full of birdiness, but tending to work a little closer to the gunners by instinct. Many of these make excellent pheasant dogs because of the inclination of these birds to flush wild. In this respect pheasants are unlike their more tight-sitting cousin, the bobwhite quail. In recent years, however, southern quail have become increasingly inclined to run, flush wild, and hide out in the densest thickets and swamps. Pheasants, however, require a fast-moving, positive and staunch pointer, rather than a ground-scenting, hound-type worker who will flush many more birds than he will point. Perhaps most of the hunting done on this continent calls for a medium-range, yet fast-moving dog, so we would recommend the English Setter, who also has a better coat for the northern climates. There are also many good medium-ranging Pointers who will do an excellent job under these circumstances. Also, Pointers which are wide rangers can frequently be broken to range within acceptable foot-hunting distance.

A breed that should not be overlooked among the medium rangers is the Brittany Spaniel. These dogs, although not very large, have good legs and a lot of endurance. They will get out and do the job along with many of the best Pointers and Setters. There are some German Shorthairs and Weimaraners who make good medium-range pointers, but most of them work rather closely, thoroughly and tend to take a good deal of their scent from the ground rather than from the air. This will result in many flushed birds that are stumbled onto by the dog. Frequently, specimens of the German pointing breeds will learn to take air scent, and thus control the tendency to put game into the air before the gunners arrive, but rarely do they possess the speed and cunning to pin down our wary, fast-running upland birds, especially the ringneck pheasant.

In very heavy cover, such as much of the ruffed grouse and woodcock country of the East and the Northeast, the close-working dog is needed. Any dog who ranges much out of gun range (60 yards or so) will be constantly lost in this country, and will often point birds in places where the hunter can neither see nor hear him. Even with the close workers, it is often necessary to hang a small bell around the dog's neck so that you will know, when the bell stops ringing, that he is on point. A few of the Gordon Setters that are still used for hunting should make good close workers, as are some English Setters, and most German Shorthairs and Weimaraners. Most Pointers have too much "go" for this kind of work, although there are individuals of the breed who work very closely. However, this is not the nature of the Pointer, and we would suspect any representative of this breed who did not get well out of gun range of being lazy, unless he was expressly trained to stay in close. Most of the German pointing dogs possess an added quality that recommends them for heavy cover: they seem to like to hunt dead game, often having a stronger instinct for retrieving than do the Pointers and Setters. The Brittany Spaniel also has a natural inclination for retrieving as do the rest of the spaniels. If you can find a pup of this breed from close-working parents, you might have a good dog in the thickets.

Another consideration that is important in selecting a pointing breed is coat. The long, comparatively heavy coat of the setters and the Brittany Spaniel offers better protection against cold and wet than the very slick, close coats of the pointer breeds. Yet these longer coats also pick up burrs, thorns and other debris that the close-haired dog will easily repel. While the argument for warmth in the longer coat is doubtlessly true, we have not noticed that short-coated dogs had any trouble staying warm while they are working, unless they have been exposed to a lot of ice water, which is not likely when hunting most upland game. The element of appearance and beauty is also to be considered, and if, for reasons of aesthetics, you prefer either the long- or the short-coated dogs, pay heed to your inclination and you will be a more contented dog owner.

RETRIEVERS

While there are officially six breeds of dogs which may be classified as retrievers, only three of them exist in the United States in sufficient number to warrant making general statements about their qualities. These are the Labrador, Chesapeake and Golden Retrievers. In terms of what is expected of these breeds, and from the fact that they compete in the same field trials, it might be said that the retrievers are more uniform as to type and ability than some of the other groups. Still, there are some differences in the way these dogs perform and the best uses to which they can be put, according to breed.

Probably the most important trait of the retriever is ruggedness, and a willingness to endure the toughest hunting conditions for long periods of time. The waterfowl season, even in the southern United States, is frequently marked by very cold weather and cold water. There is nothing more irritating than a retriever who cannot stand cold water and cringes every time he is ordered to retrieve a duck. There are also many very aggressive water dogs who take to ice water willingly who are not physically equipped to stand it, and are in extreme discomfort when exposed to these conditions. With due respect to the many great field-trial champions in the retriever breeds, there have been several of them who could not cut the mustard in ice water. We know of one excellent Labrador who finished in several National Championship trials, almost winning at least one of them, who became completely paralyzed after a few retrieves from the ice water on North Dakota sloughs and could not complete the day's hunting. To our way of thinking, a retriever must not only be a good water dog, but a good ice water dog as well. Many Labs are excellent ice water dogs, both the black and yellow; there is no difference in the working qualities of these color variants. We have owned several Labs who were a little on the weak side when the going got really cold, although they were good retrievers in every other respect and always came home with the bacon, even if they were uncomfortable.

The best cold-water workers we have known have been Chesapeakes. We have known several of this breed who would stand in a slough several hours with ice water over their backs and show no sign of discomfort. The Chesapeake's coat is wonderful for this purpose because it is extremely oily and dense, more so than that of the Lab or Golden. Golden Retrievers have a reputation for weakness in the cold water but many of them we have seen are very tough, aggressive water dogs with excellent woolly undercoats that protect them from the cold. These dogs look soaked when they come out of the water but one good shake dries them almost completely. We would especially recommend a dog of field-trial breeding when looking for a Golden, since these dogs all have to be good water dogs, at least in the summer.

It is absolutely essential that a retriever have an excellent nose, or he will not be able to find game knocked down in heavy cover, no matter how well he marks the fall. Comparing the three breeds of retrievers, we have seen nothing which would indicate that one breed had any better noses than the other. As a matter of fact, the quality of the scenting faculties of these dogs never seems to cause anyone in the retriever world much concern, undoubtedly because they are almost all adequate.

A good retriever must handle the birds gently enough so that he does not damage the meat. Most strains of retrievers pose very little problem in this respect, but some of the more aggressive Labs and Chesapeakes, if not trained carefully on birds when they are young, will develop a tendency toward hard-mouth. One of the better lines of Labs, emanating from a famous National Field Trial Champion, is known for this characteristic, and several of the better Chesapeakes have had similar tendencies. Do not let the presence of this trait in the bloodlines of a pup you want deter you, however, as the fault can almost always be corrected satisfactorily, if the pup is started young enough. Most Golden Retrievers are entirely free of a tendency toward hard-mouth. On the other hand, many of this breed are overly gentle with game, and it tends to slip out of their mouth over and over again as they bring the bird in. Often they have a slow pickup and a sloppy delivery as well.

Tractability, or willingness to please, is a trait which has been bred into all of the retriever breeds, perhaps with the Labs at the head of the list here. Many authorities say that Goldens are the most tractable, but we think they are merely soft, not being able to take punishment and go right back to work. Most soft-dispositioned dogs tend to sulk when punished, and frequently quit working altogether. A dog of this type is harder to train than a real hardhead whom you have to crack down on frequently with harsh physical punishment. Many Chesapeakes are very tough, have a mind of their own, and are almost too intelligent to train easily for some of the more mechanical maneuvers of retriever work. Some of them, however, are very bold and aggressive, yet tractable. These, of course, are the most pleasant and productive to work with. We have also seen a few Chesapeakes with dispositions like Golden Retrievers; big, tough, strapping fellows with the heart of a rabbit. These dogs broke down completely under pressure. A dog of this disposition may work out well in time, but it takes an expert several years to get anywhere with them. They are usually not worth the trouble.

Since many of the best lines of retrievers are used extensively in field-trial work, a sport which requires great speed, drive, intelligence and style, you should consider some of the probable faults of dogs bred solely for this sport. Among field-trial bred Labradors, the chief objection is that they are too high powered. They will not sit still in a blind or boat, they may constantly whine in anticipation as flocks of ducks approach and they are just too jittery for a pleasant day's outing. Unless kept under constant pressure, these dogs are very difficult to train to be steady to shot. Chesapeakes are less likely to have this fault. Most of them sit quietly in the blind until they are called up to retrieve, otherwise you rarely notice that they are there. Most Golden Retrievers are exceptionally pleasant to be in the blind with, rarely exhibiting the uncontrolled enthusiasm of the Lab.

Marking ability and memory for multiple falls seems to be developed to a high degree in all three retriever breeds. We have seen wonderful work in this department by each of them. The important thing here is to be sure that your pup is from good marking parents.

FLUSHING DOGS

A variety of breeds might be used to good advantage as flushing dogs, as the main prerequisite here is that the dog quarter back and forth in front of the guns, flushing any game birds in your path. We have seen a number of retrievers, and even some farm shepherds, do a creditable job of flushing, yet there are specific breeds developed for this job that have a natural aptitude for it. A general mark of all these breeds is the tendency to work very close, but energetically, and to be extremely birdy.

By far the most well-known of these flushing dogs is the English Springer Spaniel. This breed is without doubt the most used among the flushing dogs in North America. The Springer is very fast, eager and close working by instinct. He is also an excellent retriever under all but the coldest conditions, and for this reason, has found a place in the hearts of many hunters who seek a variety of game birds, both upland and waterfowl. Perhaps the best reason for selecting a Springer as a flushing dog is that there are so many good ones available, and you stand a much better chance of finding a good Springer than any other spaniel breed.

The Welsh Springer Spaniel can also be an excellent dog, and has much the same working characteristics as the English Springer, though they are a shade smaller. They are so rare in this country, however, as to make finding a pup of top working bloodlines a most difficult task. For our money, there is not enough difference in the qualities or physical characteristics of the two breeds to warrant the extra trouble and expense of the search for a Welsh Springer, unless you just want to be different. We find the Field Spaniel in a situation very similar to the Welsh Springer with regard to its availability.

Among the smaller breeds of flushing spaniels, the American Cocker is the most widely used, although even these are seen with comparative rarity in the field today. The best of this breed have working characteristics similar to their larger counterparts, the Springers, and can do an excellent job. A major criticism of the American Cocker, and the rest of the small spaniels for that matter, is their size. These dogs tire very quickly as they are not built for a hard day's hunt in heavy cover. However, if you are not a very hard hunter yourself, and like to go for only short periods in relatively light cover, a Cocker may be your best choice.

The Clumber, Sussex, Field and English Cocker Spaniels pose at least as great a problem of availability as the Welsh Springer does, and we can hardly recommend them for that reason. We have seen a couple of excellent English Cockers in the field though, and owing to their larger size compared to the American Cocker, they may present some advantages over that breed. The Clumber and Sussex Spaniels, when you can find them, are very heavy and rather slow, clumsy movers. These breeds are bred far more for show than for hunting. The Field Spaniel is a large, fast, aggressive breed but is hard to find in the United States.

RABBIT HOUNDS

The Beagle is the most likely choice for the rabbit hunter. Beagles have been selectively bred for many hundreds of years specifically for rabbit hunting, and most of them can do the job well. They have the voice, drive, nose and the instinct to handle their game correctly. Very little training beyond basic obedience and exposure to game is necessary to make a pleasant and efficient hunting companion of them. The Beagle has an added advantage in being large and fast enough to keep his game moving, but not so large as to push his game to ground. For the serious rabbit hunter, there is no better choice.

The Basset Hound, while it is not so widely used as the Beagle, is also a good dog if he is of hunting stock. Many of this breed, like many other breeds, are bred strictly for show, and built so heavily and low to the ground that they are useless for hunting, to say nothing of chasing fast-running cottontails through deep snow drifts. For the hunter who does not move too quickly or too far, and wants to hunt the open fields, a Basset may be a good choice.

The Harrier is an excellent hound, although there are not very many of them available in this country. They are built along the lines and coloration of the Beagle, but are larger. Generally speaking, these hounds are too large and fast for cottontails, pushing them so hard that they run down a hole or under a brush pile. For work in deep snow, or for larger, faster rabbits and hares, however, they offer some advantages over the smaller Beagle.

AMERICAN FOXHOUNDS

Among the foxhound breeds, as in most other breeds, there is one sub-breed which stands out in competition and in the field. This is the Walker Foxhound. It seems to have more speed, stamina, track sense, voice and guts than the other strains of American Foxhounds. These qualities have put him in the forefront of practically every formal foxhound competition in recent years. Still, we think it must be admitted that the Walker breed is really nothing more than a strain within the larger category of American Foxhounds, and you may find the hound of your choice among some of the other well-known strains. All of the strains in this breed are highly developed as hunting hounds.

Among the other strains of foxhounds, the Trigg is the most popular. Their adherents claim that the best of them will do the job with the best Walkers, often with something to spare. These arguments as to the best breed could go on forever, though formal competition should prove something, if the tests are really a measure of the dog's ability.

Most of the other subdivisions of the Foxhound breed have become relatively obscure, or have been absorbed into the predominant strains. In their day, such strains as July, Buckfield, Robinson, Birdsong, Redbone (which has now been developed into an outstanding strain of coonhound), and Goodman were well known. Most of these subdivisions got their names from the man or family chiefly responsible for their development. In the early days of the sport of foxhunting in this country, each strain of hound was jealously guarded family property, and several generations of hunters within the family conducted careful, selective breeding programs, helping to make the foxhound what it is today. Doubtlessly some examples of hounds rich in the blood of the above strains still exist, but the purity of their breeding is open to question since there has been so much cross breeding of hounds of all varieties in recent years.

Perhaps the best advice as to the selection of a foxhound is that you should look first to the large, well-known breeders of the leading strains (Walkers and Triggs), hunt with the parents of your prospective pup, compare, and make your choice. As in other breeds, it will pay you to look at the field-trial records of the ancestors, especially in the first three generations of the various breedings you are considering.

COONHOUNDS

There is a wider variety of working characteristics among the coonhound breeds than either the foxhounds or the rabbit hounds. It must be taken into account that, while the fox and rabbit hounds are bred merely to run a track well, the coonhounds must do not only this, frequently working in water and generally tougher terrain, and on colder tracks, but they also must have the ability to tree their game and stay at the tree. For this reason, a good coonhound is a rarer thing than a good fox or rabbit hound.

The advocates of a particular breed of coonhound (there are six recognized by the United Kennel Club, and one by the AKC) like the working qualities of that breed. Some hunters, for example, are willing to sacrifice voice for speed, some want consistently long chases and don't mind catching few coons, others want a fairly hot-nosed, semi-open dog who will bag a lot of game. All of these considerations should be weighed before you decide on a breed, or individuals within a breed. Needless to say, there is a great deal of variation within the individual breeds. The propositions we make here will be based on our reactions to the performances we have seen by the best representatives of these breeds.

Black and Tan

The Black and Tan coonhound is the only breed of coonhound recognized by the AKC. They are, with the Bluetick, the houndiest of the coonhound breeds. They have the longest ears, coldest noses and the most melodious, drawn-out bawl voices. The AKC strain of Black and Tans is more extreme in these respects than the UKC Black and Tan, which has been bred to be a medium-eared, faster hound. Even though the modern Black and Tan has been bred for more speed, and is not quite so much the old, slow, heavy-headed Bloodhound type that he used to be, he is still very houndy. If you want a cold-nosed "track straddler" with a beautiful voice, you are most likely to find one in this breed.

Our experience with this breed as tree dogs has been generally good. Many of them, however, do seem to have so much trailing instinct that they will always move a track rather than tree. There is one advantage to a hound of this type; he will rarely false-tree, since he always checks the area around a tree very carefully to see if the game has jumped out. This kind of hound will not score highly in most competitive night hunts, but his work is often more consistent than the hotter-nosed, faster, quicker tree dog, and he is by far the best for tough tracks, frosty nights and dry terrain. We have also found them to be more efficient in water and heavy underbrush.

Bluetick

We would put the Bluetick, for hound-like quality, nose, voice and trailing instinct, in a class with the Black and Tan. Except for some strains, which have been developed into a much faster, less cold-nosed type of hound, they are generally colder nosed, and have better bawl voices than most of the other breeds. One outstanding quality of the Bluetick breed is their treeing instinct. By far the hardest tree dogs we have seen have been Blueticks, and many of them will really knock themselves out at the tree. Often this quality is coupled with the very desirable trait of sticking to the tree for many hours. Many hunters claim that they don't like a dog to "starve at the tree," but if we had a hound that would stay at the tree for two or three days, we would consider ourselves lucky, although we doubt that this is ever done.

English Coonhound

The English Coonhound was the original Bluetick and Redtick before the Bluetick branched off as a distinct breed. For this reason, you will always find, if you go back far enough, registered English in a Bluetick pedigree. The English breed of twenty to thirty years ago was similar to the present-day Bluetick. The difference between the blue and red coloration is merely a color variant and has no bearing on working qualities.

In recent years, however, the English breed has adopted a new direction of giving little concern for color, and admitting a great number of grade (unregistered) coonhounds to their stud files. This has included Walkers, Blueticks and Redticks. As a result, the English breed has shown a diversity of hounds which are short-eared, long-eared, cold-nosed, hot-nosed, big, small and with a good or bad voice. Some run like Walkers; others are cold-nosed, careful trailers. We will not argue that there are not many excellent coonhounds in the English breed, perhaps some of the very best; still, to recommend a breed for specific qualities, we could not recommend the English, primarily because it has lost any really identifying characteristics. Buying one of them is little more certain today than buying a grade dog; you just have to depend on the parents and their qualities.

Plott Hound

There are two distinct types in the Plott Hound breed: the longer-eared, cold-nosed type; and the short-eared, fast, hot-nosed type. The extreme examples of the first type are often very good cold-nosed hounds. The lion's share of the credit for the perpetuation of this type of Plott, in recent years, must go to Dale Brandenburger of Millstadt, Illinois, and his great long-eared Plott, Brandenburger's Pioneer Drum. In the early part of this century both the long-eared and short-eared types were kept in the hunting packs of the Plott family. These long-eared Plotts, at their best, are nearly the equal of the Black and Tans and Blueticks for voice, and usually surpass them in speed and fighting qualities. For these reasons, the Plotts are often favored for bear, wild boar and other big game. They also have been used effectively on mountain lion, coyote, wolf and wild cat, and are supposed to excel in hunting any game that runs and fights.

The smaller, short-eared Plotts lack nothing of the larger hounds' determination, and often are faster. They tend to be less open on track, although this is by no means an invariable rule. We had a Plott of the short-eared variety a few years ago, and he was very open on track and had an excellent nose. The main sacrifice you will make in picking a Plott of this type is voice. Very few of them have good voices, and many of them are downright irritating to hear. However, if you want a dog with lots of guts, speed and good treeing instinct, and if a bag full of game is more important to you than hound music, the short-eared Plott may be just what you need.

Redbone

We call the Redbone the "in between" breed. Some of them go to the very cold-nosed, houndy type of dog, and some to the short-eared, hot-nosed type. However, the majority of hounds we have known of this breed were good medium cooners. They had enough nose to handle a fairly tough track, were reasonably houndy in appearance, had good, if not spectacular, bawl voices with a good deep chop at the tree.

Many old-timers have told us that the Redbones were good dogs, but tended to be mean with strangers and other hounds, and were hard-headed. We have found the opposite to be true. We have seen very few Redbones who were quarrelsome with other dogs in the woods, and the most tractable hounds we have known have been Redbones. In general, they seem to be very intelligent animals. Unlike some of the more independent Black and Tans and Blueticks, they have a strong sense that they are hunting for their master, not just for themselves. There is some justification for the assertion that Redbones are surly with strangers. Most of them are good watchdogs, and may bite an intruder, but are not vicious when their master is around.

Treeing Walker

The Treeing Walker is basically a foxhound breed that has been developed through selective breeding for its treeing instinct. Walkers do, however, retain some of the old foxhound characteristics. They take scent higher off the ground than the other coonhounds, are generally faster, have great endurance, drift on track, rather than retracing every step their quarry has taken, and are inclined to chase hard-running game such as deer, fox and coyote.

When well-trained, Treeing Walkers often make excellent coonhounds, and frequently are hard to beat in competition. Their speed, range and tendency to tree quickly have often helped them to surpass the slower, more methodical breeds in building up points in formal night hunts. Still, most of us hunt for pleasure, and these qualities which will definitely help to win in competition, and which may produce more game under most conditions, may not furnish you the kind of sport you want. It should be taken into account that, while some Walkers have beautiful voices, many of them have very bad squealing voices, or unpleasant sharp chop voices that sound more like a Terrier than a hound. If voice is very important to you, be careful when picking a Walker.

A few general recommendations should be made with respect to the selection of coonhounds. First, select a hound suited to your personal wants and limitations. For example, if you have little endurance, don't get a wide-ranging coonhound; he will spend most of his life lost in the woods. If you love a good chase and lots of music, don't be fooled by the semi-silent trailer who will bring in a truckload of coon hides season after season. Know what you want, and insist on nothing less. Second, if you plan to build up a pack of three to five dogs, keep them similar as to working quality. A fast dog will often discourage a slow one, or a cold-trailer may convince a hot-nosed dog that he can't smell anything, and he won't hark to the cold-nosed dog's strike. Hounds who are alike in nose, voice, speed and general ability will "pack" together better, and will give more enjoyable hunts than a collection of nondescript and dissimilar hounds. Finally, buy only from a breeder of excellent reputation who will hunt his breeding stock for you. In this way you can make sure not only of the authenticity of your dog's pedigree, but you will have first-hand knowledge of the working quality of his parents.

6

Guide to Selecting the Best

CHAPTER 5 was concerned with which breed to buy. This chapter assumes that you have already picked a breed and are not ready to consider selecting a particular animal from that breed. How do you go about selecting?

There are several important factors that will be discussed.

1. Age—puppy or adult dog?
2. Training—trained or untrained?
3. Physical conformation, health, disposition.
4. Pedigree—bloodlines.
5. Parents—working qualities and characteristics of parents.
6. Breeder—reputation and reliability.

AGE AND TRAINING

The first important question is how old should your dog be when you buy him? Should you buy a puppy or adult? If a puppy, how old should he be? If an adult, how much training?

Whether to buy a puppy or adult dog is determined by: 1) your preferences; 2) your pocketbook; and 3) your willingness to train an animal yourself. Only you can decide whether to consider a puppy or adult dog. Good trained adult hunting dogs are very expensive. Fully trained pointing dogs or retrievers that are excellent animals for hunting, but are still not good enough for the fine points of field-trial championship work, may run from $750 to $3000. Field Trial Champions of these breeds will sell for $5000 to $15,000. Fully trained hunting spaniels come a little cheaper than pointing dogs or retrievers, but well-trained animals still cost from $500 to $2000, with Field Trial Champion spaniels costing $3000 and up. Good hounds are the least expensive of any of the hunting breeds. Fully trained rabbit, coon, or foxhounds may be purchased for $100 and up, although you will find a tremendous difference in capability of $100 hounds. The best hounds—those that have proved themselves in field-trial competition—may cost $300 to $500 and up.

The prices quoted above will vary from region to region and from breed to breed. Hunting dogs are usually sold for as much as the buyer can get, so it is difficult to predict prices ahead of time. But beware of buying bargain dogs—the so-called "natural" hunters—which have had little or no training. Only by paying good prices can you expect to buy well-trained dogs. Why? Primarily because it takes a minimum of two years of regular training to develop a well-trained hunting dog. To develop a field-trial dog takes three to five years of daily training—assuming one has the best possible prospect to work with. No man in his right mind is going to spend two years or more training a fine animal and then sell him to you for several hundred dollars. Your first consideration, therefore, is: Do I want to spend the money to get a good trained adult?

You have to consider also whether or not you want to devote the necessary time to train a puppy yourself. Actually, if you are willing to devote fifteen minutes daily to training your dog, and are willing to keep at it for several years, then by all means buy a puppy. But if you don't have time, or are not willing to spend the time, then it is better to buy a trained animal. There is nothing worse or more frustrating than an untrained animal in the field. He is more nuisance than help.

What about buying a puppy and then having a professional train him? This is fine, but also very expensive. You have to pay a good professional a minimum of $3 to $5 daily plus training equipment (shells, birds, etc.). So figure it out. If you keep your puppy in a trainer's hands for a year, it will cost you approximately $800 to $1200 training expenses. And even then your dog may not be fully trained!

A more economical practice is for you to do your own training of your puppy until he is at least ten to twelve months of age, then put him into the hands of a professional for about twelve months and you should have a fine animal, assuming you had a good prospect to start with. But you will still have about $1500 or more invested in your dog before you are through.

Personally, we would rather train our puppies ourselves from the time they are young. We enjoy the exercise and like working with our dogs. But unless you are willing to train your puppy, or have him trained, you will do better to buy a trained animal, even if you have to purchase him on a time payment plan.

If you buy a puppy, how old should he be? As long as he is weaned, then the younger the better. The ideal age is to get him by the time he is seven weeks of age. Earlier is a little young, but this is preferable to a puppy considerably older. If he is over seven weeks of age, and the puppy has not been socialized by his owner, he is likely to be much harder to train that he would be if you got him younger. Never consider buying a puppy two months of age or older who has not had close and regular contact with people from the time he is young. The hardest dogs to train are the animals that have been kennel raised, with no close socialization with people, and with no regular training from the time they are young. For additional information and explanation, see Chapter 11, Training Fundamentals.

The worst prospect to buy is an adult dog who has never been trained. If you want an adult, a young adult or even an older puppy, get one who has been regularly socialized and trained. Otherwise you will have a most difficult animal to work with, or even one who may be untrainable.

PHYSICAL CONFORMATION, HEALTH, DISPOSITION

Many buyers look for particular physical qualities and characteristics in the animals they buy: a certain coat color, head, body or leg conformation. If you are concerned about physical appearance, the best procedure is to study the physical standards for the breed and to try to get a puppy or adult who conforms as closely as possible to the standards. Actually, it is very hard to tell what a young puppy may look like when grown, but you can look him over to examine general body structure, head and skull shape, neck, shoulders, ears, muzzle, mouth, teeth, eyes, chest, ribs, back, forelegs, hind legs, feet, tail and coat. Adults, of course, can be selected according to physical conformation, if desired.

We are not too particular about the details of physical conformation as long as the appearance is acceptable. We are more interested in the working possibilities and qualifications of hunting dogs. There is no point in buying a beautiful dog if he won't hunt or can't be trained to hunt—unless of course one just wants a dog for bench shows or to look pretty around the house. Our advice is to put working ability first and physical appearance second. Of course, it is nice to have both a beautiful dog and a fine working dog.

Certainly you want an animal in perfect health. The seller ought to provide you with a health certificate signed by a veterinarian after a complete physical examination. At the time you receive your dog have your vet examine him completely if there seems any doubt about health, and advise the seller immediately of any problems. Be particularly sure the dog is free of heart worms.

All dogs should be immunized against distemper, leptospirosis, hepatitis, and kennel cough. What shots should your puppy or adult have at the time you buy him? This depends upon his age. At 8 or 9 weeks of age permanent shots are administered. You will have to find out from the seller whether or not your puppy has had shots and whether or not shots are included in the purchase price. Adult dogs should have had all permanent shots already administered at the proper periods before they are sold. But you should get a record of which shots were given and when at the time you buy an adult dog. Rabies shots are given only to animals six months of age or older, and should have been given to all dogs over this age before sold.

Also, whether buying a puppy or adult, find out what worms the animal may have had and what treatment has been administered. Most puppies have round worms. These are not serious, but failure to treat them will impair health. Whip, tape, heart or hook worms are much more serious and such ought to be treated immediately. The only way to tell for certain what worms your puppy or adult dog has is by a microscopic examination of the stool for round, whip, tape and hook worms, and by an examination of a blood sample for heart worms. Dogs in the southern part of the United States are more likely to have heart worms than dogs in the north.

In the larger breeds especially, be certain to select puppies from parents who are free of hip dysplasia. Adult dogs ought ordinarily to be shown to be free of hip dysplasia before being sold. Whether to buy or sell adult dogs with very mild cases of hip dysplasia that do not substantially impair the working qualities of the dog is a matter for debate. Certainly, dogs with hip dysplasia, should not be used for breeding purposes, nor should one ever be bought or sold without the buyer having full knowledge of the condition.

An important factor to look for in dogs you are going to buy is disposition. A puppy should have a merry, lively, effervescent disposition. All dogs should be free of excessive nervousness, shyness and skittishness. Some puppies and adults seem to exhibit a calm, placid disposition, others seem to be very high strung, even from the time they are young, so decide what sort of disposition you want and look for this. Also, get acquainted with the parents of the puppy you are thinking of buying to determine some things about disposition. However, remember that each puppy in a litter is different, and there may be individuals completely different in physical appearance and disposition from the sire and dam.

PEDIGREE

Most knowledgeable buyers go more by pedigree and bloodlines than anything else. A purebred animal is always accompanied by registration papers, included with the sale. Every litter of puppies should be registered with the AKC or UKC. When the owner of a litter registers it, he receives one application for registration form for each puppy of the litter. When each puppy is sold, this application for registration form is filled out by the seller, transferring ownership to the buyer, who then selects a name for his puppy, fills out the form and sends it in to the AKC, or UKC (for some hounds). Or, the owner of the litter may not only register the litter, but he can name and register each puppy in the litter by filling out the application form for each puppy. In this case, the buyer of a puppy would receive the permanent registration paper with the name, assigned registration number, and parents' names on it. The same holds true for an adult dog. A permanent registration certificate accompanies the dog at the time sold. There is no extra charge for supplying "papers." This should be included with the purchase price since it costs the seller almost nothing to supply the paper.

Never buy a puppy or dog either without the registration application form *or* without the permanent registration certificate. This is the only guarantee you have that your dog is a thoroughbred and of the parentage claimed.

Although not ordinarily supplied by the seller, ask to see the pedigree, or bloodlines, back four or five generations. By an examination of the pedigree you can determine the ancestry of your dog. Good hunting stock should have some field-trial champions in their bloodlines in the first two or three generations. Wherever you see an FC in front of a Retriever's name, this means he is a Field Trial Champion, earning his championship at licensed trials in the field. A Ch. in front of the name means he is a Bench Champion (a show dog, not necessarily a good hunter). A Dual Ch. means he is both a Field Trial Champion and a Bench Champion. An NFC means he is a National Champion. A CNC means a Canadian National Champion. A CFC means a Canadian Field Trial Champion. An AFC means Amateur Field Champion and NAFC means National Amateur Field Champion.

In selecting the best dog to buy, try to get one with at least one parent a Field Trial Champion, and as many FC in the ancestry on both sides of the line as possible. The sire and dam each contribute half of the heredity. The grandsires and granddams each contribute a quarter. The great-grandsires and great-granddams each contribute an eighth. The great-great grandsires and great-great granddams each contribute only a sixteenth, so don't get too excited about any generations beyond the great-grandsire and great-grand-dam, since each individual animal beyond this point contributes so little to the total heredity. For additional information on breeding see Chapter 9.

PARENTS

When buying a puppy or adult dog, it is helpful to get to know as much as possible about the parents—both the sire and dam—since each contributes half of the total heredity. Are the parents trained working hunters? Field-trial dogs? What type of a hunter or field trial dog is each? What are his general style, disposition, hunting aptitude and working characteristics? What are his strengths? Weaknesses? What faults?

Many times you will find that the sire is a field-trial dog, but the dam is not. Many females are raised strictly as brood bitches and never trained. If, however, the bitch comes from good working stock as indicated by the fact that at least one of her parents is a field-trial dog, then you are assured of getting better prospects in puppies. We would never buy a dog whose dam and sire both had never proved themselves in the field.

During the past five years, we have raised over 100 puppies (mostly Labs and various hounds), most of them sired by Field Trial Champions and many by National Champions. The bitches themselves have all been trained, and from the best field-trial stock that we could obtain. Most of the puppies have been fine hunters, some have been exceptional field-trial dogs. Occasionally, even in the most careful breeding program, you will find a real dud —usually a throwback to an unworthy ancestor. So if occasionally you have bought a puppy that doesn't measure up to expectations, it may be you were unlucky enough to get a dud, so don't blame the poor breeder. He is trying his best to provide you with a fine dog. But he doesn't have complete control over nature. Of course, how a dog turns out depends at least 75 percent on training, so there is always a possibility you need an expert to examine your training technique.

BREEDERS

Always try to buy a dog or puppy from a reputable breeder whom you trust. He doesn't have to own a large kennel. He can be a private owner who en-joys raising one litter a year but who is the kind of person on whom you can depend. Of course, many of the large-scale breeders produce some mighty fine dogs, so they are possibilities too, but don't overlook the small operator who tries to breed only the best.

The following information is supplied to help you to find out about out-standing breeders for each breed of hunting dogs.

Pointers and English Setters

Both of these breeds are given extensive coverage in the *American Field* periodical, American Field Publishing Co., 222 West Adams Street, Chicago, Illinois 60606. Look for information on field-trial breeders and inquire of them whether they are developing medium or wide-ranging individuals.

German Shorthaired Pointers

The main publication of this breed is *German Shorthaired Pointer News,* Box 188, St. Paris, Ohio 43072.

Brittany Spaniels

Full information may be obtained from the periodical *The American Brittany,* American Brittany Club, Route #3, Box 14, Sherwood, Oregon 97140.

Weimaraner

Write to the Weimaraner Club of America, Box 351, LaCrosse, Wisconsin 54602.

Retrievers

A complete and up-to-date account of the field-trial performances of these breeds as well as interesting articles and ads of prominent breeders, may be obtained through a subscription to *Retriever Field Trial News,* 4213 S. Howell Ave., Milwaukee, Wisconsin 53207.

Springer Spaniels

Write to: *Springer Back,* P.O. Box 187, San Leandro, California 94577, for the periodical on springers and to find out information on breeders.

Tree Hounds

Excellent information on the tree hounds and the various breeders can be had through a subscription to *American Cooner,* Sesser, Illinois 62884, editor, George Slankard, or *Full Cry,* Box 190, Sedalia, Missouri 65301, Mrs. Estelle Harris Walker, editor. These two periodicals cover the subject of coon and big-game tree hounds very well, and are invaluable for their information on buying puppies and trained hounds of the various breeds.

American Foxhounds

The main publication in the foxhound world is: *The Chase,* The Chase Publishing Company, 152 Walnut Street, Lexington, Kentucky 40507.

Beagles

The periodical *Hounds and Hunting,* I. W. Carrell, editor, Bradford, Pennsylvania 16701, carries much information on breeding, hunting and training the Beagle hound.

Bassets

Much care must be exercised in selecting a Basset hound so as to avoid getting a pup of purely show breeding, which many are. The chief Basset hound publication: *Tally Ho,* official organ of the Basset Hound Club of America, c/o Norwood Engle, Box 207, Liverpool, Pennsylvania 17045.

7

Housing and Feeding

THE KENNEL

No hunting dog should be permitted to run free. Many people are convinced that penning a dog is cruel, but dogs who are properly kenneled, and who get plenty of regular exercise hunting and training, are by far the happiest and healthiest members of the canine species. Any dog who runs loose will inevitably get into trouble, either by destroying a neighbor's property, or picking up foods unfit to eat. The risks of getting hit by a car, shot by a farmer or killed in a dog fight are also great. Further, the dog who is not confined will not have the energy and enthusiasm when he is taken out for hunting or training that a penned dog will. For these reasons, we strongly recommend that suitable kennel facilities be set up before your new dog or pup is brought home.

The individual run need not be large. Most experts agree that a run 12 feet long and 4 feet wide is adequate for a large hunting dog. If two dogs are to be kept in the same pen, an additional 2 feet can be added to the width, making the size 12 feet long by 6 feet wide. I do not recommend kenneling more than two dogs together, and these of different sexes, if possible, since if two of the same sex are penned together, the probability of fighting and injury to a dog is great. The kennel fencing should be 6 feet high, and should be constructed of heavy-gauge, small-mesh wire. One-by-two-inch mesh is excellent, as it keeps the dog from breaking his teeth by biting and chewing on the wire. Woven fabrique cyclone fencing is probably the best material for the sides of the kennel, as it is very strong, but it is also very expensive. This fencing now comes in 1-inch mesh which is very strong and offers positive protection against chewing. Metal fence posts are by far the most satisfactory because the dogs cannot chew them. Creosoted cedar poles make a reasonable second choice. The posts should be set in cement so the tightly stretched fencing will not cause them to bend. The easiest fence to

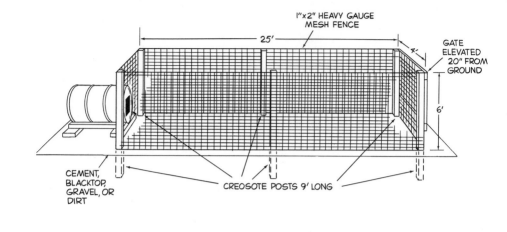

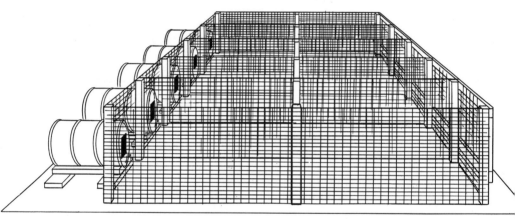

Oil-drum house and run of wire mesh is a good arrangement for keeping a dog comfortable and out of trouble (top). For keeping several dogs, a multiple kennel enclosure (bottom) is the best solution.

assemble is the cyclone, or chain link, which consists of prefabricated panels. The panels sit on the concrete surface and remain in place by virtue of their own weight. It is advisable to roof your kennel runs with close-weave fencing similar to that used on the sides. The purpose of this is to keep your dogs from jumping out, to keep other dogs from jumping in, in case your female is in heat, and as an added protection against theft. A sturdy gate with a strong locking device and a padlock will complete your kennel enclosure.

Next, the run surface should be considered. Perhaps the simplest and cheapest solution is dirt. We have had good luck with the health of dogs raised on dirt. For that reason, we like it. It has many disadvantages that one should consider, however. Dirt runs become sloppy and muddy in wet weather and are comparatively hard to clean. Dogs may also dig deep holes in the dirt run, sometimes out of boredom, and sometimes in an effort to escape. It is necessary in all cases where the dirt run is used to set the fencing at least 2 feet into the ground in order to prevent the dogs from digging it out.

A variation on the dirt run is gravel. This material is famous for conditioning the dog's feet, and it may well do this, but we have never had any trouble with dogs raised on concrete. The main advantages of a gravel surface are that dogs are less likely to dig in it, and drainage is exceptionally good. When shoveling up the stools on any dirt or gravel surface, a small amount of the run material is taken with each scoop, and eventually must be replaced or the run will become low and wet.

Blacktop makes a very good run, but has the disadvantage of getting extremely hot when exposed to the direct rays of the sun. It is easily cleaned, however, and seems to offer a high resistance to the development of worm larvae and other parasites. If you can locate your kennel in a well-shaded spot, or if you live in a very cool climate, the blacktop surface is a wise choice.

Concrete runs are used by more professional dog breeders, boarders and veterinarians than any other surface. It is, of course, very durable and can be kept clean and free from offensive odors more easily than any other surface. We have had excellent results keeping mature dogs on concrete and can see no basis to the claim that it causes splay feet. We do not, however, like concrete for raising litters of puppies. These youngsters are so active, and do so much urinating and defecating, that the runs are constantly dirty and wet. This condition seems to breed pneumonia, distemper and other puppy disorders. On gravel or dirt, the moisture has a better chance to soak in and dry out. The best solution for puppy raising is to keep them on fine mesh a foot or so above the ground. For all around neatness and minimal upkeep, though, concrete is the best solution for adult dogs.

There are a number of excellent solutions for the kennel box (dog house), depending on the size of your dog and how many will use the box at once. An excellent and economical solution for the single dog box is a barrel—either a wooden vinegar barrel or a large oil drum with a flap on the door mounted on a solid wooden rack. These are very windtight and waterproof, and if kept well-filled with good bedding make excellent quarters. If you live in a cold climate, kennel boxes should be made double-walled and insulated by stuffing the walls with crumpled newspaper or other insulating

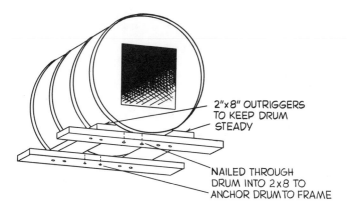

2"x8" OUTRIGGERS
TO KEEP DRUM
STEADY

NAILED THROUGH
DRUM INTO 2x8 TO
ANCHOR DRUM TO FRAME

Oil-drum house should be mounted on 2-by-8s to keep it steady. Drum is nailed to boards from the inside.

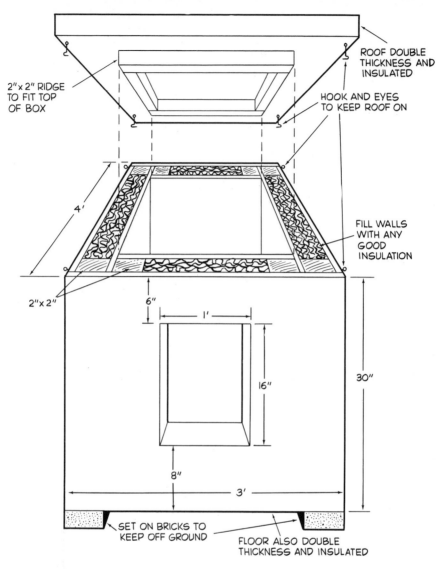

ROOF DOUBLE
THICKNESS AND
INSULATED

2" x 2" RIDGE
TO FIT TOP
OF BOX

HOOK AND EYES
TO KEEP ROOF ON

FILL WALLS
WITH ANY
GOOD
INSULATION

4'

2" x 2"

6"

1'

16"

30"

8"

3'

SET ON BRICKS TO
KEEP OFF GROUND

FLOOR ALSO DOUBLE
THICKNESS AND INSULATED

For cold climates, a kennel box can be built of ⅜" exterior-grade plywood treated inside and out with Firzite sealer and painted. The house is double-walled, with 2-by-2s being used as a frame for nailing. Walls are filled with newspaper or other insulating material.

material. This is necessary only if most of the winter nights in your area are below freezing. The oil drum or barrel house can be insulated by piling straw bales over the entire shelter. An arrangement of this kind will keep dogs warm in any weather. We have raised a litter of coonhounds in the dead of North Dakota winter (the temperatures there in January and February are commonly 20 to 25 below zero) in a straw-covered kennel box with a flap over the door, and they did beautifully.

Bedding is an important aspect of your dog's comfort. A hard surface is not only cold and disagreeable to the dog, but wears patches of hair off his elbows, haunches and belly, sometimes causing callous-like growths similar to proud flesh frequently seen on horses. There are many good bedding materials. Straw is perhaps the most commonly used because it is readily available and inexpensive. Straw tends to break down very quickly, however, and must be replaced often if it is to be much good. Hay is generally a poor choice, particularly if it contains much alfalfa or other dusty varieties which might irritate the dog's nasal passages and eyes. Some clean meadow grasses which are often cut as hay are very good. Coastal Bermuda hay, found throughout much of the South, is clean, dust-free, and tough. You should be sure, whenever using hay, that it contains no hay-needles (small, barbed, very sharp seeds). These can penetrate the dog's skin and cause discomfort and serious infection. Fine, hard slough grass is perhaps the finest of the natural beddings as it is clean, durable and extremely comfortable. Farmers often bale a quantity, which is cut from the slough bottoms after they have dried up late in the summer. A few bales of this will tide several dogs over the winter, and it is not expensive. Usually cedar shavings are recommended because of their pleasant odor and the repellent effect they have on various insects. This material is very expensive and comparatively scarce. If you use shavings, ensure that they are high-grade, rather than mere chips, which release dust that can irritate the dog's eyes and nose. For these reasons, we do not consider this material a practical solution to the bedding problem. Bedding should be checked often. As long as it is dry, clean and reasonably resilient, it is all right. When it loses these qualities, it should be replaced.

FEEDING

Contrary to popular belief, it is not expensive to feed even a large dog, if the problem is approached intelligently. Many dog owners feel that they save money by feeding table leftovers. This idea is erroneous, since human food is far more expensive than the costliest dog foods and is generally less nutritious than good dog food. Your dog's diet should be planned around a high-grade dry type of dog food; then genuine surplus from your table that isn't utilized for human consumption can be added to his feed. We recommended dry dog food not only because it is far more economical, but because it is more convenient and, in the better grades, more nutritious than canned foods. If you have only one dog, feeding the best of these foods will cost only five or six dollars a month at present prices.

If you are keeping a pack of hounds, or a number of dogs, you will want to cut these feed costs as low as you can and still provide a maximum of nutrition for your dogs. In this case you should buy your feed in large quantities through a wholesale milling company. Often, if you order a sufficient amount you can receive free home delivery. Some feed companies offer special discounts under kennel plans for owners of more than a certain number of dogs. And these plans help reduce feed costs greatly.

The feed should be of fairly high protein content (21 percent or more). It should also contain about 8 percent fat and should be listed as a complete diet for dogs. We prefer the completely kibbled, baked food rather than the cold-pressed pellets because the kibbles contain a larger percentage of digestible food.

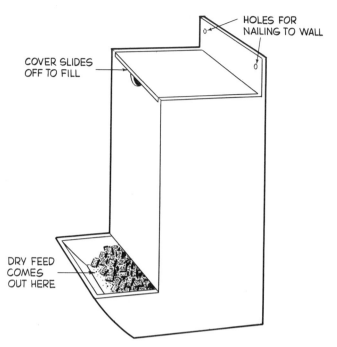

HOLES FOR
NAILING TO WALL

COVER SLIDES
OFF TO FILL

DRY FEED
COMES
OUT HERE

Self-feeder of galvanized iron does away with dishwashing. To prevent your dog from gorging himself, fill the hopper each day with only as much food as he needs.

We feed our adult dogs slightly moistened feed once per day. And when working dogs in cold conditions, we favor a light morning feeding. For campaigning field-trial dogs, and for hard hunting, we up the protein by adding a handful of raw hamburger to each feeding. Though the quantity recommendations on the feed bags are basically sound, nutritional needs among dogs of the same size can vary. A dog that tends to be fat should be fed less than the recommended amount, and a lean dog should be fed more. Generally, dog food manufacturers recommend slightly more than most dogs need.

The excitement a dog generates over his food and his personal contact with the owner at feeding time, help develop closer rapport between dog and owner. Feeding times should be kept regular, peaceful, and pleasant for the dog. A dog should not have to fight for his food, so dogs that are possessive of their feed should not be fed with other dogs in the same kennel run.

A liberal supply of fresh water must be kept at the dog's disposal at all times. This is especially true if no water is mixed with the feed, as dogs will not eat dry food unless water is available. For puppies under six months of age, and bitches that are nursing puppies, keep a self-feeder full at all times. Their demands for food are much greater than a mature dog's and they should have a continuous nutritional supply.

Don't worry about your dog's needing fresh meat as a steady part of his diet. A good commercial feed will supply all the nutrients your dog needs. He will live a long, healthy life on this food, and will perform at peak efficiency as a result of a constant, fully adequate diet.

8

Health Care

ANY DOG worth owning deserves to be taken care of and to be kept in the best possible health. Providing a good diet, clean, comfortable living quarters, protection from physical harm, practicing preventive medicine and taking your dog to a veterinarian for periodic check-ups are the best assurance of health protection.

HEALTH INDICATORS

There are a number of general ways you can check on your dog's health.

1. His personality—Normal activity, alertness, temperament. Any sudden change in his normal behavior such as listlessness, apathy, unwarranted trembling or excitability may indicate illness.

2. His coat—Normally ought to be healthy looking and shiny. A dull, dry, rough coat, or excessive dandruff or shedding may indicate poor diet or disease symptoms.

3. Skin—Watch for lesions, reddening, possibly associated with loss of hair, change in color, dryness, flakiness.

4. Eyes—Ought to be bright and clear. If eyes become dull, clouded, bloodshot, photophobic (extremely sensitive to light) or contain accumulations of gummy matter, you ought to check for trouble.

5. Nose—Warmth or coldness of nose is not an indicator of normal or abnormal temperature. Watch for runny nose or nose clogged with gummy mucus.

6. Coughing—Could indicate a cold, sore throat, something stuck in the throat, beginnings of distemper-type disease, or irritation from worms migrating to the lungs.

7. Gums and tongue—Ought to be a healthy pink. Watch for pale, bluish or even bright red colors.

8. Vomiting—All dogs vomit occasionally, sometimes just to reject food or as an expression of mild upset. If vomiting is continuous or chronic, however, or associated with blood, pain, disorientation, apathy, trembling, weakness or shallow breathing, it becomes serious.

9. Stool—The color and consistency will vary some with diet. Color may vary from light tan to dark brown. Reddish colors are obtained with some commercial dog foods. Black colors come from a lot of horse meat or iron in the diet. Normal consistency should be firm but not hard, although sudden changes in diet will cause mild diarrhea. Watch for marked changes in color or consistency without a change in diet. Chronically loose, watery or bloody stools indicate trouble. Bleeding in stomach or upper intestine causes a black or tarry stool; bleeding from lower intestine or rectum causes bright red blood in the stool. Orange to yellow stools may be an indication of infectious diseases.

10. Urine—Watch for marked change in color from light to dark, with strong odor, or blood.

11. Appetite—Dogs, like people, are hungrier sometimes than others, but lagging appetite over a period of time is one of the best symptoms of trouble.

12. Scratching, biting—Indicate possible external parasites, or, if aimed at a particular spot, may indicate pain in that area.

13. Temperature—Normal temperature is 101.7°. Puppies tend to run a little higher on the average (102.5° for some puppies would be considered normal). Temperatures vary some from pup to pup, season to season, and with time of day, but if the temperature gets to 103° or higher, even in a pup, begin to suspect trouble. A temperature of 106° indicates a very serious condition and requires prompt action. Temperature should be taken with a rectal thermometer.

14. Obvious symptoms like local pain, convulsions, and others are self-evident indicators of trouble.

Actually any one symptom may indicate only a mild disorder, but it may indicate something more serious; therefore, be alert for other symptoms and don't hesitate to call your vet.

EXTERNAL PARASITES

The most commonly found external parasites include fleas, lice, ticks, ear mites, sarcoptic mite (mange mite) and demodectic or follicular mite (also a mange mite).

Fleas can be an annoyance both to the dog and his owner, particularly if the fleas get into carpets and furniture in the house. Fleas bite and inject toxins that irritate the skin and cause summer eczema. They can be easily killed on the dog with ordinary antiseptics such as 1.25% Lysol (3 tablespoons to 1 gallon water), 1.25% Creolin, and 1.25% soluble pine oil, or antiseptic soaps. Various flea powders containing rotenone, DDT or benzene hexachloride are safe when used according to directions. Sevin Dust is effective against fleas and ticks.

But after the dog is free of fleas, the life cycle of the fleas must be broken by removing eggs and fleas from bedding and other areas where the dog stays. This can be done by thoroughly cleaning and vacuuming after liberally sprinkling with flea powder. Fleas will hatch out in one's own house in the absence of your dog, so adult fleas and their eggs must be killed and removed. After de-fleaing the dog, quarters and house, let the dog in his quarters again to attract spare fleas that remain; deflea him and everything else again, and remove powder and fleas from his quarters and from your own house with the vacuum. Sometimes a good insecticide that is harmless to animals will help to kill fleas or their eggs in or around his quarters or in your own house.

Lice are of two kinds: biting and sucking. Biting lice are light brown, move about and eat skin scales, causing itching, scratching and thickening of the skin. Eggs may drop off onto the ground or dog's bed and cause re-infestation. Antiseptic baths and powders ought to be repeated weekly.

The blue-colored, blood-filled sucking louse feeds on the dog by burrowing into the skin and sucking blood, causing itching, anemia and even death. Lice are killed by antiseptics, but the nits or minute white eggs, attached to the hairs, resist antiseptics so must be killed with pyrethrin solutions. Vinegar will detach nits from the hairs.

Wood ticks which attach themselves deeply in the skin must be anesthetized or killed before removal to prevent leaving a sore. Newer powders, such as Sevin Dust, are effective in removing ticks.

Ear mites cause a dog to shake or scratch his ears, and always leave a brown residue inside the ear. The mites can be seen by the vet with his special lighted magnifier and ought to be treated with special oil drops over a period of weeks until the life cycle is broken.

Both sarcoptic and demodectic or follicular mites, which cause mange, are hard to diagnose and treat. The sarcoptic mite is microscopic and burrows into the skin, causing red pin-point nodules or spots, thickening of the skin, severe itching, scales and scabs. The skin condition will spread from one part of the dog to another and from one dog to another. Diagnosis is made by microscopic examinations of skin scrapings from infected areas. Treatment should be recommended by a vet.

Demodectic or follicular (red) mange mites are microscopic and live in the hair roots, follicles and in the skin. The disease is characterized by loss of hair (permanently in advanced cases), reddening and thickening of the skin, and development of pustules. Vigorous treatment should be undertaken under the direction of a vet. Wherever pustulation occurs, no new hair grows back, but over 90 percent of early cases can be treated so areas again grow hair. Early treatment is therefore important. Some dogs have a constitutional weakness for mange and can never be cured.

INTERNAL PARASITES

The most commonly found internal parasites include: roundworms, tapeworms, whipworms, hookworms, heartworms and coccidia. Of all these worms, roundworms are the most common and the most easily treated. A positive diagnosis is made by finding adult worms in the dog's feces or by examining a feces solution under a microscope to find eggs which show up as round discs with a rim around the outside. The adult worms which live in the stomach and intestines are long and rounded, much the shape of spaghetti. Treatment is with Piperazine compounds given orally, repeated at intervals of two to three weeks (if needed) under a veterinarian's direction. Reinfestation comes by way of the mouth by the dog eating fecal matter or any foreign matter contaminated with infective eggs from the ground. After being swallowed, the eggs hatch into larvae, which burrow through the bowel wall and get into the blood stream. From there they circulate to the vital organs, particularly the lungs, where they reach an air sac, are coughed up, swallowed and hatch out as adults in the stomach and intestines. There they mate and lay eggs which pass out to the ground to start the cycle over again.

Other symptoms of roundworms are: distended abdomen with leanness or emaciation in other areas, loss of appetite, dull, shaggy coat, pale gums and mucous membranes, chronic digestive disturbance with diarrhea, constipation or vomiting, or a hacking croupous cough.

Tapeworms are collections of flat, white worm segments joined together, each segment capable of movement and life independent of the total worm. When fertilized, the mature segments, located at the rear of the worm, drop off, are ingested by an intermediate host such as fleas or lice, and, after development, become infective for the dog. A dog with tapeworms usually has a voracious appetite, but remains thin with a poor coat; he seldom is anemic or has constant diarrhea. Diagnosis is made by seeing white, live, mobile segments in the stool, or dried up, brownish, rice-grain segments attached to the hair of the buttocks, or tapeworm eggs in a fecal sample (under a microscope).

Whipworms are slender, hairlike worms with a thick hind part. Infestation is through direct ingestion of the eggs or larvae, which reach the dog's appendix, or caecum, where they become adult. Symptoms of whipworms are chronic, profuse, watery diarrhea, general emaciation and nervousness. Most positive diagnosis is finding whipworm eggs in a fecal sample under microscopic examination.

Hookworms are small, gray to reddish parasites about a half inch in length, which puncture the linings of the stomach or intestines to suck blood. Since the worm injects a substance into the wound which prevents blood coagulation, the dog may lose a lot of blood, develop severe anemia and iron depletion, and eventually die. Symptoms are anemia, pale mucous membranes, weakness, stunted growth, dull, harsh coat, bloody mucous-filled stool or black, tarry stool. A positive diagnosis is made microscopically by finding hookworm eggs in a stool sample. If the ground of the dog run is kept dry, and treated with common salt, the larvae die and reinfestation may be controlled. The dog is treated with special worm medicine; in severe cases he may need a blood transfusion, liver injection, or iron tonics.

Heartworms are the most commonly encountered blood and circulatory organ parasites in the United States. All sections of the country have the parasites, but they are much more frequently found in the South. The mature worm is white, threadlike and from 6 to 10 inches long. The normal habitat is the right ventricle of the heart, but the worm may be found in the large lung arteries or the posterior vena cava. An infestation of larvae comes by a bite from an infected mosquito or flea. Eight to ten months are required before mature worms appear in the heart. A positive diagnosis is made by microscopic examination of the blood to find microfilariae.

No specific symptoms always occur. Heavily infected hunting dogs sometimes exhibit minor or no symptoms. Sometimes, however, the dog tires easily, hesitates to exercise, shows lameness, a cough, chronic and dry eczema with loss of hair, anemia, stiffness of limbs or a stiff, arched back (indicating a kidney inflammation). Regular blood examinations ought to be routine in areas where heartworm disease is active. Treatment with new drugs destroys both the larvae and the mature worm but requires careful examination prior to and after treatment, so the dog is usually hospitalized. Heartworm infestation can be prevented by daily doses of medicine designed for that purpose.

Coccidia are bacterial organisms which invade the intestines, causing diarrhea, with watery, bloody, mucous-filled stools. Severe infections are very dangerous, especially to young puppies, and can cause death. Other symptoms are a slight cough, discharges from the eyes and nose, emaciation, dehydration, fever, loss of appetite and unthriftiness. Diagnosis of coccidiosis can be made by a microscopic examination of a stool specimen. Treatment must be handled by a vet who administers sulfa drugs and/or antibiotics.

Many types of worm medicine are sold. Some, such as Tri-worm Capsules (for roundworms, tapeworms and hookworms), require some fasting before administration. Others require complete fasting for twenty-four hours prior to ingestion, or a puppy might die from the worm medicine. Therefore, follow fasting instructions to the letter. It is best to worm your dog only under the directions of a veterinarian.

DISTEMPER

Distemper is the most serious virus disease of young dogs. It is highly contagious, with the fever reaction usually beginning on the fourth day following exposure. The virus is transmitted airborne, or by direct contact with an infected dog or his secretions. Onset of the disease is accompanied by watery discharge from the eyes and nose, loss of appetite, fever, and lassitude. Initial temperature may rise to 105°F or more, last about two days, followed by two or three days of nearly normal temperature, followed by a secondary temperature rise for several weeks. The dog feels terrible, is very depressed, vomits, develops severe diarrhea, often mixed with mucous and blood; pneumonia may occur; skin eruptions or nervous symptoms may appear. Dogs that develop muscular spasms or seizures may be damaged for life. The death rate averages about 50 percent. The best treatment is prevention through the administration of distemper vaccine.

Modified live vaccines of ferret origin (originally known as the Green Distemperoid vaccine) require a single injection, and generally cause a reaction about the fifth day. Modified avianized distemper vaccine which has been cultured on embryonating chicken eggs requires a single injection without noticeable physical reactions and ordinarily requires no booster vaccinations.

It must be remembered, however, that better immunity is obtained on strong, healthy, well-nourished dogs free from parasites, and of two months or more of age. Pups vaccinated earlier ought to be revaccinated after three months of age. Dogs vaccinated only with killed vaccines generally require three injections, periodic booster vaccines, and usually do not develop permanent immunity until exposed to a live street virus.

HEPATITIS

Infectious canine hepatitis is a virus disease, almost universally distributed, but most often picked up in congested areas through direct contact, or contact with the urine, feces, saliva or nasal discharges of an infected dog. While found in dogs of all ages, it is most common in dogs under a year and a half. Contaminated areas can be disinfected with soap and water followed by a diluted bleach solution, such as Clorox.

Symptoms vary somewhat, but usually there is a rapid onset of symptoms: listlessness, loss of appetite, intense thirst, initial high temperature rise (104° to 106°F), followed by a dropping off and even a subnormal temperature, labored, shallow breathing, depressed pulse, depression or coma, toxic, bluish mucous membranes, opacity of the cornea of one or both eyes, low white blood cell count, soreness around abdominal region, swollen liver, and humped appearance, rapid loss of weight, vomiting of yellowish liquid, tarry stool, and enlarged, inflamed tonsils. Mortality averages 10 to 25 percent, death occurs in several days, or the dog recovers within two days to two weeks. One attack gives solid immunity, but immune dogs may still spread the virus.

The best treatment is prevention through administration of anti-infectious hepatitis serum to young puppies (immunization lasts two weeks) and Canine Infectious Hepatitis Vaccine to older puppies and dogs. Generally the serum and vaccines are combined and administered with distemper serums and vaccines.

LEPTOSPIROSIS

Canine leptospirosis is a kidney disease caused by organisms known as spirochetes. Transmission comes through contact with the urine or excretions of an infected dog or of rats. Symptoms include change in color of urine to deep yellow or orange, chronic vomiting, muscular stiffness and pain, marked dehydration and thirst, and congested and/or jaundiced eye and mouth membranes. Penicillin will kill the organism in the bloodstream but leaves them active in other parts of the body, making an active carrier of a cured dog. The best protection is through vaccine which gives protection from only six months to a year, so must be repeated.

RABIES

Rabies is a viral disease transmitted by a bite (or injection of saliva) from an infected animal. It is nearly always fatal to humans as well as animals, once the disease develops, but only 30 to 50 percent of dogs bitten by rabid animals eventually develop the disease. The virus attacks the nervous system, causing nervous excitement (such as the desire to bite any object in sight), increased irritability, avoidance of noise and light, staring eyes and dilated pupils, refusal of favorite foods, inability to drink, a change in voice due to paralysis of the vocal cords and throat, excessive salivation (foam around the jaws), high temperature, increased urination, diabetes, increasing depression, spreading paralysis, convulsions and finally death. A human bitten by a rabid dog ought to bleed the wound thoroughly and then cleanse it immediately and thoroughly with a strong tincture of green soap solution, strong vinegar or absolute alcohol. To prevent the disease all dogs ought to be vaccinated after six months of age. Brain tissue vaccine provides protection for two years, avianized vaccine for thirty-nine months.

OTHER DISEASES

Dogs are also subject to other diseases such as various respiratory diseases (colds, pneumonia), hard pad, tonsillitis and others. Dogs may also develop tumors, hernias, prolapse of the rectum, and other problems which require special veterinary care.

HIP DYSPLASIA

Congenital hip dysplasia is a specific hereditary disease characterized by a dislocation of the hip joint, with malformation of the socket of the hipbone and the ball or head of the thigh bone. The weakness is associated with a lack of pelvic muscle mass and is most common in the larger breeds of dogs. Incidence of the malformation may run as high as 70 percent in some breeds of dogs, such as the Chesapeake Bay Retriever, Labrador Retriever, Golden Retriever, English Setter, Gordon Setter and Weimaraner, and to a lesser extent the Springer Spaniel and Foxhound.

Clinical, morphological and radiographic signs of congenital hip dysplasia are not present at birth and dysplastic changes do not become radiographically detectable until the affected pups are at least eight to sixteen weeks of age. In some instances the dog may be close to a year old before a positive diagnosis can be made radiographically. The disease is present about equally in both sexes.

Evidence is lacking that the disease is traceable to or limited to any particular family or strain within a breed. The occurrence is influenced, however, by a number of traits associated with (a) lack of inherited pelvic muscle mass, and (b) early rapid growth and weight gain. Therefore, heredity plays an important part and it has been shown that litters from sires and dams with normal hip joints have less dysplasia than dogs from litters of affected parents. All parents used for breeding purposes should be shown to be free of the disease. Also, since puppies which are heavier than average at sixty days of age have a higher incidence of the disorder, some buyers prefer to avoid very large puppies.

The only positive way to diagnose the disease is through hip X-ray examination. Some dogs with the disease seem to walk, work and perform almost normally, but such dogs usually have a lower tolerance for exercise and experience greater fatigue than do those with normal hip joints. Some dogs may endure two to seven years of hard work before performance is subnormal. Many dogs kept as pets will perform soundly throughout life, yet have some hip malformation.

The only way to eliminate the problem is through careful breeding programs. Mature hunting dogs that are only mildly affected may prove very valuable as working dogs, but such should not be used in breeding.

ACCIDENTS

Dogs that are hunted are exposed to a variety of wounds, punctures, fractures, and to snake bites. Any dog may be accidentally burned or poisoned.

Puppies especially may swallow foreign objects which catch in the mouth, stomach or intestines.

Any wounded animal should be muzzled with a cord, necktie or handkerchief (to prevent his biting) before he is moved. Bleeding should be controlled with a clean pressure bandage. Dogs with fractures should be moved carefully to avoid further injury. Shock is treated with application of heat or by covering the dog. A dog suffering burns may have to be treated for shock. Five percent tannic acid solution or crude cod liver oil may be applied if the burns are not too severe. Burns from acids may be neutralized with diluted ammonia or bicarbonate of soda.

Emergency treatment for poisoning consists of induced vomiting with simple emetics such as powdered mustard made into a paste, soap suds or washing soda. In cases of collapse administer stimulants such as hot strong coffee or tea.

If a dog gets foreign objects such as bones, sticks, pieces of metal, pins or needles stuck in his mouth or throat, sometimes they may be removed by the owner with his hands or pliers. If they cannot, or if the dog swallows the object, immediate veterinary care is needed.

Dogs bitten by poisonous snakes quickly show swelling around the bite, followed by vomiting, convulsions, weak pulse, difficult breathing, collapse and, perhaps, death. Emergency treatment consists of applying a tourniquet between the bite and the heart and incising the wound and expelling as much blood as possible. The tourniquet ought to be released every thirty minutes to prevent gangrene, and the dog should be rushed to a vet where serum and other aid is administered.

In all cases of accident the best treatment can be given by a qualified vet, but some emergency care by the owner may save the dog's life.

SKIN AND COAT CARE

The best way to insure a healthy skin and coat is to give your dog an adequate diet (proper vitamins and enough fat helps to maintain a shiny coat) and keep him free from parasites and disease. In addition to doing these things, however, give him a regular combing with a hard rubber curry comb and a good brushing with a stiff brush. If your dog picks up burrs or other objects in his hair, these should be combed out. Matted, snarled hair can be combed and brushed smoothly in place. If your dog returns from hunting all muddy and wet, wipe him clean with a damp towel, then dry him with another towel and brush him thoroughly before leaving him in the kennel. In warm weather take him swimming regularly in your favorite lake or stream and he will stay remarkably clean and odor-free. If he is kept in the house, an occasional bath may be necessary, especially when outside weather prevents a dip in the lake. Generally, however, wiping and brushing him clean is all that is needed. Certainly he should never be left dirty and wet in the outside kennel, no matter how rugged you think he is. Keeping him clean and dry is little enough payment to him after a hard day's hunt.

FOOT CARE

Hunting dogs are especially susceptible to puncture wounds, cuts, thorns and abrasion of the pads and feet. Even a small puncture or laceration, once infected, can put your dog out of commission for a good part of the hunting season, so the feet ought to be regularly inspected and immediate attention given to any sore spots. Hydrogen peroxide can be used to cleanse wounds, antiseptic dusting powder is good for abrasions, lanolin helps to soften dry, cracked pads. Antibiotics or sulfa drugs may be prescribed by your vet to fight infection. Sometimes a tetanus shot is given when there has been a puncture wound. A dog with a sore foot ought to be kept in a dry, clean, restricted area until the foot heals.

Additional suggestions for foot care include the following:

1. Keep your dog's feet in tough working order through regular exercise, especially before the hunting season.

2. Toenails that become too long ought to be trimmed carefully, making certain not to cut too short and into the soft, sensitive quick. Generally the quick is darker in color on white nails and can be seen through the nail. On black nails, trim carefully a little at a time; usually only the sharp, slender hook part that grows out and downward from the larger part of the nail should be cut. Nails may also be filed smooth.

3. Dewclaws, if removed at all, are best removed from pups at three to five days of age. To remove them on older dogs requires surgery. If present, the nail should be kept clipped to prevent growing into the leg. Occasionally, a dog with dewclaws will snag one on a piece of brush tearing the appendage partially from the leg. For this reason, we like to remove dewclaws on all working dogs.

EYE AND EAR CARE

The eyes of hunting dogs are constantly subject to bombardment from dust, dirt, weeds, grass, brush and even sticks. Dirt and debris ought to be removed with a bit of dry, clean tissue or cotton. Clean water is the best material for washing eyes, although boric acid in maximum strengths of no more than 5 percent may be used cautiously as recommended by your vet. Special drops are also sometimes prescribed, but, as a general rule, don't bathe your dog's eyes regularly with anything unless prescribed. The more you leave his eyes alone when attention is not needed, the better off they will be.

Congenital defects of the eyelids or eyelashes, tumors, cysts, wounds, infections, diseases and injuries of the eye require professional care.

The ears ought to be kept clean at all times. Burrs, sharp weed awns or other foreign matter should be removed from the hair of the outer ear. Dirt or other debris inside the ear should never be removed with hairpins or match sticks; there is great danger of infections or of puncturing the drum. The best procedure is to let your vet clean the ears with a piece of cotton soaked with mineral oil. Similarly, waxy accumulations in the ear canal can be softened by a few drops of mineral or special oil, the ears gently massaged and the debris which is worked to the surface removed with clean cotton. Also, a coating of mineral oil in the ear canal will suffocate any mites that might be present.

If you find your dog shaking his head, or in other ways fussing with his ears, take him to a vet. Insect bites, inflammation from dirt, scratches or wounds, open sores, ulcers on the edge of the ear, eczema, ear mites, blood-tinged discharges or other troubles usually require a doctor's attention. Failure to pay strict attention to ear troubles may impair your dog's hearing. Your function is to be alert for problems and then to get medical advice and treatment.

TEETH CARE

Dogs, like humans, are subject to tooth trouble: broken crowns or tips, pyorrhea, loosened teeth and other problems, but rarely decay. Consequently, teeth sometimes have to be filled, extracted or treated to prevent pain, disease or blood poisoning.

The average puppy gets his teeth on the following schedule:

Canines (fangs) erupt at 3 to 4 weeks, replaced by permanents at 5 to 6 months.

Incisors (front teeth) erupt at 4 to 5 weeks, replaced by permanents at 4 to 5 months.

Premolars erupt at 3 to 5 weeks, replaced at 5 or 6 months.

First molars erupt at 4 to 5 months, second molars at 5 to 6 months, third molars at 6 to 7 months.

A normal complement of teeth is forty-two; some dogs develop two to four extra teeth to the rear of the last molars. If baby teeth are not shed in time they may cause misalignment of permanent teeth. Removal of stubborn baby teeth that do not fall out at the right time may sometimes be the best prevention.

During pregnancy and nursing, bitches ought to be given vitamin and mineral supplements to the most nourishing food available, to insure keeping their teeth and the puppies' teeth healthy.

9

Heredity and Breeding

PRINCIPLES OF INHERITANCE

The characteristics of any puppy are inherited from his parents: half from the sire and half from the dam. The inheritable factors themselves, called genes, cannot be seen even with the highest magnification, but are always present in pairs in larger bodies called chromosomes, which lie within the nucleus of every cell in the dog's body. Each cell in the dog's body contains 78 chromosomes, arranged as 39 pairs, except the sex cells which contain 39 unpaired chromosomes. At the time of conception, therefore, when a sperm cell fuses with an egg cell, the 39 chromosomes in the sperm cell come together with the 39 chromosomes in the egg cell to form the fertilized cell which grows into an embryo. Each time the fertilized cell divides, the chromosomes divide. Therefore, each cell carries with it the 39 pairs of chromosomes, half of each pair inherited from each parent.

There are countless possible combinations, however. There may be 2^{39} or 549,837,733,888 combinations of chromosomes theoretically possible. In addition, each chromosome contains combinations of genes and the genes are sometimes exchanged between the two partner chromosomes in each pair, so that in reality it is possible for still more combination products to occur. It is no wonder that it is almost impossible to find two brothers or two sisters who are identical.

SEX DETERMINATION

The chromosomes also determine sex. One of the 78 pairs of chromosomes of the body cells, the so-called sex-chromosome pair, has different partners, designated X and Y by geneticists. The male has one X and one Y chromosome while the female has two X chromosomes. Thus, the body cells of the male have 76+X+Y chromosomes, the female 76+X+X.

The sex cells are also differently equipped. The female's egg cells always contain 38+X but half of the male's sperm contain 38+X and the other half 38+Y. Whether a given fertilization results in the birth of male or female pups is just chance and depends upon whether the eggs are fertilized by a 38+X or a 38+Y sperm. It is the male, then, which determines sex.

The following combinations take place in fertilization:

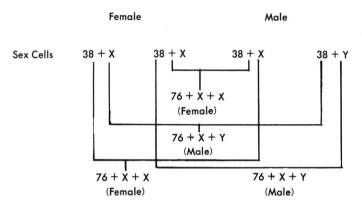

Offspring; 2 males and 2 females

Theoretically, over a period of time half females and half males would be born. In reality about 10 percent more male pups are born than female, indicating that there must either be 10 percent more 38+Y sperm than 38+X sperm or else 10 percent more of the 38+Y sperm fertilize eggs. This is nature's way of keeping equality of the sexes, however, since the chances of survival of the male embryos are less.

DOMINANT-RECESSIVE TRAITS

It is a well-known fact in breeding that some inheritable traits seem to be dominant over others. In Irish Setters, for example, true red coat color is dominant over those with blackish tinge. In Labrador Retrievers the black coat color is dominant over yellow or chocolate. In Pointers white mottling (white distributed over large areas of the body and limbs) is recessive to self-color (all one color or a white spot on the chest or on one or more paws).

Inheritable factors, or genes, always exist in pairs. In some cases, however, both of the paired genes are exactly alike so are called homozygous. In other cases the paired genes are unlike, so are called heterozygous.

In designating dominant-recessive traits, those genes which are dominant are given a capital letter; those which are recessive are given a small letter. Homozygous genes would both have either capital letters or both small letters. Heterozygous genes would have a capital letter and a small letter. This can be illustrated in the case of coat color for Labrador Retrievers.

Let: B represent dominant gene for black coat.
b represent recessive gene for yellow coat or chocolate coat.
BB—Black Lab is able to produce only black Labs, regardless of mating. Homozygous genes.
Bb—Black Lab with heterozygous genes is able to produce only black pup-

pies when crossed with a BB. Can produce $\frac{1}{4}$ yellow or $\frac{1}{4}$ chocolate when crossed with a black Lab with heterozygous genes (Bb). Can produce $\frac{1}{2}$ yellow or $\frac{1}{2}$ chocolate if crossed with a yellow or chocolate (bb).

Thus:

BB × BB = All BB puppies, black.
BB × Bb = Two BB puppies, 2 Bb puppies, but still black.
BB × bb = Two Bb puppies, 2 bB puppies, but still black.
Bb × Bb = One BB puppy, 1 bB, 1 Bb, all are black.
One bb puppy. May be either yellow or chocolate, depending upon whether b gene is for yellow or chocolate.
Bb × bb = Two Bb puppies, black. Two bb puppies, yellow or chocolate.
bb × bb = Four bb puppies, either all yellow or all chocolate, depending upon whether parents are yellow or chocolate.

By looking at a black Lab one cannot tell if he possesses homozygous or heterozygous genes for coat color. This can be discovered by mating to a yellow or chocolate Lab (either of which obviously possesses homozygous genes), or to another black Lab known to have heterozygous genes for coat color.

The important point to remember is that a recessive gene in a heterozygous condition may be carried unnoticed for generations, because it is masked by the dominant gene of the pair. Furthermore, most parents are heterozygous for many genes, unless they are inbred for several generations to develop homozygous strains.

The examples given are applied only to coat color for Labs. Predicting coat colors for setters, pointers and other breeds with mottled colors becomes very complicated indeed. And trying to predict temperament, body conformation and hunting ability as evidenced through various traits is extremely difficult because of the millions of combinations possible and because only a few inheritable traits have been isolated enough to be studied to the point where prediction is possible.

The prospective breeder or buyer, therefore, cannot be absolutely certain that he will get a good hunting or field-trial dog, even from a mating of National Field Trial Champions, although such breeding is certainly more certain than less desirable parentage. Each pup inherits half of the traits of the sire and dam in any mating, but whether each pup gets the "good" half is not always certain. Sometimes one gets a real dud, even from the best of breeding.

Some sires and dams, however, seem to have the ability to impress, with consistency, their good characteristics upon their offspring. This ability is known as prepotency and is why some stud dogs consistently sire Field Trial Champions, while others, equally good themselves, never seem to, regardless of the dam to which they are mated. Similarly, some dams consistently whelp outstanding dogs, while others never do. This is why the sire and dam must be selected with extreme care, not only by a thorough study of the pedigree and ancestral background, but by a study of the offspring from previous matings, if such exists. Prepotency is not transmittable from parent to offspring, but is more common to intensely inbred lines where there is a high degree of homozygosity, or where the desired characteristics are dominant.

SYSTEMS OF BREEDING

Inbreeding is breeding closely related individuals to develop dogs with homozygous genes who will transmit their outstanding characteristics to their offspring. Inbreeding varies in intensity depending upon the closeness of the relationship and the number of generations it is carried out. The following examples show the blood fractions produced through inbreeding relatives. The examples are listed in order of decreasing intensity of the relationship.

	Percentage of Blood
Full brother to full sister	100%
Parent to offspring	75%
Aunt or uncle to blood related niece or nephew	75%
Grandparent to grandchild	62.5%
Half brother to half sister (For example, same sire but different dam)	50%
First cousins	50%

While inbreeding may result in fixing certain desired characteristics in a strain, it also brings out many recessive genes which may be undesirable, and so may lead to the degeneration of the breed, especially if carried on for several generations. Degeneration shows up as a decline in vitality, decrease in size, extreme nervousness, reduced fertility, abnormal individuals or birth of some dead puppies. Any breeder who starts a program of inbreeding, therefore, must be willing to destroy inferior animals and to breed only the most promising, robust individuals. Generally it is unwise for any but the most experienced, knowledgeable breeder of hunting dogs to produce puppies with more than 50 percent blood of any individual (for example, half brothers and sisters or first cousins). Even breeding this closely may occasionally result in problems.

The following show examples of inbreeding over several generations that produce more than 50 percent blood from a certain individual (A).

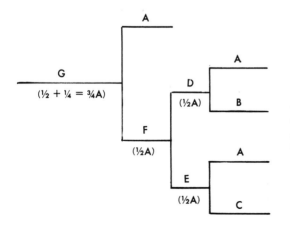

In this case, D & E (half brother and sister), produce F (maternal and paternal granddaughter of A) who was backcrossed to the grandsire (A) to produce G (¾A).

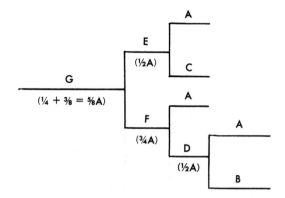

In this case, D was bred back to her sire (A) to produce F (both a daughter and granddaughter of A) who was then bred to E (son of A) to produce G (⅝A).

The next system of breeding is called linebreeding. It is a very popular breeding system and really only a modified, low-intensity inbreeding system. Its purpose is to keep all descendants of a line closely related to a desirable ancestor. In this system parents are used that are closely related to a desired ancestor, but are not related through any other ancestor to each other. Since the sire and dam are related through a common ancestor, some inbreeding does take place.

The following is an example of low-intensity line breeding.

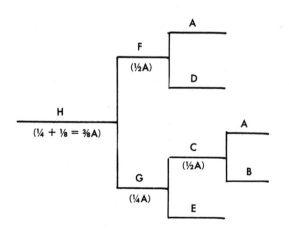

In this example it is assumed that B, D, & E are not related through a common ancestor to each other or to A. F (son of A) is bred to G (granddaughter of A) to produce H (⅜A).

The diagram on the next page illustrates higher-intensity line breeding.

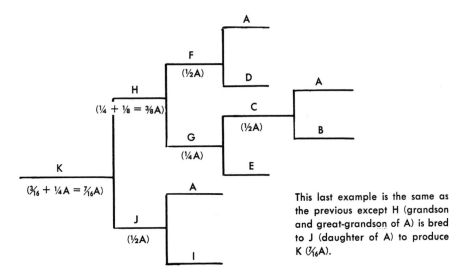

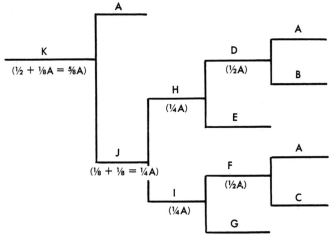

This last example is the same as the previous except H (grandson and great-grandson of A) is bred to J (daughter of A) to produce K ($\frac{7}{16}$A).

Sometimes inbreeding and line breeding can be combined to produce a fairly high-intensity breeding yet without so much risk of degeneration. The following is an example of moderately close breeding that combines the best features of both line and inbreeding.

In this example H (grandson of A) is bred to I (granddaughter of A) to produce J (paternal and maternal great-granddaughter of A) who is then backcrossed to A to produce K ($\frac{5}{8}$A).

The last system of breeding to be discussed here is outcrossing. In this system the parents are unrelated and so of different families within the same breed. This system can be used successfully if these parents and their ancestors have shown themselves to be exceptional hunting dogs or Field Trial Champions. While this system produces heterozygous genes, undesirable characteristics are eliminated by breeding only to the best individuals generation after generation. This is the system we are now using in breeding Labrador Retrievers and many of our puppies are exceptional retrievers.

The following would be a perfect outcross breeding if such could be accomplished.

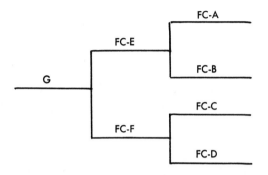

In this case FC represents a field of champions. All of the parents and grandparents are Field Trial Champions yet unrelated by blood. Theoretically then G would possess the full heredity of Field Trial Champions.

The following illustrates good outcross breeding because so many Field Trial Champions are in the bloodlines.

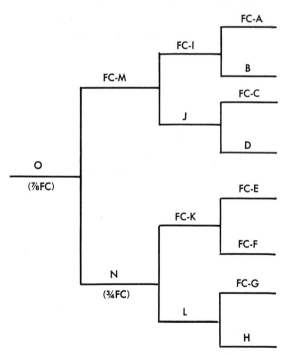

In this example M is the third generation of Field Trial Champions. N (while not a Field Trial Champion herself) has ½ the heredity of FC-K plus ¼ the heredity of FC-G or ¾ the heredity of Field Trial Champions. Theoretically then O would have ½ + ⅜ or ⅞ the heredity of Field Trial Champions.

One real problem with the above examples is that it is practically impossible to find both sire and dams with this many Field Trial Champions in the bloodlines. Another problem is that even by breeding to Field Trial Champions, sometimes undesirable traits of those champions may be inherited rather than the good ones. But by always selecting only the best individuals over several generations, the possibility is minimized. The serious breeder should not overlook this system of breeding as it produces many fine dogs.

The following show the pedigree of two recent National Field Trial Champion Labrador Retrievers. Both cases are outcrosses, but with a maximum of Field Trial Champions in the bloodlines for several generations.

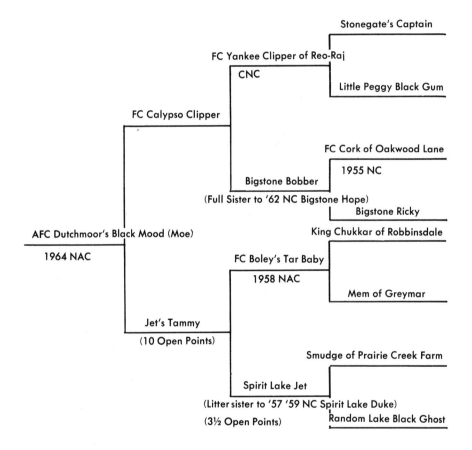

In Moe's pedigree his sire, paternal and maternal grandsires were Field Trial Champions. His paternal granddam was a full sister to a National Champion. His dam was a field-trial dog who had enough points to be a Field Trial Champion but who never won a first place, which is also required for a championship. No dogs are closely related on either side of the line, a full outcross breeding.

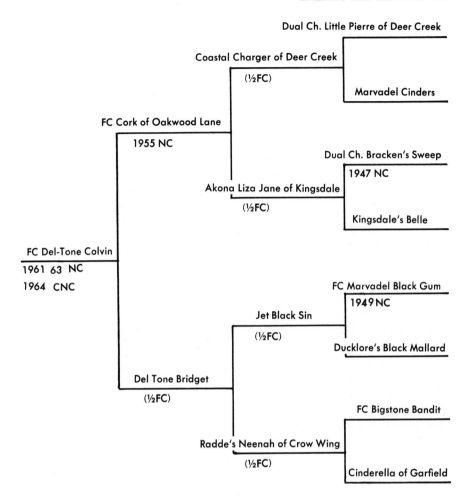

In the above pedigree of Del-Tone Colvin, every sire in the 4th generation back was a Field Trial Champion. There weren't any Field Trial Champions in the 3rd generation back, but each of these inherited half the characteristics of Field Trial Champions. Cork of Oakwood Lane was an outstanding Field Trial Champion and stud dog with prepotency, the ability to impress his characteristics upon his offspring. He was known for siring outstanding field-trial dogs. The only dogs at all closely related on both sides of the line are Black Mallard, who is a daughter of Little Pierre of Deer Creek. But Colvin inherits only $\frac{3}{16}$ of the blood of Little Pierre, really too small a fraction for this to be considered line breeding.

10

Mating, Whelping, and Raising a Litter

THE MECHANICS OF MATING

Assuming that you have selected the stud dog and the bitch, when should the mating take place? The average bitch comes into heat twice a year. The progress of the heat period is as follows:

1st day: Discharge of bright red blood begins.

5th to 8th day: Discharge gradually changes to light pink or straw color, accompanied by a marked swelling of the vulva.

9th to 14th day: Bitch becomes playful, interested in males, then eager to accept males for copulation. Ovulation usually takes place from about the 10th to the 13th day, which is usually the best time for mating. Usually the later in the period mating occurs, the more eggs are present and the larger the litter.

16th day: Bitch begins to reject males, conception may still be possible.

The 17th to 21st day: Bitch vicious, snapping at males to drive them away. By the 20th day conception is usually impossible.

The above schedule is average, it may be off by two or three days for your bitch, so you ought to guard her carefully during the full period to prevent unwanted conception.

Generally it is best to put the bitch with the stud for awhile, since some dogs require a short time to get used to one another. If the bitch or stud is inexperienced, it is best to supervise the breeding to prevent either dog from biting or scaring the other. If ovulation has taken place, the bitch will usually stand by herself with the vulva drawn up and her tail to one side. If the stud is aggressive, he is usually able to climb on, begin pumping and insert the penis without difficulty. Sometimes an inexperienced bitch will have to be held. An inexperienced stud ought to be protected from being bitten or scared by the female. Some handlers prefer to muzzle the bitch. If the stud has trouble making connection, even after vigorous pumping, the bitch might be shifted to a position up or down hill to get a better angle, or the bitch's tail drawn aside, or the vulva tipped up slightly with the fingers.

Once a tie has been accomplished, the male will pump for awhile, then stand relatively still during ejaculation. It is necessary for the male to be tied to the female while the sperm are "manufactured" and semen ejected from the testes into the bitch. This may take from several minutes to 15 or 30 minutes or longer. Actually, at the time he enters the female, the male has not yet achieved an erection. A bone in his penis enables him to copulate, but after entry erection begins and large swelling occurs on the posterior part of the penis. It is this swelling which keeps the male tied or locked to the bitch during the production and ejection of the semen. Unlike the human male, the male dog has no seminal vesicles and no sperm are stored ahead of time. It is best for the handler to hold the dogs still during the tie, permitting the male to slide one front leg over the back of the female and to stand by her during the tie. By keeping the dogs still, and preventing each from snapping at the other, possible injury or a premature parting may be prevented. Generally, the tie will be broken after ejaculation and as the erection gradually subsides. The handler ought to encourage the tie as long as possible to make sure ejaculation has occurred and to prevent undue and premature pulling.

After parting it is best to put the dogs in separate pens and then to repeat the breeding within 36 to 48 hours. The dogs ought to be mated at least twice, because if the male has not been used at stud for two weeks or more, the first breeding may produce only a few if any sperm. Also it is always possible that additional unfertilized ova are present which need to be fertilized to complete the conception of the whole litter.

WHELPING

A bitch will usually whelp between 58 to 64 days after conception. Actually, 60 to 62 days is the usual gestation period. During her pregnancy the bitch ought to be given regular exercise daily. Her ordinary high protein, high mineral diet ought to be supplemented with vitamins, minerals and extra protein. We have found that powdered milk added to the regular dry dog meal mix, plus some meat, plus vitamin-mineral pills pushed down her throat is more than adequate.

A whelping box of half-inch plywood, about 3 by 4 feet in size, with sides 10 inches high, works well. The best bedding is plenty of newspaper which the bitch will tear up to make a nest. The paper absorbs any embryonic fluids, blood or liquids during whelping, and can be changed so that a fresh bed is provided for the bitch and puppies. Hay, straw, shavings or cloth material gets messy and has to be changed anyhow. Besides, there is a greater chance for a puppy to get covered over and smothered.

It is important that whelping be planned in a moderately warm place (70° is adequate), not so much for the bitch, as for the puppies, which are born soaking wet and need a lot of warmth in the first two weeks or so of life. A severe chilling breaks down a puppy's resistance to bacterial infection. Also, the whelping spot ought to be private, yet accessible to you, but away from distracting noises, people and disturbances which tend to excite the bitch excessively, possibly causing her to step on or lie on a puppy, with possible injurious or fatal results.

As the 58th to 60th day approaches, there are several signs that whelping is approaching:

1. The bitch loses her appetite for food usually 12 hours before whelping.

2. Colostrum, then later milk, begins to fill the mother's breasts, and can be expressed by hand. This usually begins about a week before whelping.

3. Nest building becomes more pronounced.

4. The bitch's temperature drops from normal (100.5° to 102°) to 99°, then may go back up again for several days to 100° or even 101°, then drops again to 98° or 97°. When the temperature gets this low, whelping may be only a matter of hours or minutes.

5. Sometimes a bitch begins to act as though she has some pain near her rear, wincing, moving her head suddenly to lick the vulva. This may be a sign that labor has started.

Once labor begins, the bitch will hunch up and start to strain with each pain. If she is in labor for four hours or longer without results, call your vet. The bitch needs help. Sometimes a bag of water breaks; there is no trouble usually, since this often happens as the cervix dilates, but if a puppy does not emerge in an hour or two, call your vet.

Ordinarily, hunting bitches whelp very successfully and take care of everything themselves. As each pup emerges the bitch begins to lick it, chewing the cord in two, licking and eating the membrane that surrounds the puppy and then the afterbirth when it arrives. The bitch ought to lick each puppy until the mucus is away from the face and head and until the puppy begins to breathe and to cry. The bitch may roll it around very roughly, which is fine, and this starts the puppy breathing. She usually continues to clean it and the mess in the box until dry. Usually by the time one puppy is cleaned up, the next one may start to arrive. Occasionally several hours elapse between births, which is no cause for alarm, provided everything seems to be normal. Usually the best thing the owner can do is nothing. Let the bitch handle things herself. Just make sure she doesn't step on a puppy, or lie on one, while she is having another.

Certain situations, however, may call for veterinary help:

1. If the bitch is in labor four hours and doesn't whelp.

2. If the puppy is stuck in the birth canal. If the puppy's head is already out, but is stuck for a minute or longer, pull the membrane and mucus off the face to allow the puppy to breathe, provided the bitch doesn't do it herself. Don't pull the puppy; allow it to come out by itself. If it doesn't, call the vet. If he is not available, simply hold the pup after each spasm, preventing it from slipping back in the distance the mother has pushed it out. Never hold straight out, but in the direction of the bitch's hind feet. If the puppy is out three-quarters of the way, but the hind feet are stuck, you may use a little traction, never out, but in the direction of the bitch's hind feet.

If a puppy comes out backward and is stuck, with the hind feet and tail part of the way out, wait a minute before doing anything. If nothing happens, grasp the legs with a clean towel, handkerchief or newspaper, holding them, even bearing down a little, in the direction of the hind legs of the mother. If the pup is not pushed out, increase the traction gently. When the hips are out put your other hand around the hips and get the puppy out (but gently) as quickly as possible. If the cord is pinched the puppy will start to breathe while in the birth fluid and so may drown.

One warning, no matter where a puppy is stuck, never put your fingers in the mother's vagina; you may cause infection.

3. If a bitch does not voluntarily remove the membrane, or chew off the cord, you or your vet will have to remove the membrane by hand. (Do this first so the puppy can breathe.) To start the puppy breathing hold it upside down between a towel, shake it and rub it vigorously. If it still doesn't breathe, give artificial respiration by alternately pulling on the umbilical cord, then pressing on the chest, all the while with the puppy's head down. Every couple of minutes rub as before, then go back to the artificial respiration.

After the puppy is breathing, cut the cord a couple of inches from the navel. It is not necessary to tie it with thread unless it bleeds more than several drops of blood.

4. If all of the afterbirths, one for each puppy, do not come out, then call your vet. Ordinarily, each comes out with each pup. One may be separated from its umbilical cord and come out with the next pup. By the time labor ceases, however, all of the afterbirths should be out.

Ordinarily the emergency measures prescribed above never need be taken. Let nature and your bitch do it all if they will and can. If they don't, call your vet. If he is not available, the measures prescribed may save a puppy's life.

CARE OF THE LITTER

Soon after birth each pup will begin to nurse by itself. This nursing further stimulates contractions and speeds along the birth of subsequent pups. If a pup has trouble finding a nipple, put him to the breast, even putting a nipple to the mouth if necessary.

The bitch does all of the work for four weeks, nursing the pups, cleaning them and cleaning up their messes. All the owner has to do is keep them in a warm place, feed the bitch a good diet, including plenty of water, and occasionally change the bedding, since this keeps the ammonia odor to a minimum.

By four weeks or so, as the puppies get their baby teeth, the bitch begins to grow more impatient, and to drive them away. Then the owner must begin feeding the pups preparatory to weaning. Begin with warm milk, perhaps with a little meal mixed in. To teach the puppies to lap the milk, put their noses in it. After a time, they will begin lapping up the milk. We gradually increase the amount of meal in the milk as the puppies learn to eat. After they begin eating well, feed them three to four times daily. Ordinarily they can be completely weaned and taken from the bitch, usually by six weeks of age. Sometimes, also, you will have to supplement the milk by giving water in a shallow dish. We also give supplementary vitamins and minerals. By four months of age, you can cut down the feeding periods to twice a day, depending upon whether the pups continue to gain in weight and are getting enough nourishment.

At five to six weeks of age, take the pups to a vet to check them over, including a microscopic stool examination for parasites. The vet will also want to give temporary serum or Gamma Globulin for distemper, hepatitis and leptospirosis, repeated at two-week intervals until three months, at which time permanent vaccine is administered. If worms are discovered, worm the pups according to your vet's directions.

Any time after weaning, from six weeks on, the pups (if robust and healthy) can be sold and placed in the hands of their owners. Before delivering them, we generally move the pups to an outside, unheated kennel, sometimes at two to three weeks of age, depending upon the weather. We have a small, insulated dog house (with only a small door to cut down cold air entry) inside our kennel shed, and put plenty of straw in the house. Also, it is a good idea during very cold weather to put a canvas flap over the door of the house, provided the bitch will not tear it off. These measures insure that the body heat of the bitch and puppies will keep the dog house nice and warm. Puppies ought to be acclimated to cool climates gradually. Usually by eight weeks of age our puppies are going in and out of the shed to the outside run.

11

Training Fundamentals

How you get started with your dog will determine to a large extent your future success in training him. This sounds drastic, but it is true. You can either help or permanently ruin your chances of making your dog into a wonderful hunting companion during his first few months of life. It all depends upon the kind and quality of the relationship which you develop with him in the crucial period from about five to sixteen weeks of age. But let's start at the beginning.

In recent years a number of articles appeared describing the results of studies on dog training which were conducted at the Roscoe B. Jackson Laboratory in Bar Harbor, Maine. The director, Dr. J. P. Scott, and his associate geneticists, biologists, zoologists, anthropologists, physiologists, and psychologists have been making intensive studies for fifteen years to determine important influences in the training of dogs. Scott and his associates have come up with some conclusions which are all-important to you as a dog owner.

According to Scott's findings, there are 5 critical periods which occur in a pup's life before he reaches 16 weeks of age.

Period One: Birth to 3 weeks. During this period the young puppy is almost immune to outside influences. His eyes are closed for approximately 2 weeks; he is born deaf, and hears nothing at all for 3 weeks. His brain doesn't really begin to function much until the 21st day. He needs warmth, food, sleep and his mother, but is fairly immune to emotional shocks and disturbances.

Period Two: 3 to 4 weeks. His eyes have opened; the puppy is hearing, and his motor and sensory skills are developing. The puppy begins to explore and to respond to his outside world. This is the period when he needs the warmth and companionship of his mother. It is poor psychology and unwise nutritionally to take a puppy from his mother during this period.

Period Three: 4 to 7 weeks. This is the most crucial period in your puppy's life and the time when socialization with humans should begin. By the end of the period he should be weaned, separated from his mother and litter mates and put into the hands of his permanent owner. But most important, it is during this time that he should have daily, close, pleasant contact with people. Keep your puppy in close contact with you or other members of the family. He needs gentle fondling, playing and a lot of companionship.

In one experiment at the Jackson Laboratory, puppies were isolated in fenced fields with the bitch and taken out individually at various periods up to 14 weeks, played with by handlers and returned to isolation. The results showed that those who were socialized between 5 to 8 weeks of age developed the strongest attachment to man. Those who were not socialized until after 14 weeks never got over being timid and wild and were extremely difficult to train. It was found that many of the differences in temperament between dogs were developed during this crucial period.

This means that if you are buying a dog to raise and train yourself, you should get one between 5 and 8 weeks of age. The puppy can be older, but only if he has been given a lot of personal attention by the breeder to insure easier training later.

Period Four: 7 to 12 weeks. The rapport you have begun to establish with your puppy at an earlier age should be strengthened by close and friendly contact. This is the age to begin play training. Begin teaching simple obedience commands: "No," "Come," "Sit," "Down," "Stop that noise," "Charge," and so forth. Also, you can begin making trips into the field with your dog and to start training in retrieving. You should make the training sessions pleasant, short (about ten to fifteen minutes daily) and informal during this period, avoiding all firm or harsh discipline and making the training period fun and joyful.

This is the time to begin housebreaking your dog since he will begin wanting to avoid messing his quarters. Here also avoid harsh training methods at this early age.

Period Five: 12 to 16 weeks. This is the period to start serious training and to begin demanding that your dog obey commands. Any punishment should still be mild, but this is the time to establish who is boss. If this period has been preceded by intensive socialization and by pleasant play training, it should not be necessary to be very rough with your dog to establish discipline.

The important principle is this: Get your puppy young, establish a close relationship with him; begin training early and continue regularly, seldom interrupting the training or your socializing for protracted periods, and you will find that your dog is much easier to train and that he is a pleasant, loyal companion.

BASIC PRINCIPLES OF TRAINING

A good hunting dog has been carefully bred for generations for the proper characteristics and instincts. Thus, the urge to chase a thrown object is instinctive in most well-bred retrievers. Bird interest is bred into good pointing, retrieving and flushing dogs. Interest in a variety of fascinating animal scents is partly instinctive in well-bred trailers.

One purpose of training is to bring out and further develop the proper hunting instincts which drive the dog to locate birds or game. Thus, waving a retrieving dummy in front of a young retriever's nose and throwing the dummy a short distance away will further enhance the pup's natural desire to chase a thrown object. Or waving a bird wing at the end of a long pole and out of reach of a pointer pup further stimulates the dog's desire to chase after, or even to creep up on, a bird. Similarly, teasing a hound pup with a coon's tail or a piece of rabbit fur, and dragging the lure along in front of the dog, further stimulates a natural desire to follow a particular scent or animal.

But even though the desire to chase birds or animals is instinctive in well-bred bird or hound dogs, the control and refinement of this desire which are necessary in hunting are not instinctive. They must be taught.

For example, even though a good retriever pup has an instinctive drive to chase a thrown dummy or bird, the desire to return the bird to you or to hold it gently without chewing it is not instinctive. Although some pups retrieve to hand much more readily than others, these things must be taught. Similarly, a good pointing or flushing pup will instinctively want to chase birds. But a pointer's ability to classically point a bird it smells, and to remain staunch on that point while you flush the bird, is not instinctive. These habits must be taught. In fact, every hunting instinct in the pointer tells him to rush in and to try to catch the bird. The point is more of a sneaking up action, with capture being the ultimate purpose. Similarly, a flushing dog may have a natural instinct to search existing scents and to flush birds, but this instinct must be further developed through practice. And certainly the ability to sit or drop at shot until the command to retrieve is given is not instinctive. These refinements must be taught. Finally, hound dogs are bred with a well-developed sense of smell, but the ability to follow an animal's trail by scent does not come at once. It must be developed through experience and practice. And certainly the desire of a straight coonhound to follow only a coon's trail and not the trail of another animal is a desire that is developed through conditioning, discipline and practice.

The point is that you may have a good animal with all of the proper instincts, but those instincts will not put game in your bag unless you are willing to spend some time developing the right desires, and tempering the wrong tendencies with obedience and training.

Dogs learn through conditioning, repetition and experience. Conditioning means that a dog has been taught to respond in predetermined ways to certain words, whistles, horn blasts, gun shots or other stimuli. Thus, a dog learns to sit by associating the word "Sit" with the proper action. The action is taught by pushing the dog's rear end to the ground while repeating the command "Sit." Through repetition the dog learns that the word means to sit, and that compliance brings pleasure and verbal rewards, while disobedience brings reprimand. Thus, in training any dog to do anything, you somehow have to show him what you want him to do, and then to train him to do it in response to a spoken word, whistle command or a horn blast (used only with hounds). Responses are trained into your dog through conditioning, and further developed through practice, repetition and experience. Dog training is simple in theory but requires patience and persistence, even if only for a few minutes a day.

A dog is conditioned to respond to your commands primarily by your showing pleasure or displeasure. A hunting dog does not need to be rewarded with tidbits of food, but he does need to be rewarded by a pat on the head or by finding game. The best stimulus you can give him to hunt is for him to find game. The best stimulus you can give him to respond as you desire is to praise him verbally or to offer a pat on the head when he does well.

Needed, but less effective, is the displeasure you show through your angry voice or physical restraint when the dog disobeys. If your dog has been properly socialized when young, he will want to please. If he has been properly taught, he will learn that the proper response brings game and praise, and improper conduct brings nothing but rebuke. If enough practice is given, your dog should eventually, and nearly always, do the right thing—but this takes practice.

Of course your dog is not a machine; the smarter he is the more he will try to think for himself and figure out situations. Sometimes this gets him into trouble, but a dog with a good head is needed to respond well to your training. In other words, your dog will never respond to your commands like a robot to a pushed button. He is a living creature, highly intelligent, with marvelous physical assets for the task of hunting (especially the sense of smell), so don't expect him to respond in a mechanical way. He will make mistakes, plenty of them, but it is your job as a trainer to see that he doesn't get by with them after he knows better.

It is generally agreed that training progresses fastest with a young puppy by training him for periods of about fifteen minutes daily. Don't overdo the training by working your dog for longer periods or too often. Ten minutes of intensive training is far superior to an hour of indifferent, sloppy work. Try not to miss any days, even in bad weather. If you have to miss a day now and then, no great harm is done, but the most consistent results are obtained by short, daily training sessions. As your dog gets older, you can gradually lengthen the training periods, but if your dog gets indifferent, you are pushing him too hard or too long, so ease up. By the time your dog is eighteen months old you will enjoy formal training periods up to thirty minutes (longer if actually hunting, of course), but only if the total time is interspersed with short rest periods.

Training is also a step-by-step process with fundamentals to be mastered before difficult work is to be expected. Therefore, try to follow the general order of training suggested for each type of dog in this book, but feel free to vary the specific order of things whenever conditions warrant it. Contrary to the suggestions in some books, it is not necessary to master one lesson before introducing a new one. You will usually be working on several things at once. Thus, while you are still teaching your dog basic obedience, you may also be working on training him to retrieve, flush, point or trail, depending upon the type of dog. However, don't expect your dog to do graduate work before he has mastered the fundamentals. Let your dog develop confidence and get a lot of praise in doing a few things well before you introduce new lessons which he is sure to fail and for which he may require some scolding. The best sign of whether you are moving too fast or slow is your own dog. If he consistently does the thing you are requiring, move on to the next stage of training. If he continually fails, you are pushing too fast. Every lesson ought to be partly pleasurable to both dog and trainer with the dog being praised a lot more than he is punished. Also, try to end each training session on a pleasurable note by romping and playing with your dog after the formal lessons are over. When severe correction is required, however, put the dog up as soon as the desired result has been achieved and the punishment has been administered. The following period of sleep will set the idea in the dog's mind. You have, literally, let him "sleep on it."

12

Training Equipment

DOG COLLAR

The best and most common collar to use in training is a chain "choke" collar, one that tightens when the dog is on leash and pulls against it. Don't be frightened by the word "choke" collar. The collar will never be used to choke or punish your dog. There are two reasons for using this collar: it will not accidentally slip off your dog's head, and it is the most effective way of restraining your dog on a leash so that he will not pull your arm out of the socket.

Buy a collar of suitable length which is long enough to slip over your dog's head. The loop in the collar is formed by doubling the chain and passing it through a ring at one end, the doubled-up portion forming the loop. The loop is adjustable as the chain slides easily through the ring, and will always fit your puppy as he grows. However, you do not want the chain so long that the loose end dangles too far out, so get one of reasonable length.

A stout leather collar is also used by most hunters under actual hunting conditions. An identification plate bearing the owner's name and address should be attached to the collar in case the dog is lost. Many hunters fear that a chain choke collar will become tangled in the brush when a dog is hunting and prefer the leather collar whenever the dog is in the brush. It is wise to have both types. Properly trained retrievers are always in sight of their owner. So they need no collar in the field or for advanced training. No collars are allowed in advanced retriever trials.

DOG LEASH

Get a strong one of heavy leather, nylon rope or chain with a stout snap at one end. Some trainers prefer the double, short-leather leash which can be snapped to your belt; others prefer the stout chain or nylon rope. Select what you like, but that small, playful puppy will soon be a dynamic hunk of muscle and bone, so get a strong leash now or else you will have to buy another later.

CHECK CORD

In addition to the short leash, you will need a long check cord. Fifty feet long is about right. We prefer a strong, thin polyethelene rope to which a snap is tied. We usually make our own according to our needs. This check cord is handy in teaching a dog to come, in steadying pointers, flushers or retrievers, or in dragging scented lures for hounds to follow. Its use will be described later.

DOG WHISTLE

Get a small whistle used primarily for sporting purposes. The "Acme Thunderer," either of metal or plastic, is a good standard model for many trainers. Whistles can be obtained in either metal or plastic with a cork ball inside. The Roy Gonia plastic whistle is an excellent model. It is usually best to carry two whistles on a lanyard since one is likely to jam.

Don't use the silent dog whistle; whistles you can hear are better training aids. A whistle will be an important part of training from the beginning, so get one now. You will also use it constantly in the later stages of training when you teach your dog to respond to hand and whistle signals.

HUNTER'S HORN

This horn is used only in training and hunting hound dogs. The horn is usually a cow horn, cleaned up and polished, and cut off a little at the small end so that it can be blown like a bugle. The horn seems to add to the romance of hunting hounds and is also an effective way of calling far-ranging dogs. These horns may be purchased completely finished from various dog supply houses.

BAMBOO POLE, FISH LINE

For training pointers, flushers, or hounds. Its use will be described in subsequent chapters of this book.

RETRIEVING DUMMIES

You need two sizes: A small one for puppies, about 1½ inches in diameter and 8 to 10 inches long made out of a rolled up piece of carpet, terry cloth, or other material, and secured with rubber bands, and full-sized ones about 2 to 3 inches in diameter and a foot in length. The most practical dummies are made of molded vinyl plastic with knobby textures so that the dog can hold them more easily.

Canvas-covered dummies filled with granulated cork, kapok, and other flotation materials are still available from some sources, but are rapidly being replaced by plastic. Both cork and kapok will become waterlogged in time and will rot out from the inside as well as becoming soggy, heavy, and unpleasant for the dog to handle.

A dozen dummies is not too many. Even with one dog, when you set up a triple mark with three throwers, and you may want to repeat it three or four times, it will take that many. Having plenty of dummies saves time and leg work as well. Good plastic dummies can be ordered from all of the dog supply houses today.

PISTOLS, SHOTGUNS

These are needed when you introduce your dog to the gun. They should not be used at the beginning of his training. We prefer a blank pistol for most training, using the standard .22-caliber blanks, since they are easier to obtain than the imported .22 "caps" and have a louder report. In the long run it will pay you to buy the blank pistol. A shotgun is too loud to begin with and shells (even blanks) are too expensive. It can be used in the later stages of training, however, after your dog is used to blanks.

When first introducing your dog to any kind of gun, you can use a toy paper-cap pistol.

LIVE PIGEONS

These are used in all stages of training a pointing dog, flusher or retriever, when you introduce your dog to feathers, but it is wise to begin discovering sources of supply now. Usually, you can buy live pigeons for about $1.00 each, compared to about $3.50 for live pheasants and about $4.00 for live ducks. These hardy birds are the cheapest to use in training. After your dog gets used to handling dead birds gently, you can clip the wing feathers off of one wing of a live bird and use live birds from this time on, thus avoiding shooting up all of your birds. We once bought twenty-four pigeons to use for all of our retriever training. We were training five dogs at the time. By carefully rotating the pigeons, housing them indoors, and feeding them well, we managed to have sixteen birds left after four months of constant use with our dogs. Some dogs are much rougher, however, and losses can run quite high.

LURES AND SCENTS

Various types of lures are helpful training aids, depending upon the type of dog to be trained. Bird wings are useful in training pointers, flushers and even retrievers. Various types of furs, animal tails or pieces of hide are useful in training hounds. Thus, you will need a coon's tail or hide for training coonhounds, a fox tail or piece of fox fur for training foxhounds, a piece of rabbit fur for training rabbit hounds, and a bobcat or lynx hide for training cat hounds.

We have never felt the need for liquid scents for training bird dogs (pointers, flushers or retrievers), but they are wonderful for laying trails for hounds. Breaking scents are also useful with hounds in developing "straight" hounds (those who will hunt only a particular type of animal). Deer scent, skunk or other odors can be used on your hound to break him of running that type of game.

DECOYS

Used in training your dog to retrieve through decoys in the water so that he can get used to them before the waterfowl season opens.

ELECTRONIC DOG TRAINERS

These are expensive training aids, but nevertheless useful in some training situations if used wisely and sparingly. The dog is outfitted with a special leather collar to which a shock coil is attached. A battery-operated electronic transmitter is carried by the trainer. At the push of a button on the transmitter, the shock coil on the collar is activated, giving your dog quite a jolt.

We have used such a trainer in training pointers and retrievers, but *a good dog can be ruined quickly if shocked too often.* We were called in by a friend to break his German Shorthaired Pointer of running off in the woods. The first time the pointer did not come when called, we gave him a short shock. The dog leaped into the air, obviously bothered by the shock, but he continued hunting. After the second whistle blast, and after he still refused to come, we shocked the dog a second time, then called him again. This time he came in meekly with his tail between his legs. This completely cured him of disobeying, but for a few minutes the dog refused to go out at all to look for birds. Only after some persuasion would he go out. This story illustrates the need for caution in the use of the trainer.

Hound-dog trainers use electronic trainers in breaking hounds of running forbidden game, but the same caution must be used in this situation or else a hound will refuse to run any game.

Retriever trainers use shock devices to get an overly aggressive dog to sit on whistle when some distance from the trainer, or to steady a dog on the line and in some cases to make a reluctant dog go. One shock associated with the whistle command to sit or the verbal command to stay is usually enough to get the most obstreperous retriever to obey the commands.

The above list of training equipment includes all of the items you will need for training every type of dog. As indicated, some items are used only for certain types of hunting dogs. Of course, live birds or animals of various kinds are useful in training dogs on particular types of game. For example, shackled ducks can be used in training dogs to retrieve. Pheasants can be used for any type of dog that hunts birds. Live rabbits or coons are used in training hounds. But the foregoing list includes the essential items (the electronic trainer is certainly optional) without involving much expense.

13

Obedience Training

THE OBEDIENCE COMMANDS

Basic obedience training ought to begin early—between seven and twelve weeks of age. (For a complete discussion of training fundamentals see Chapter 11.) This early training ought to be businesslike, but without harsh discipline. Serious training in which you demand obedience is begun between twelve and sixteen weeks of age.

The basic obedience commands are simple, and there are only ten of them, but they should be mastered as thoroughly as possible.

"NO"—Used whenever you wish your dog to stop doing what he is doing or to refrain from doing what he is about to do. The best way to teach this

Never let your dog be a nuisance. Give a sharp "NO" command to forbid undesirable behavior such as raiding a garbage can.

command is just to use it whenever needed. Be consistent, however, and use it firmly and under the same behavior situations. Do not overuse this command, especially with a young pup, because it might destroy his confidence.

"SIT" ("Hup" is used for flushing spaniels)—To teach this command hold your dog by the collar with one hand and push his rump down with your other, saying "Sit" ("Hup" for spaniels) in a quick, firm tone. Repeat this procedure until your dog learns to sit on command. When he responds willingly, try moving farther and farther away from him, scolding if he tries to move from his spot. Gradually increase the time you require him to sit without moving until he will do so for periods up to five minutes.

After he has learned to respond to the spoken command, teach him to sit at one blast on your whistle. To do this say "Sit," then immediately blow the whistle one short blast. If needed, push down on his rump for the first few times until he learns the whistle means sit. From this time on, alternate between using the spoken and the whistle command. You will need both commands as training progresses.

To teach your dog to sit, put one hand under his head, the other on his rump, and push his rear-end down, giving the command, "SIT." Each time he tries to stand up, push his rump down again, repeating the command, "SIT." The whistle signal to sit is one sharp blast. Say "SIT," blow the whistle, and push him down until he responds to either the word or the whistle.

"STAY"—This is the command for your dog to stay in whatever place he is standing, sitting or lying down when you give the command. The command is used mostly to tell your dog to remain quietly beside you until sent to retrieve, hunt or play. The best way to teach this command is to say "Stay" in a firm voice whenever you want him to stay put, and to scold him if he disobeys. If the dog moves after the command has been given, take him back to the original spot and say "Stay," then move away again. Practice this until he will not leave the spot without being ordered to do so. Once he learns the meaning of the command he should be reprimanded if he disobeys.

"COME"—This is the basic command for your dog to come to you. Have

After teaching your dog to sit, point your finger at him and give the command, "STAY." If he tries to move, put him back on the same spot and in the same position and repeat the command. Make him stay for longer and longer periods in one spot until told to move.

To teach the command "COME," run away from your dog, clap your hands and shout the command. The proper whistle signal is several short blasts. Give the command and then blow the whistle. Never chase your dog; always make him follow you and then pet him when he obeys.

him sit near you; you then turn and run away slowly, clapping your hands, saying "Come, Come." Ordinarily a puppy will try to chase you and will gradually learn to associate the word "Come" with going to you. When your dog does come to you, praise him, pet and fondle him and let him know that you are pleased. Avoid punishing your dog when you have told him to come or else he will hesitate to get near you for fear you will reprimand him. After he is older, if you do have to punish him for disobedience, but can't reach him, it is better to shoot him in the rump with a sling shot, a low-powered **BB** gun, or shock him with an electronic dog trainer. He will soon learn to respond instantly to your commands. Such firm measures should only be used on older dogs who deliberately disobey.

An even better way of breaking your dog of the habit of ignoring "Come" is to put the long check cord on him and say "Come." If he doesn't respond, jerk slightly on the cord and say "Come" again. A few jerks on his choke collar is usually enough to convince even the most stubborn animal that he should come when called. This is the best and quickest method to teach your dog what "come" means.

After he responds to the spoken command, introduce him to the whistle command for come, which is usually several short, staccato blasts. (Hounds are trained to come to a long blast on the horn.) In teaching this command say "Come," then blow several staccato blasts on the whistle. Repeat this process until he learns to come to the whistle alone. In the beginning your dog may get confused about whether to sit (one blast) or to come (repeated blasts), but verbal urging will help him to learn to distinguish the two commands.

"KENNEL"—This is the basic command to use whenever you want your dog to go into his yard, through a door, into the car, into his house or into the boat. Every time you put him into his sleeping quarters, have him sit, then point to the door and say "Kennel." If necessary push him in, repeating "Kennel, Kennel." Your dog will soon learn that "Kennel" means to go in. You will have to repeat this procedure in introducing him to something new, like getting into the car, crate or boat, but he will soon learn to respond to your command. If he wants to stall, procrastinating like a stubborn child refusing to go to bed, try rolling up a newspaper and whacking him on the

"KENNEL" is the command to use whenever you want your dog to go into the pen, house, boat or car. To teach your dog to kennel, point toward the opening of the particular enclosure you are using, repeat the command, "KENNEL," and push him inside. Do this each time you put him inside until he does it voluntarily.

rear once or twice. Incidentally, as your puppy gets older, the rolled news-paper is a good means of discipline. It is noisy, it doesn't hurt, and it is effective yet harmless. Another good device for an alarming but relatively painless swat is a child's toy "whiffle bat." These are available in most department stores.

"CHARGE"—This is the basic command for your dog to lie down. It is used primarily rather than "Lie down" so it will not be confused with "DOWN." "Down" means for a dog to quit jumping on you or to get off the furniture. To teach "Charge," ask your dog to sit, then pull his front legs forward while you repeat "Charge, Charge." Urge him down a few times in this way and he will soon get the idea. If you want him to remain lying down, then combine this with "Stay" after he is down.

"CHARGE" is the basic command to use when you want your dog to lie down. To teach this command, first make your dog sit. Then pull his front legs forward and give the command.

"DOWN"—This means stop jumping up, or get off the chair or couch. The command is used whenever you don't want your dog to jump on people

Your dog should be taught not to jump on people or furniture. When your dog jumps on you, grab his front paws and squeeze, giving the command, "DOWN." Use the same command indoors when he jumps onto furniture.

or on particular places. It is annoying to have a dog jump on you or your guests, especially if he is dirty, or if you have a loaded shotgun in your hands. Also, your dog makes a better house pet if he is never permitted on the furniture. If he jumps on you, you can slap him with your hand, or plant your knee in his chest, or step on his hind paws. Another effective way is to grasp his front paws and squeeze them.

The best way to teach your dog to stay off the furniture is never to permit him to develop the habit in the first place. Say "Down" if he does, scold him and push him off until he learns what down means.

"HEEL"—This command is the hardest of the obedience commands to teach, since it requires more firmness and patience. The command means that your dog should walk beside you with his head even with your heel—either your left heel or right heel, depending upon your own preference. We prefer to have our dogs walk on our left since we shoot right-handed. To teach this command, attach your leash to the ring of the choke collar, holding the leash fairly close to the dog with your left hand so the dog has to walk by the left heel. If your leash is long, hold the excess in front of you with your right hand. Now, walk briskly along keeping the dog's nose near your left side. At first your puppy will be afraid of the leash and may hang back, refusing to move. Don't drag him; rather take him in your arms and comfort him, then put him down again and pull in short, mild jerks on the leash to indicate he is to walk. Don't ever keep tension on the leash with the collar tight. He will soon learn to get over his fear and follow along willingly.

Heeling lessons are begun with your dog on a leash. Keep him by your left heel with his head just even with your left leg. Every time he lags or runs ahead, pull up gently on the leash and say, "HEEL." After your dog begins to obey the command while on a leash, try him without a leash. Pat your leg and give the command, "HEEL. HEEL."

After he goes willingly along let him know with short, mild jerks on the leash that you don't want him to get ahead of you or to lag behind. Practice this until he will follow you all over the neighborhood without straining the leash. Then remove the leash and practice with it off. To help him know that you want him by your left heel, pat your left leg with your left hand and say "Heel." After your dog gets very good at walking at heel with the leash off, practice near distractions (other dogs, children playing, cats, barnyard animals and so forth), first with the leash on, then with the leash off. Perfection may require some weeks of patient practice, but you will be rewarded by a well-behaved dog if you persist.

"HIE ON"—This command means never mind heeling, go run, go hunt, go play, go do your business. Begin teaching this command before your dog learns to heel properly so he won't get the idea that he is never to run or hunt out ahead of you. Also, use this command at the end of a training session to let your dog romp around, as long as he doesn't get out of complete control. Try to let him have a bit of fun every day, but never give him the run of the neighborhood. Also, don't let a flushing dog get more than 25 to 30 yards away from you unless on a retrieve. By keeping him within range even during play, it will be easier to limit his range under hunting conditions.

"STOP THAT NOISE"—This command is not usually taught hounds but is very necessary for retrievers (who must remain silent in a blind), pointers or flushers. Barking dogs are an annoyance to owners and neighbors alike. The easiest way to teach this command is to begin when your puppy is young. Whenever you want him to stop barking put your whole hand around his muzzle and squeeze lightly, saying "Stop that noise." If your dog persists in barking as he gets older, you may have to resort to a severe spanking to break him of the habit. Some dogs bark while tied on a leash, in the kennel run or shut up in a strange room, garage or on the porch. Whenever the dog is reprimanded for barking, squeeze his muzzle, repeating the command at

"HIE ON" is the command for your dog to start hunting or to run and play. The command should be accompanied by a wave of the hand. Teach this command before your dog has mastered heeling, otherwise he may not obey for fear of disobeying the command to heel.

Do not allow your dog to acquire the habit of barking, especially if he is a retriever. A barking retriever doesn't attract many ducks. Every time he barks, clamp your hand over his mouth and give the command, "STOP THAT NOISE." This command is *not* taught to hounds.

the same time the reprimand is given. Perseverance is needed to break some dogs of a habit already established. Hounds are excluded, of course, or you may develop silent trailers.

The ten commands mentioned above are the basic ones to use. All that is needed for a perfectly behaved dog is to teach these commands carefully. Other hunting commands are discussed in the chapters on training and hunting.

In teaching obedience always expect your dog to respond immediately and with enthusiasm. He will test your authority repeatedly, but once he knows what a command means, don't let him break it without very good reason. You will get the kind of obedience you demand, but you have to be patient yet firm.

What methods of discipline should be used? Certainly the methods depend upon the age and disposition of your dog. Your methods must be less harsh on a puppy who is just learning than on an experienced dog who has deliberately disobeyed. Expect your dog to mind between twelve and sixteen weeks of age, but use only very mild discipline in your training. After four months, begin to be more firm in your methods, resorting to a good spanking when needed. Occasionally you may have to give an adult dog a few hard swats on the posterior with a leather strap or stick, but this is only for a hardhead that has refused to mind when he knows better.

Every dog is different in disposition and temperament. Some are so sensitive that a harsh word is a sufficient reprimand. In general, try to stimulate your dog to proper behavior through praise and practice, rather than punishment. If you haven't taken your dogs training for awhile, they make many more mistakes for which they need a reprimand. The lesson is obvious: punishment, no matter how severe, will never take the place of regular practice. We certainly don't like to punish our dogs more than is necessary, but we don't hesitate to if they need it. That is about all the advice we can give you. Avoid cruel methods, or those which might injure your dog. It is unwise for a hunter to resort to shooting his dog with a shotgun, except in the hands of a pro who understands range and effect perfectly. Most such instances occur when a hunter never trains his dog before the season opens and expects him to mind perfectly, without practice, when he first takes the dog hunting.

Also, make certain your dog knows what he is being punished for. This means you have to punish him the instant he disobeys. Five minutes after the rule is broken is too late. There is no use using discipline unless by so doing you are teaching your dog what is right and what is wrong.

HOUSEBREAKING

Your hunting dog ought to be housebroken even though you kennel him outside. There will be times when you want to let him in your house, a motel suite or a hunting cabin.

Housebreaking a young puppy may be easy or difficult, depending upon your particular dog. Some dogs seem to take to training easily, others persist in messing or piddling for a long time. However, there are certain principles you can follow which will help with any dog.

1. Don't give your dog a chance to make a mistake. This means that you have to let your puppy out every half hour or so in the beginning. Each time you let him out say "Hie on" and wave him on with a reminder: "Do your business." Gradually he will learn to go each time you let him out.

2. Never start training him to go on a newspaper in the house, or he may also mess on your Sunday paper when you leave the paper on the living room floor. Besides, you will have to break him of going on the paper anyhow, but this is harder to do if the habit is already established. Papers are a real mess to pick up daily and usually some of the urine soaks through to your floor.

3. Let your puppy out after each meal; this is the period of the day when he is most likely to have to go.

4. Watch for signs that he has to go. Most dogs will begin running around in circles looking for a spot. When your dog starts to do this, take him out quickly before he goes on the floor. After he begins to be housebroken he will start whining, going to the door, or scratching to get out. If you watch for such signs and let him out promptly, he will be more likely to continue to tell you when he does have to go.

5. Whenever you catch him making a mistake, say a firm "No" and take him out immediately. If he messes without your seeing him, take him over to the mess, put his nose near it (not in it), and say, "No." Do this several times until he learns to associate the feces with the "No." This helps him to learn that he has done wrong by going in the house.

6. Cut down on his liquid intake whenever he will have to hold his urine longer. This means take his water dish away before bedtime or before leaving him in the house.

7. He will be less likely to mess at night, or while you are away, if you tie him on a short leash or shut him up in a small pen, box or dog house. No dog likes to mess near where he sleeps. Confining him to a small area is an added incentive for him not to go.

8. When you do let him out to go, train him to stay off the neighbor's lawn by calling him to you if he should ever go on. Nothing is more unneighborly than letting him go on someone else's property.

9. If he persists in messing, take him to the mess, say a firm "no" and give him several whacks with a rolled up newspaper.

10. Don't expect results immediately. Give him time to learn. Usually he will learn to hold his bowels before he learns to hold his urine. Even when

fully trained, your dog may make an occasional mistake, usually because you have forgotten to let him out. Therefore, don't expect him to do the impossible.

CHASING CARS

There are several ways to keep your dog from chasing cars: Keep him penned up when you are not training, exercising or playing with him. Keep him under voice control at all times when you have him out of the pen or house. Never let him start the habit in the first place. If he should ever try to chase a car, bicycle or motorcycle, catch him immediately, tell him "No," and punish him if necessary.

If he has already developed the habit, you have more of a problem, since you will have to break him of something he has learned to do. One way to break the habit is to have a friend drive by in his car and to really frighten your dog if he starts to chase the car. The dog can be frightened by throwing a bundle of tin cans at him, throwing water bombs at him (balloons filled with water work nicely), or having your friend stop the car, jump out and chase him home, or wallop him with a big stick. Another good way to break the habit is to give him a good shock with an electronic dog trainer each time he chases the car. Or, if you can catch him in the act, tell him "No," call him home and shut him up each and every time. Or, if this doesn't work, give him a good walloping before shutting him up.

Usually car chasing is a habit a dog develops because the owner is careless. A dog should not be allowed to run loose and develop the habit in the first place. If your dog does run loose, he should be under voice control at all times. A dog that doesn't mind is worthless as a hunter. And car chasing is one result of disobedience and shows sloppy training. So resolve that your dog has to learn to obey at all times.

RAIDING GARBAGE CANS

If your dog is kept penned up or under control when you have him out, you can call him away from raiding cans, or punish him when he does. If he is allowed to run loose as a scavenger, there is really no way to keep him out of garbage. Even a well-fed, over-fat house dog will get into garbage if allowed to; therefore, the best protection against garbage-can raiding is not to let him run loose unsupervised. If you find the neighborhood dogs getting into your cans, the simplest way to prevent it is to have the can shut up in a covered wooden box or in a closed garage.

If your dog gets into your garbage in your own house or garage, you have two alternatives: keep the garbage can out of his reach, or break him of the habit of getting in it. The most direct way of breaking the habit is to catch him in the act and tell him "No" and to punish him.

CHEWING RUGS, FURNITURE

Most puppies like to chew on things, especially when first teething, or when they are losing their baby teeth and their adult teeth are coming in (about four to six months). The best solution is to keep your puppy outside in a pen, except when you are supervising him in the house. Unsupervised indoors, any pup will chew up something. If he does start to chew on your good rug or furniture, snap his muzzle with your finger, saying "No." If more extreme measures are required, swat him with a rolled newspaper everytime he starts to bite something he shouldn't. Also, it helps to have a large piece of suet, or a dog meal bone on which he can chew. Don't give him artificial rubber, plastic or metal bones, or sticks, balls, old rags or other things of this sort to chew on. Most puppies can bite off small pieces and will eventually swallow them. Such pieces are bad for the digestion and potentially dangerous. A good rule to follow is never to give him anything to chew on that you do not want him to eat.

Sometimes puppies chew on things that are dangerous to their lives: electric cords, pieces of glass, metal or plastic, or poisonous substances. The best cure is prevention. Keep such things out of his reach, or keep him shut off from the hazards.

STEALING FOOD

Have you ever had the experience of your dog stealing the pot roast, the hamburger, the butter or the whole pie from the kitchen table? If you never have, you are part of a small minority. Most dogs will try to steal food some time or another, and will eventually succeed if left to their own devices.

Here again, the best cure is prevention. Don't leave food around to tempt your dog, or the dog around where he will be tempted. As the dog grows older and more able to reach food on counter or table tops, tell him a firm "No" whenever he starts to sniff around food that you do not want him to eat. If you catch him in the act, punish him immediately, and shut him up in his pen, box or dog house. Also, don't feed the dog at the table; this only encourages him to take food when you are not around.

GETTING ON FURNITURE

The best way to teach your dog to stay off the bed, couch or good chair is never to let him get into the habit of getting on them in the first place. If he does jump on the furniture, tell him "Down," and point to the floor at the same time. If he doesn't know what you mean, push him off while you say "Down." Once he knows he is not supposed to get on the furniture, reprimand him, or even punish him severely, if he persists in disobeying.

We have heard dog owners complain about their dogs getting on the furniture, but also have noticed that such owners usually permit their dogs on the furniture at times, or even call their dogs onto the furniture. Such inconsistency is confusing to any dog. You can't let him sleep on your bed or couch all night and expect him to stay off all day. If you want to teach your dog to stay off, never let him get on. If he tries to get on, reprimand him or punish him for disobedience. Even the hardest-headed dog will do what you want him to do if you know what you expect and force him to abide by your wishes.

14

Training and Hunting the Pointer

HUNTING BEHIND a good pointing dog can be one of the most thrilling experiences of any sport shared by man and dog. However, it can be the most frustrating if the dog is not properly trained, or if he lacks ability. He should have real potential if you have selected your pup wisely. Any good pointing dog must be trained though. While we have seen some individuals who have worked fairly well with little or no formal training, we would be the last to recommend that you proceed on the assumption that your pup will mature into a fine bird dog on his own hook.

BEGINNING TRAINING IN POINTING

The younger you begin your pup's training, the better. It will give your prospect confidence in you at an early age, if you don't overdo force, and it will awaken his hunting instincts. Both of these points are extremely important and should never be overlooked in an effort to get a good gunning dog in the shortest possible time.

While your pup is still a mere baby, six to eight weeks of age, he will have started developing the instinct to go after moving objects and, in the manner of a pointing dog, will creep up on his quarry. This is the instinct from which the act of pointing arises; the dog is actually sneaking up on the game, hoping to get close enough to grab it before it can get away. When this is brought under control so that the dog will not break in after game, but holds the point until his handler comes in to flush, it is known as a point. While your pup is still very young, eight to ten weeks is ideal, you can begin playing a game with him that will set the foundation for all of his work as a trained hunting dog.

To begin this training procedure, all you need is a bamboo pole, some fish line, and the wing or skin of an upland game bird. The procedure is as follows: Dangle the feathers from the end of the pole in order to attract the pup's attention, first in the air to get him excited, then on the ground where he thinks he can catch them. Do not let the pup catch the lure and chew it up, however, but keep it constantly out of his reach. Quickly the pup will learn that he cannot catch his game by barging in on it and will begin to adopt a quiet, sneaking approach. When he does this you can reassure him by gently saying "Whoa" to him, letting him know that you approve of his actions and giving him confidence. The amount of pointing instinct in a puppy will vary, but any pup worth training should respond to this approach quickly. In time, assuming that you practice this game daily, the pup should be approaching the lure, freezing on point when he gets a few feet from it, and holding staunchly, since he knows it will jump out of his reach if he goes closer.

TRAINING IN RETRIEVING

When you have your pup approaching the lure carefully and freezing into point, you are ready to introduce him to the second phase of the game, retrieving. Many dogs will become indifferent to this training routine if they are never rewarded by being allowed to catch their game. As has been pointed out, you cannot allow your pointer to rush in on the game and catch it on his own. You must gently hold him back and say "Whoa" to him while a helper walks into the lure, picks it up quickly and throws it in the air, shouting "Bang!" At this point you should release the pup, saying "fetch" to him, and allow him to run over and pick up the lure. Now call the pup back quickly so that he will bring the lure to you. He cannot run away with the lure because it is still tied to the bamboo pole. Some dogs are more inclined to retrieve than others, but if your pup is started young enough you have a better chance of convincing him that this is an enjoyable part of the game than if you wait until he is older and you have to force train him. For a complete discussion of training in retrieving see Chapter 15.

OVERTRAINING

The above method of training can be continued until the pup is five or six months of age, gradually increasing the complexity of the problem, in terms of heaviness of cover and the length of time you allow him to hold his point, according to his progress. At this early age, make sure that you never go beyond the point where it is really fun for the pup or you will run the risk of his going sour. Overtraining has ruined many fine prospects. If your pup begins to show any indifference, stop and play with him a bit and put him back in his kennel.

INTRODUCTION TO THE GUN

Sometime during his first few months of life, you should introduce your dog to the sound of a gun. Some authorities say that you should shoot over your pup while he is being fed. We have never agreed with this since we can see no sense in relating the act of eating to the sound of a gun, even though they are both positive things to the dog. We prefer to follow the method of having the helper shout "Bang" when the lure is in the air. Then progress to a blank pistol, and finally a shotgun fired at some distance from the pup to begin with and then brought closer. In a short time you should have your pup responding very well to the sound of a gun, perking up his ears and looking about expectantly whenever he hears a shot. A hunting dog will become so enthusiastic about guns, since he relates them to hunting, that merely seeing one or hearing the action of a repeater worked will send him into fits of ecstasy.

USING LIVE BIRDS

When your pup is doing perfectly in the first phase of training, is retrieving the lure nicely to hand and has overcome all fear of firearms, you are ready to move on to the second phase of his training: working with a live bird. We have always liked ordinary domestic pigeons for this, since most dogs seem to respond to them fairly well. They are easily available and are similar in size to many of our upland birds. Basically, the routine followed here is a repetition of the method used with the feather lure and the bamboo pole. The main difference is that the bird is no longer attached to anything but planted with its feet tied together and one wing clipped so that it cannot move. The dog, now about six months old, is walked into the area downwind of the bird so that he may catch its scent. The dog should be tied to a 50-foot check cord during this operation. When your pup winds the bird and moves in to point, you simply reassure him with the command "Whoa." If he offers to break in on the bird, pull him back with the check cord, repeating the command "Whoa" more firmly. If he seems to be fairly staunch, you can freeze him into a really solid point by pushing him gently toward the bird. By using these two methods, in accordance with the nature of your pup, you will soon have a staunch pointer on planted pigeons. After several repetitions of this you should have your dog freezing on point when he is able to wind the strong body scent of the pigeon.

The next step is to move in ahead of your dog's point, reach down, pick up the bird and throw it into the air, holding your charge by the check cord as the pigeon flutters to the ground. A helper is of advantage here and should be used in the same capacity as in the previous training program. Now release your pup and give the command to retrieve simultaneously. You may find that your pup will be hesitant to retrieve the pigeon on the first try, due either to the fact that the bird is alive, or simply because it is different. Don't be discouraged if this is the case. You can probably correct this by killing the pigeon, teasing the dog with it, throwing it out a distance and telling him to "Fetch." If this does not work, gently place the bird in his mouth and tell him to "Fetch." A little time spent in this way every day will soon have your pup running after the pigeon, picking it up and retrieving it to hand just as he did with the lure earlier in his training.

Variations of this training method can be employed until the pup's first hunting season, which should not be before his first birthday. By this time you should have your pup completely under voice command, his obedience training having been done concurrently with his hunting training (see Chapter 13), and he will be reasonably steady on point and steady to wing and shot. The check cord must have been kept on him until he no longer breaks when the bird is flushed, thrown in the air and the blank pistol fired. Eventually, your pup will be allowed to range out, pick up scent of planted pigeons under more difficult circumstances, point steadily and make his retrieves in fine style.

HUNTING WILD BIRDS

Even though your dog has been well-trained on the lure and the live pigeons, don't expect him to do a top-notch job on wild birds his first year or so. It takes a great deal of experience to learn to handle wild birds; they can be depended upon to do the unexpected, and young dogs will go through a considerable period of confusion before they get used to them. The best idea is to take the young dog to a game preserve which holds the type of bird you will be hunting in the wild, and see how he does for the first few hunts. When your young pointing dog is first introduced to wild game, he may lapse into some of the problems he was having in the earlier phases of his training. He may move while he is pointing or, due to the excitement, may temporarily become unsteady to wing and shot. Hunting wild game is always more exciting than training no matter how closely you try to simulate the hunting situation. In these instances you will have to go back to some of the training devices used earlier in your pup's career. For instance, if breaking on wild game really becomes a problem, you must put him on a check cord so you can restrain him with force and the command "Whoa" as you walk in to flush. You will find that working a hunting dog from a check cord takes practically all of the fun out of the sport, but it is necessary if your young dog is to be corrected before an incipient problem becomes an incurable fault.

RESTRICTION OF RANGE

Once you have your dog hunting boldly, making good solid points, obeying your commands and retrieving to hand, you will have what most people call a perfect dog. There are still some improvements you can make on the per-

Months of training are rewarded in the field when your dog scents a game bird, then moves slowly in on point and holds staunchly.

Leonard Lee Rue III

formance of your dog that should not be overlooked if you wish to get the most out of his potential.

Perhaps most important, you should train your dog to restrict his range in keeping with the kind of terrain you hunt and your ability to follow a dog on foot. If you are a field trialer, have plenty of open country and do most of your hunting from horseback or truck, you will have little interest in this. Most of us, however, hunt in heavier cover and smaller fields and cannot afford to keep a stable full of horses for hunting purposes. If your dog is taught to come when you call or whistle him in, he can be reminded when he is getting out of range by those methods, and frequent reminders of this kind will often suffice to establish in him the willingness to stay within range.

Many dogs, however, are very hard-headed in this department, and when they think they are out of their master's reach will "take off for the hills." Much of this can be avoided by correct early obedience training. If it does become a problem, though, the check cord may be used to keep the dog within range, although this is extremely awkward in cover. Perhaps the most positive method of breaking a dog to correct range is through the use of an electronic shocking collar. With this device you can deliver a harmless but painful shock to your dog's neck by remote radio control. If your dog refuses the command to check back closer to the guns, a jolt from the electronic trainer will assure him that he cannot get away with his defiance, and quickly convince him of the wisdom of obeying your commands. The main danger in the use of these is that they may be easily abused. Applied too severely, they may well break a dog of any desire to hunt. One short jolt is usually sufficient, and the rule should be followed that as little punishment should be meted out as will do the job. Don't regard punishment as revenge you are taking on the dog, but as simple cause and effect; in order to avoid pain he will behave according to your commands.

There are individual pointing dogs and entire breeds which tend to work within restricted range. In some cases this is very good, if a close ranger is what you desire. On the other hand, this is often a result of laziness in the dog. Hard-working, close-ranging dogs are usually tractable and like to remain close to the gunners. Most of these are Pointers, English Setters and especially Brittany Spaniels, who seem almost always energetic and hard going, as well as being comparatively close workers.

HANDLING

If you have accomplished everything up to this point in training your pointing dog, you have just one more thing to do in order to make him a completely polished performer. This is handling. Many hunters hold that a handling dog is strictly a "trick" dog and has no useful purpose in the hunting field. We heartily disagree. To have a handling dog is nothing more than to have a dog you are able to control and direct into more promising cover. Owing to the fact that the hunter, because of his higher elevation and better eyesight, can often assess the field more quickly and surely than can the dog, a good deal of time and effort can be saved by handling. Further, it puts the dog under one more element of control, making him generally easier to handle and more pleasant to hunt.

As opposed to training a really sharp handling dog in the retriever breeds, it is fairly easy to train a pointing dog to handle. Begin in the yard with an object or bird the dog can see. Simply make him sit and stay, then wave him toward the object using a vocal command—"Over" to make him go to one side, or "Go back" to make him go farther out. Once this has been repeated several times in all directions and the dog seems to have some idea of what you are trying to communicate, you can take him to a field where you have planted birds. To begin with, get the dog fairly close to the location of the bird, then attract his attention by voice or whistle and wave him over in the direction of the bird. The important thing here is to make sure that within the first few tries you put hm on game very quickly, preferably with just one wave of the arm. If you do not do this, he will quickly lose interest and begin to ignore your signals. It takes a long time to perfect this aspect of the pointing dog's work, and you will profit from it according to how well he obeys your commands. Some dogs will learn over a period of time to take long casts at the signal of the handler. Many of these will take a 200-yard jog to the right or left on command. Others never learn to do this well and are constantly diverted from their cast to hunt out covers along the way. It is well to understand that there are certain limits beyond which each individual cannot be trained. Try to find out what that limit is for your dog, and avoid needless frustration, both for you and your dog, by not pushing him beyond his potential. Some men are so driven by pride that they can never be satisfied with what they have and insist on performances from dogs of which none are capable. In many cases this is a result of ignorance on part of the handler; he does not understand a dog's capabilities. More often it is a result of impatience, selfishness and lack of concern for the animal's well being. Such a man would be better off never to own a dog since he will never be happy with his dog's work, and his dog will never be happy while in his care.

HUNTING BOBWHITE QUAIL

The classic game-bird hunting with a pointing dog is for bobwhite quail. By their nature, and the terrain they inhabit, these birds seem the best suited to hunting with pointing dogs. Many upland birds have a marked tendency to run from the dogs rather than to sit tight, making them very difficult for a dog to point. This is less true of the bobwhite quail. He will generally sit tight rather than flush wild. Although, through natural selection, the bobwhite is becoming increasingly inclined to run. Another consideration is the kind of terrain bobwhites often inhabit—the big, open fields of the Atlantic coastal states, the Carolinas, Georgia and Florida, providing an ideal habitat. Many of the best quail dogs come from those areas. In this kind of country a "big going" class pointer can be used to advantage, especially if you have some means other than foot power to follow your dog.

Much of the terrain, even in those states just mentioned, and certainly in the Central states which have good quail populations, are characterized by smaller fields and heavier thickets. In these areas a closer worker is a necessity if you wish to avoid constantly losing your dog.

If you have a really hard-working pointing dog, you must be careful, especially in warm weather, not to overwork him. A good dog has so much hunting instinct that he often will go beyond his physical capabilities. Heart attacks and heat stroke are not uncommon when a dog is pushed too hard, especially if he is out of shape, as he is likely to be at the beginning of the hunting season. It is always a good idea to give your dog a month's roadwork previous to the hunting season. Five miles per day on a country road behind a bicycle or car will do wonders for him, and may save his life.

HUNTING PHEASANTS

Perhaps the second most widely hunted game with pointing dogs is the ring-neck pheasant. Twenty-five years ago almost any reasonable pointing dog could do an excellent job on these birds, as they would sit tightly in the brush, much in the manner of quail. The heavy hunting pressure in recent years, however, has caused them to evolve into a much smarter and more wary bird. The result has been that very few pointing dogs can handle pheasants well. If a dog is slow and methodical, pheasants will easily run away from him. If the dog is too fast and bold, moving in too hard on his points, the pheasants will almost invariably flush before you are within gun range. If your pointing dog ranges too wide, you will not be able to get close enough to the birds for a shot because they have learned not to sit still that long. The best pheasant dogs we have seen in recent years have been those that combined speed, caution with positiveness, and moderate range. We do not believe the very close ranger is much good because the pheasants are constantly unnerved by the gunners tramping through the brush. A medium ranger will usually be in close enough so you can get to him before his birds flush out of range. He is fast enough to pin down hard-running cock pheasants, and he is cautious enough so that he will not constantly "bump" his birds into flushing wild. It's hard to say how to go about getting a dog that will handle pheasants really well; but a good, fast, medium-range quail dog of the Pointer or English Setter breeds should be ideal. A first rate Brittany Spaniel also is hard to beat on this game.

HUNTING RUFFED GROUSE

Some of the most picturesque and pleasurable hunting over a pointing dog can be had on ruffed grouse. Ruffed grouse are found only in the heavily wooded, hilly sections of the country. They sit very tightly, often in the branches of trees and in thickets. This is one game bird that requires a close, methodical worker. Perhaps the ideal ruffed-grouse dog would be practically worthless on any other game bird except woodcock. Certainly they would not do as a quail or pheasant dog. Occasionally, a very old dog who has lost the speed and desire to range out after quail and pheasant will work well on ruffed grouse. A dog who lacks the energy and bird interest to make the wide casts required of an acceptable quail dog may also prove adequate. In general, stay away from all but the closest-working setters and pointers for this work. The German pointing breeds are admirably suited to these birds because of their excellent noses and their tendency to work closely.

If a dog ranges out in ruffed-grouse country, he will soon be out of sight. Some hunters solve this problem by attaching a small bell to the dog's collar. If the dog stays within reasonable range you will be able to hear the bell ringing constantly, except when he strikes a point. Then you can walk to where you last heard the bell ringing. This device may be employed in other forms of bird hunting where the cover is so heavy that the dog will be spending a good share of his time out of sight.

HUNTING SHARPTAILED GROUSE

There are many other kinds of quail, grouse and other upland birds on which the hunter may use a pointing dog. While we can by no means treat all of them here, the sharptail grouse is worthy of mention. The sharptail, while it is not widespread over the United States, is perhaps the closest to quail in its inclination to sit tightly. These birds are found largely in the northern part of the United States and in the Canadian provinces. They offer some really superb gunning. Due to the fact that sharptails sit so well, and because they are found in open prairie country, a wide-ranging pointer can do an excellent job on them. A wider range would be more tolerable in a sharptail dog than in a quail or pheasant dog. We have hunted sharptails in North Dakota both with and without a dog, and the amount of walking you have to do without a good pointer is staggering. In that country you can see for miles in any direction. Unless you know the particular terrain you are hunting very well, your guess as to where the birds may be is no better than any other similarly experienced hunter's. Perhaps the best solution in this kind of country is to study the terrain very carefully with strong binoculars, spotting your birds from a distance, and moving directly to that location with your dog. This may sound absurd to the southern quail hunter, but in the Dakotas and Canada this is often done. Sharptails make themselves very obvious in the morning while feeding. This is the time to spot them.

HUNTING HUNGARIAN PARTRIDGE

Hungarian partridge may also be hunted successfully with the pointing breeds. These little partridges, found throughout the northern prairie states, are an excellent game bird and are hard to hit, resembling quail in their explosive take-off. They pose the difficulties, however, of being very widely scattered, and they are very jumpy when approached by man or dog. There are times, though, when they sit very tightly. Then they provide good sport with a pointing dog. Even though the chief game bird, bobwhite quail, is not to be found over the entire United States, keeping a pointing breed may be justified by hunting one or a combination of the following: pheasants, sharptailed grouse or Hungarian partridge. In some areas, such as southern North Dakota and parts of South Dakota, Minnesota and Montana, all three of these birds are found in good supply in the same areas, and one may go out after a mixed bag of upland game with some assurance of success.

HUNTING WOODCOCK

In all probability, the most specialized of all game-bird sport with a pointing dog is the hunting of woodcock. In all respects, this game bird demands the very close-ranging qualities of the ruffed-grouse dog. In addition, the dog must have the comparatively unusual trait of liking to hunt woodcock. Many pointing dogs who are otherwise very good dogs, simply do not have any interest in woodcock. Others will hunt them fairly well, but refuse to pick them up. Perhaps there is something in the smell of a woodcock that repels most dogs. Still, the extremely heavy cover that woodcocks stay in during the daylight hours makes them difficult to hunt without a dog. More than the ruffed grouse, these birds will hide in the very densest thickets during shooting hours, venturing into the open to feed on angleworms only after dark. They also sit very tightly, so it is hard to flush them without knowing exactly where they are. Considering the fact that woodcock and ruffed grouse inhabit similar terrain, and that a close-working dog is required for both of these birds, it would be wise for the prospective pup buyer to select his pup only from good woodcock-working parents if he wants to hunt these birds. Almost any good dog will go crazy over the smell of ruffed grouse just as he will pheasant or quail.

CHASING OTHER GAME

All of the game birds hunted with a pointing dog, with the exception of woodcock, belongs to the order of gallinaceous fowl (chicken-like, short-beaked, pecking fowl). These birds all smell somewhat alike to a dog, and you should have no fear that you will ruin your dog if you work him interchangeably on these species. We have, however, seen many otherwise good dogs who, if the correct game is scarce, point everything from shypokes to rabbits and will often chase them when flushed. Make every effort to break a dog of these very bad habits, especially if it amounts to his chasing every rabbit, fox or deer into the next county. We had an Irish Setter that insisted, during his first season, on disappearing over the horizon after every jackrabbit he saw. This really became irritating, but we corrected him promptly with a lustily applied cornstalk. Before the season was out, this dog would pay no attention whatever to a rabbit. The same treatment early in his career taught him that we were not thrilled with his chasing chickens and cats. A good hunting dog of any breed is going to chase almost anything that moves until he finds out what you want to hunt. He will be more fun to hunt with, will produce more game for the gun and will be far happier once he knows which game is permitted and which is taboo.

15

Training and Hunting the Retriever

We have learned from experience that the younger you can begin training your dog to retrieve, the better. This means you can start training at the same time you start obedience training: any time after your dog is seven weeks of age. Such training ought always to be kept playful and fun, never harsh, so that both you and your dog will enjoy the training sessions. If you get angry and punish a puppy, you may dampen his natural enthusiasm or even spoil him completely, so resolve to do everything to stimulate his eagerness and enthusiasm and to avoid dampening his spirit.

After your dog is twelve weeks of age, you and he should both take the training more seriously, but even then keep the sessions short and fun. Never use severe discipline on any dog less than six months of age. Between four and six months of age your methods can be firm, but discipline must still be mild. Your dog is the best guide. If he is sensitive, take it easy. If he tries to be a hardhead and deliberately disobedient, you will have to use firmer methods, but only when you are sure your dog understands what you expect.

BEGINNING TRAINING IN RETRIEVING

Your first task in training your dog to retrieve is to get him interested and enthusiastic about chasing a thrown dummy. Begin your training in the house, garage or in a small closed pen so that you can catch your dog easily. Wave a small dummy around in front of his nose, talking excitedly to him to try to get him to want to grab the dummy. When he seems interested in it throw the dummy out 6 feet or so in front of him, saying the command to retrieve, which is "Get back" for retrievers and "Fetch" for pointers and flushers. If the dog's enthusiasm has been aroused, he will run after the dummy and either sniff it, stay and bite it or pick it up and run with it. If he gets the dummy in his mouth at all blow the come signal with your whistle (four or five staccato blasts), say "Come," clap your hands and begin running slowly away. Never go toward your dog or give him the idea you are chasing him, or else he will want to play and run away from you. As you move away your puppy will come to you. Then is the time to take the dummy from him as he passes. The only trick is being able to grab the dummy easily. From the very beginning, try to get your dog to deliver to your hand as you move away, getting the dog to give you the dummy as soon as possible.

If he drops the dummy don't make any fuss over it now. You will be teaching him to hold on to it later. The important thing is to keep practicing in succeeding sessions until the dog chases after the dummy excitedly and starts back with it when you say "Come." It also helps to pat the ground with your hand while you call the dog to you.

By the way, now is the time to decide how you want your dog to deliver: while standing or while sitting at heel. (Spaniels are usually taught to sit in front of the handler.) Don't require any fine delivery in the beginning, but later on, after you have taught your dog to hold on to the dummy as long as you want him to, you will want to work also on his delivery. Both the standing and sitting delivery are acceptable for retrievers. To make your retriever sit to deliver, tell him to "Heel," then when he's at heel give the sit signal by blowing one sharp blast on the whistle. He will soon learn to do this automatically. If he stands to deliver, just wait until he comes right to you and reach down with both hands and gently take the dummy. Praise him every time he does an acceptable job.

One of the hardest tasks is to get your dog to bring the dummy to you rather than running around you with it or running away from you. As has been mentioned, never chase your dog, always back up or run away and he will be more likely to come. Sometimes, however, such tactics don't work. Your dog will pick the dummy up and run past you just out of reach, or occasionally he may run off with it. The basic trouble here is that he isn't coming when called. If he is completely obedient to "Come," or to the come whistle, he will come to you whether carrying a dummy or not. If he isn't coming right to you then work some more on basic obedience "Come," but without the dummy. Continue practicing "Come" on successive days until he responds promptly, then go back to practicing retrieving. As was suggested in Chapter 13 on obedience training, you may have to resort to a long check cord snapped to his collar.

Another good way to practice "Come" is to have your dog "Sit" and "Stay," and then back slowly away while the dog remains seated. If he gets up, put him back on the spot. Back away 10 to 20 feet, then call "Come," blowing the come signal with the whistle at the same time. Practice walking farther and farther away before you call your dog to "Come." After a lot of practice he will "Stay" when ordered to do so, but will come promptly when called. If he doesn't do both, practice until he does.

HOLDING AND RELEASING THE DUMMY

After you have your dog going out after the dummy with enthusiasm and returning promptly (with practice this can be accomplished by the time he is six months old), it is time to work on holding, carrying and releasing the dummy smoothly. If your dog has been dropping the dummy, then work on holding and carrying first. For this command use the word "Fetch," which means "Hold on to it" or "Pick it up." (For pointing and flushing dogs fetch also means retrieve.) The easiest way to teách "Fetch" is for you to hold solidly to one end of the dummy, holding it in a horizontal position near your dog, talking excitedly and moving the dummy back and forth. As the dog tries to grab the dummy, give the command "Fetch" and let him have it. If he will not take it and hold it, then put one hand over his jaw, squeeze your finger on either side of his mouth, forcing the dog's jowls between his teeth to open his mouth. Then place the dummy in his mouth with the other hand. If he tries to spit the dummy out, or to drop it, put it in again, each time saying "Fetch." Repeat until he will hold it indefinitely.

The next step is to get him to hold onto the dummy while he walks. Most dogs who have learned to sit or stand and to hold the dummy will drop it when they try to walk with it. Have your dog "sit," with the dummy in his mouth ("fetch"), then back up 6 feet and call your dog: "Come." If he drops the dummy, take the dog back to the original spot, say "Sit" and "Fetch" and put the dummy back in his mouth. Say "Stay" and back off slowly, then call him again. Each time he drops the dummy put it in his mouth again and repeat the procedure. Eventually he will learn to "Fetch" and "Come" at the same time. When he has mastered that, put him on a leash, put the dummy in his mouth and let him practice walking beside you at heel while he holds the dummy. If he takes a sloppy hold, place the center of the dummy in his mouth to show him how you want him to hold it and say "Fetch" at the same time.

After you have him obeying all the foregoing commands, put a dummy on the ground, take your dog over to it, command him to "Fetch." If he refuses to pick it up, put it in his mouth and say "Fetch." Do this until he will pick it up voluntarily.

This whole procedure may take several weeks, the time depending upon your dog, but practice only ten to fifteen minutes daily, repeating each day until the lesson is well learned and your dog never drops the dummy until told to do so.

After you have taught "Fetch," then teach the command "Leave it," which means "Let go, give it to me." As you take the dummy say "Leave it." If your dog hesitates to let go take the dummy from him by force, repeating the command. Practice this until he knows that "Leave it" means to give you the dummy. Repeat until he does it willingly.

SINGLE MARKED RETRIEVES

As you progress in your training, send your dog after longer and longer retrieves until he is doing single marked retrieves on bare land at distances up to 175 yards. Have a friend throw birds for you at distances beyond which you can't throw yourself. Then teach your dog to mark and look for the dummy by beginning with short retrieves in medium cover, gradually lengthening the retrieves as your dog learns to search for each dummy. Increase the length of the retrieves and the denseness of the cover until he will do over 100-yard retrieves in fairly thick cover—tall grass, brush-covered fields and uncut hay fields. In fields with a lot of flowers or alfalfa, the competing scent is very strong so it's harder for your dog to smell the dummy. This type of cover takes a lot of practice.

The average young dog will have a tendency to hunt short in the beginning. If he can't find the dummy, go out and throw it in the air so that every time you send him for a dummy he brings one back. Repeated failures will make your dog indifferent; do not make the work too difficult.

It is not necessary to put any scent on the dummy unless you want to get your dog used to particular bird scents. If you desire, you can rub the dummy thoroughly with a live or dead bird. However, just rubbing your own hands on the dummy is enough to give the dummy sufficient scent.

STEADYING

Up until now you have sent your dog after the dummy as soon as it was thrown. The important point has been to get him to go after it with enthusiasm and to retrieve to hand. Only after this has been accomplished should you go on to the next step, which is to require your dog to be steady; i.e. to sit and wait to retrieve until sent. Retrievers are taught to sit and stay at heel; flushing dogs to sit where they flushed the bird. If you require steadiness too soon, you will dampen your dog's enthusiasm. If you wait too long to begin teaching this, he will be so used to buzzing after the dummy as soon as it is thrown that you will have a hard time breaking him of the habit. Many trainers may disagree, but we feel that you should begin steadying your dog as soon as he is retrieving with great enthusiasm to hand. If the steadying is taught gradually, you need not dampen your dog's enthusiasm. If you find him refusing to retrieve, then you can be sure you are making him wait too long before you send him, so go back to sending him immediately until you build up his enthusiasm again.

To teach your dog to be steady, put him on leash at heel. Say "Sit," and "Stay." Throw the dummy and wait an instant before you speak the retrieve command, "Get back" ("Fetch" for pointers and flushers). As soon as you throw the dummy your dog will start to run out to get it and be caught up short on the leash. Tell him to "Heel," then unsnap the leash and send him as quickly as possible. Repeat this lesson until the dog is steady while on leash. Then try the same thing with the dog off leash.

From this time on, each time before you throw the dummy say "Sit" and "Stay" and give the dog a couple of jerks on his chain collar before you send him to retrieve. If he "breaks" (goes after the dummy before being sent) when the dummy is thrown, say "No," and "Leave it" before he reaches the dummy, call him back and send him over again. If he goes out after the dummy and manages to get it before being sent and ignores your "No," call him to you without reprimand. Certainly never punish him for retrieving or he may refuse to go after the dummy at all. The idea is to let him know you never want him to retrieve until you send him. The best way to do that is to not let him get the dummy until you send him. If he continues to break, reprimand him each time, trying to prevent him from getting the dummy. Run after him if necessary, hollering "No," "Leave it," "Come" or "Heel," which ever seems appropriate.

Actually it is very difficult to steady a dog who has a lot of drive and

Sending a retriever in the right direction after a bird—called "giving a line." Use the hand on the side at which the dog is heeling and move it back and forth alongside the dog's head in the direction you want him to go. Train your dog to do this while retrieving dummies.

Courtesy American Chesapeake Club

instinct for retrieving. It may take several months to get him steady on dummies, and additional months on birds, but it is better to be cautious in this phase of his training than to spoil his enthusiasm. Ideally, then, you have to be tough enough to make him mind, but not so tough as to break his spirit and enthusiasm. If you are too tough, he may refuse to retrieve at all, in which case ease up on steadying him until you have him going out with enthusiasm again. If he refuses to retrieve, start over again, waving the dummy, throwing it only a short distance until he willingly goes for it.

GIVING A LINE

At the same time that you are steadying your dog, you should start giving him a line. This means that you send him along a certain direction after the dummy. To do this use the hand on your side from which you heel your dog. With your hand open, move your arm and hand along the side of the dog's head, from back to front, moving your hand out in front of the nose in the direction you want him to go. Some trainers prefer to hold the hand directly over the center of the dog's nose when lining. We feel that this might interfere with the dog's vision and still prefer the beside the head method. This hand gesture will tell your dog which direction to go as he runs out after the dummy. This is very necessary when you start training him to do double, triple and blind retrieves. From now on, always give a line when you send the dog to retrieve, repeating the retrieve command "Get back" as you make the arm and hand gesture.

INTRODUCING TO WATER

When should you introduce your dog to water? Our own feeling is that he should be started while very young, but only if the water is warm. Any time after your dog is three or four months old is a good time for water introductions, provided the water is warm. If you have to wait until your dog is six months old in order to get warm water, no great harm is done. More harm will be done if his first experiences in the water are unpleasant. A good policy for very young puppies is to wait until they go in on their own, then start their water retrieves.

Many dogs take very easily and naturally to water and no urging is needed. Others require a little urging and coaxing, sometimes even discipline. Pick a shallow pond with sloping beaches and a hard sandy or gravelly shore and put on your waders or swim trunks. Wade out into water a foot deep and call your dog. Play with him in the shallows, giving him a chance to romp around and get used to the water. Then wade out into swimming depth, calling your dog to you. He may swim clumsily and with a lot of splash, but after several sessions he should be swimming well.

After this introduction, you can throw a dummy into the shallows (wading depth) for him to retrieve, increasing the distance and depth as your dog gets used to the water. From this point on you ought to alternate between land and water retrieves, giving your dog retrieves first in open water, then in rushes, cattails and increasingly denser cover as he becomes more efficient.

INTRODUCTION TO FEATHERS

After you have introduced your dog successfully to the water, you can introduce him to feathers. Obtain some live pigeons, kill one and wrap some cord around the wings to keep them from flopping. Tease your dog with the bird until he gets interested in it, then throw it 10 feet in front of you. Tell him to "Get back" ("Fetch" for pointers and flushers). He will likely run to the bird, then sniff and muzzle it, or try to pick it up. Give the command "Fetch." In all likelihood, after several trials, he will pick up the bird and bring it to you. If he refuses to pick it up, go through the same procedure as in training the dog to hold a dummy. Pry open his mouth and put the bird in, saying "Fetch." Repeat until he will hold the bird and carry it in his mouth. From that time on you can use pigeons occasionally for training. If you find your dog growing indifferent to retrieving dummies, switch to dead or live pigeons; his interest will pick up considerably.

After he is used to dead pigeons, try live ones, each with the feathers of one wing clipped, making certain the dog never bites or mauls the birds or plays with them. The best insurance against hard-mouth (biting or crushing the game) is a careful introduction to feathers, and watchfulness on the part of the trainer. Never let your dog play with a bird; make him return it to you immediately.

PREVENTING HARD-MOUTH

If you find that your dog is too rough with your birds, hold a bird in your hand and with your hand around it offer it to your dog. If he starts to bite it, reprimand him with a stern "No." He won't bite your hand and you can let him know that you want him to handle the bird gently. It is also a good idea to have your dog practice sitting and holding a live bird, or to walk around holding one in his mouth. Usually, a dog that is very rough with birds can be cured by bringing him inside and forcing him to sit quietly holding a bird for five to ten minutes at a time. During this period the dog should not be allowed the slightest mouthing of the bird. Harsh punishment must be administered if he does.

INTRODUCING THE GUN

The introduction to the gun should also be done carefully to avoid gun shyness. It is best to begin with a cap pistol or blank pistol. (Actually, from the very beginning of training we shout "Bang" each time we throw a bird for the dog to retrieve.) The procedure in introducing the dog to the gun is simple. Have a helper throw a bird or dummy for you (a bird is probably best here, at least until the dog is thoroughly used to the gun), firing the blank pistol before the bird is thrown, so as to attract the dog's attention to the bird. Since the thrower will be a considerable distance away from you, the shot will probably not disturb your dog and he will retrieve as usual. If he should show signs of fear and refuse to retrieve, use a cap pistol the next time, and have the thrower move farther away, or have a separate person at a farther distance shoot the gun when the thrower throws the bird. It should not take long before the dog will associate retrieving with the gun shot and will perk up his ears in readiness to retrieve each time the gun is fired.

After the dog gets used to the gun, have the shooter move closer until he is shooting the gun right beside you whenever a bird is thrown. After your dog is used to the blank pistol, then introduce him to the shotgun by the same careful procedure.

DOUBLE MARKED RETRIEVES

After your dog is retrieving singles (dummies and birds both) from land and water, marking each one well and returning it to hand, you can begin to introduce him to double marked retrieves. The procedure is simple but requires a lot of practice. Begin on bare ground, throwing two dummies widely separated, some 25 feet or so in front of you. Make your dog sit and remain steady while both birds are thrown. You can fire a shot for each bird, or shout "Bang" while each is thrown. Send your dog after the last bird thrown. After he retrieves it, make him sit and then give him a line to the second bird, using the usual gesture and the command to retrieve: "Get back." (The command is "Fetch" for pointers and flushers.) Your dog may act a little confused at first; he may refuse to go out, or he may just hesitate. If you are fortunate, he will go right out and bring the second bird to hand. It helps if both birds are thrown in short grass so the dog can see them.

After the dog is retrieving both birds to hand, gradually increase the distance until the dog will retrieve at distances over 100 yards. You can repeat the procedure for double marked retrieves on water. (For long distances on land or water you will need a helper to throw the birds.)

In the beginning your dog will have trouble remembering the second bird, particularly for water retrieves, and particularly when he can't see the second bird; but practice should enable him to develop his memory. It takes a lot of practice and patience, however, before he will be doing a good job on long doubles in cover or across water. Keep the work easy enough so he can accomplish the task most of the time, gradually increasing the difficulty of the falls as the dog's skill develops.

It is good to take your dog to different fields or to different sloughs or ponds or lakes for his workouts. He needs to learn to hunt under a variety of conditions and in different places, so try to work him out in various locations.

INTRODUCTION TO DECOYS

Sometime before you take your dog on his first duck hunting trip you should introduce him to decoys. Place several decoys on bare ground and send your dog on a short single retrieve through the decoys. He may stop to sniff them at first. When he does, say "No" and "Leave it." Your dog will soon learn to ignore them. Repeat this same procedure on the water.

INTRODUCTION TO OTHER BIRDS

Also before your first hunting trip, you will want to introduce your dog to shackled ducks and pheasants. Obtain a live duck, bind the wings close to the body with gummed tape wrapped around the duck. Tie the legs together with string or a rubber band so the duck cannot swim. Tease your dog with the duck, throw the duck into the water, and send the dog to retrieve it. He will soon enjoy the duck work.

In introducing your dog to pheasants you will have to kill the bird before using it. Tease the dog with the pheasant; throw it out and send your dog. If he hesitates to pick it up give the "Fetch" command. Or put the pheasant in his mouth and make him hold it; then call the dog to you. After a few times he will pick up the pheasant and retrieve it for you. Since these birds are considerably larger and heavier than pigeons it will take a little practice before the dog learns to take a firm hold on the bird. Always try to keep him from dropping or playing with the birds. If pheasants are unavailable, small Bantam chickens are an excellent substitute.

THE FIRST HUNTING TRIP

Your first hunting experience with your retriever should be an exciting one. If your dog will retrieve doubles on land and water, and is obedient, then he is certainly ready for his first actual hunting experience. Your months of careful training should pay off. Your dog will not do a perfect job, but he will retrieve part of your birds without too much help from you. Right now don't expect him to retrieve birds he hasn't seen fall. Send him only after marked birds at a reasonable distance.

If your first trip is for duck hunting, you may have some trouble with your dog holding still in blind or boat. Or he may break occasionally and go after birds before he is sent. This is to be expected. However, if you have too much trouble you may have to tie him to you or the boat for the first few times. Reprimand him and say "Stay" if he breaks, but don't expect perfection at first. Several seasons may come and go before he is doing his best work.

WORKING FROM A BOAT

If you are going to be duck hunting from a boat, it is a good idea to introduce your dog to working from the boat before the hunting trip begins. Start the training with the boat on land or on shore. Send your dog from the boat to retrieve. Then anchor in water of wading depth and practice there. Finally, go into deep water and practice from there. It may take a little patience before your dog is hitting the water with gusto from a boat in deep water.

When the dog returns with the bird take the bird before you call the dog into the boat, otherwise the dog may drop or crush the bird in trying to enter the boat. Also, you may have to help him climb in. Once he gets his front paws over the gunwale, pull and push down on his head to help him get his hind legs in.

UPLAND GAME HUNTING WITH RETRIEVERS

If you are taking your retriever pheasant hunting or hunting for other types of upland game, it is wise to walk the dog at heel in the beginning. If you are unsure of his obedience, even put him on leash and let someone else do the shooting. That way your dog is sure to be right beside you where you can send him after shot birds. Nearly every young dog has a tendency to chase flying birds at first until he learns not to do so. Try to keep your dog under perfect control and to make him wait until sent. If he should break, whistle him back as quickly as possible. If he starts flushing birds ahead of you, keep him leashed and release him only for retrieves.

After your dog has become steady on flying birds, you can use him as a flushing dog. Begin in cover you are to hunt, tell him to "Hie on" and then don't let him move farther away than about 25 yards. He will soon learn to move back and forth in front of you. However, if you intend to use your retriever for field trials, don't let him quarter and flush birds as this will hurt his lining on blinds and long marks. For a discussion of training your dog to flush, see Chapter 16.

If you find your dog getting too excited and not minding when he gets away from you, a low-power BB gun or pistol, or a sling shot, or an electronic dog trainer helps considerably to bring your dog under control. A couple of shots in the rump should remind him to come when called or to do as he is told. Use such measures only if you have to, but this is certainly better than letting your dog ruin the hunt and develop bad habits. Remember, a good retriever should be under voice and whistle control at all times.

MULTIPLE FALLS

An advanced stage of your retriever training is to teach him to do multiple marked retrieves (up to four marked birds). The best retrievers are able to mark, remember and retrieve four birds on land or water without being handled. So after your dog is retrieving marked doubles on land and water, and in fairly dense cover, you can try triples. Here again, begin with short retrieves on open land or water, gradually increasing the distance, the thickness of the cover and the difficulty of the retrieves as your dog progresses. Some dogs are never able to remember over one bird, some never over two. If, after considerable practice, your dog doesn't seem to be able to remember over two birds, you may either have to settle for that, always helping him on more than two birds, or, as a last resort, get a better dog. However, you must remember that it takes several years of regular training before a dog is doing his best work on marking triple falls. Because on the more difficult triples and quadruples even a top field trial dog is generally "helped" to a bird by fine lining.

HANDLING AND BLIND RETRIEVES

The final stage of your retriever's training is to teach him to handle; that is, to respond to hand and whistle signals in going after blind retrieves (birds that he hasn't seen fall). Ordinarily most retrievers should be one and a half to two years of age and marking doubles and triples well before you begin blind retrieves.

Teaching your dog to handle will tax your patience and his. For a time his marking may be poor; he may even grow indifferent about the whole thing; but try to keep the sessions short enough and interesting enough so your dog is trying all of the time. If he grows indifferent and sulky, you are pushing him too hard.

Actually, teaching your dog to handle is a simple procedure, but it requires a lot of practice and patience. Here is how to do it.

First, your dog should be responding well to the basic whistle signals: one sharp blast to sit, a series of short blasts to come. If he needs more practice on these signals, work on them until your dog will respond to these from 100 yards away.

Second, he should be taking a good line now, going out at full speed in the direction you send him with your hand. If he does not do this well, continue working on it. One way to teach him to take a good line is to hide a dummy in the grass about 15 yards ahead of you; then hide another at about 25 yards, and another at 50 yards. Tell the dog to "Heel" and "Sit," then give him a line and send him to retrieve the first dummy. If this is his first experience in going out when he has not marked the fall, he may hesitate, or he may refuse altogether. If he does refuse, then place the dummy where he can see it before you send him. Then try very short retrieves; 10 yards or so with the dummy hidden. Eventually, he will learn to go out whenever you send him, whether he sees the dummy or not.

After retrieving one dummy on a certain line, send him after the second at a slightly greater distance on the same line. By gradually increasing the distance, you can get him to take a good line a long distance.

Third, you have to teach what the arm signals mean. There are three basic commands here. "Over" is used along with a right arm or left arm gesture for your dog to go right or left. "Get back" is used to tell your dog to go out. At the time you give this command, throw and point your arm straight up into the sky and say "Get back." "Come" is used to get your dog to come straight toward you. Also use the signal on the whistle and point your arm and hand straight down to the ground, moving your arm from front to back.

To teach your dog to respond to the arm signals, proceed as follows. Imagine that the ground on which you are training is a baseball diamond with you and your dog in the pitcher's mound. Tell your dog to "Sit" and "Stay." Then throw the dummy to first base. Leaving your dog on the pitcher's mound, walk to home plate. Then, throwing your right arm straight out from your right side, give your dog the command "Over." If he hesitates, tell him to "Fetch" and "Over." Eventually he will learn that "Over" means go out and get that bird on first base. After he gets the dummy call him to you on home base. Then walk back to the pitcher's mound, ask your dog to "Sit" and "Stay," and then throw the dummy to third base. Leave the dog on the pitcher's mound and then walk back to home plate. Give the command "Over," and this time throw your left arm out straight from your left side. Your dog should get the dummy on third base. Call him to you as always.

After he has mastered these two gestures (it will take many days of practice), then, starting on the pitcher's mound once more, throw the dummy to second base. Leaving your dog on the pitcher's mound, walk to home plate. Give the command "Get back"; throw your arm straight up in the air. This is the signal for your dog to retrieve the dummy which is on second base. When he finds it, call him to you at home.

After he learns to associate the vocal command and arm gesture with the direction he is to go, plant a dummy on each of the bases without your dog watching you. Ask him to sit on the pitcher's mound while you walk to home plate. Send him first to first base. After he retrieves, return him to the

Labrador Retriever shows top form in fetching a downed bird from the water.

Courtesy Del-Tone Kennels

pitcher's mound. Send him next to third base to retrieve; return him to the mound. Send him last to second base to retrieve; then call him in. Practice this until he will take a good line in any direction you send him. If he is not sure which direction to go, have him mark the birds again while you throw, then give him the proper arm signal until he begins to associate the particular arm movement with the proper direction in which to go.

After your dog learns the basic directions, plant a bird out about 25 yards and send your dog after it from a position at your heel. Try to give him a line so he will pass just downwind of the bird and scent it. If he is well trained to sit on signal, give him the sit signal whenever you want him to stop. When he sits and looks at you, give him the needed voice and arm gesture to send him in the direction to retrieve the bird.

It takes a lot of practice before a dog will handle well, but once it is accomplished it's an achievement for both you and your dog. But don't expect quick results. Some of the finest field-trial dogs require over two years of training before they will really handle well. And even the old campaigners are in training all their lives to perfect this phase of their work.

After you have trained your dog to handle on land, try handling him in the water. The same voice, whistle and arm gestures are used as on land. When you blow the sit signal, your dog will quit swimming, turn around and look at you and wait for directions before swimming on.

After the basic commands are learned, you need to lengthen the retrieves gradually until your dog will take "casts" to the right or left, or out, of distances up to 100 yards.

Some dogs may never learn to handle well. If you are having trouble, get the advice and help of a professional trainer before you discard your dog as too dumb to learn.

You can have a pretty fair hunting dog even if you never try to handle him, but the birds he does not see shot down, you will have to retrieve yourself. But it is preferable to have a dog you can teach to handle. It is a lot of fun training him, and it is a real joy to work with him once he's trained. In many duck hunting situations, where the dog is worked from a blind that obstructs his view of shot and falling birds, a dog that will not line and handle on blind retrieves is not of much use.

16

Training and Hunting the Flusher

THE PRINCIPAL flushing dogs which are referred to in this chapter are the spaniels—especially the English Springer Spaniel and the Cocker Spaniel (both American and English), since these two breeds are the most popular and the most widely used. The flushing spaniels also include the American Water Spaniel, Welsh Springer Spaniel, Clumber Spaniel, Sussex Spaniel and the Field Spaniel. The training principles outlined in this section of the book apply to all of these spaniel breeds. For a complete discussion of the flushing breeds see Chapter 3 of this book. It should be noted that since the Brittany Spaniel is a pointing dog, it is discussed in the chapters on pointing dogs and setters.

An English Springer Spaniel is put through his paces during a training session in retrieving.

In addition to the spaniels, however, two retriever breeds, the Labrador Retriever and the Golden Retriever, are frequently used as flushing dogs. These retrievers are specialists in retrieving, but they can also be easily trained as flushing dogs. Most of the principles of training flushing dogs which are discussed here, therefore, do apply to training these retrievers as flushers. If, however, you ever want to run your retriever in field trials, you should never consider training or using him as a flusher.

Occasionally even some hound dog breeds, particularly the Beagle and the Basset, are used to flush game birds, as well as rabbits or other small game. In fact we have a friend who owns a Beagle whom the owner claims to be the best dog he has ever used on pheasants. Ordinarily, though, we would not recommend trying to train hounds as game-bird flushers, especially if you want to use the same hounds on rabbits or other game. If you do succeed in training your hounds to flush game birds, you will practically ruin them for the purpose for which they are bred, since their range will become too restricted and other wrong habits will be developed.

This chapter, therefore, applies principally to the spaniels, and secondarily to the two retriever breeds mentioned. Chapter 15, "Training and Hunting the Retriever," applies principally to the retriever breeds, and secondarily to the spaniel and pointing breeds which you want to train to retrieve.

THE TASK OF THE FLUSHING DOG

The task of the flushing dog is really three-fold: 1) to seek and find game; 2) to flush it within gun range of the hunter; and 3) to retrieve fallen game when ordered to do so. At first thought, this three-fold task may seem like a simple one. A good dog who shows courage, enthusiasm, aggressiveness, a good nose and a well-developed bird instinct takes naturally to the task of seeking out game. Most good flushing dogs also have a natural instinct for retrieving. But to further develop these natural instincts, to refine and temper them with control and obedience, and to train the dog to the point where he will work for the hunter and in perfect harmony with him, requires time, patience and know-how.

Consider first the task of finding and flushing game. The flushing dog must have drive and courage to hunt all types of cover and to crash into thickets, thorns and brambles to find game. He must have endurance and stamina to be able to "beat the brush" and run for long periods of time in his search. He should show a fine style, which means he exhibits real enthusiasm for the quest as he goes about it with eagerness and anticipation. Spaniel owners describe this style as a "merry bustle," as the dog speedily quarters in front of the hunter with his tail flashing and quivering, his head often up and alert to test the wind currents for body scents of birds, and at other times with head low to investigate the scent of a track. When such a dog finds game, he dashes in with determination and vehemence, scaring birds into the air with a roar of their wings, or springing a rabbit from his covert posthaste.

A good flushing dog must have not only eagerness, drive and endurance, but also a keen nose. Since he locates game principally by his sense of smell, his usefulness depends upon his ability to find game even under dry, poor-scenting conditions. Sometimes he will be called upon to follow the trail of a wounded pheasant, or to sniff out the location of a downed bird in the heaviest land cover or in the thick rushes in the water.

The best dogs also must learn to hunt efficiently, to quarter back and forth smoothly so that the total area ahead of the hunter is covered, and to keep moving steadily, while quartering, in the direction the hunter is traveling. This means that the dog should turn away from the hunter each time the dog changes directions, and should not double back over an area already covered (unless game is found) or double back behind the hunter. Furthermore, the dog should not range out too far, either too far to the side, or too far ahead. This means that the dog has to stay within a maximum range of about 40 yards so that when game is flushed the gunner gets a shot.

Experienced dogs also learn where game is most likely to be found. They learn to hunt the clumps of grass and brush, the food patches, the thick cover by fence rows, and the likely-looking thickets which provide maximum security and protection for game.

The best flushing dogs also have to be tractable (easily trained and eager to please), since control is of the utmost importance in the field. The dog has to be under voice or whistle control at all times so that the handler can keep him in range, or direct him to likely spots. It is standard procedure also to teach spaniels to "Hup" (sit) at shot or flush and to wait until ordered to retrieve. Obviously, this kind of perfect obedience requires a great deal of training, but it also requires a dog that is willing to learn and wants to do what is expected of him.

Consider also the task of retrieving. Once game is found and flushed, the dog has to carefully mark the fall of the shot bird, and to find it when asked to "Fetch." If doubles are shot down, the dog has to find and retrieve one bird, and then remember the second fall so as to be able to find and retrieve the second. When a fall is not marked by the dog, he has to be able to take directions from the hand and whistle signals of the handler, to go out downwind of where the bird fell so he can scent it, find it and retrieve it.

Handling the game is also important. On the one hand, a dog who is too soft-mouthed, and not sufficiently trained, will repeatedly drop the bird on the way in, or will have to readjust his grip so as to be able to carry the bird well at all. Some dogs even get in the habit of dropping the bird before reaching the handler. Therefore, the dog must learn to carry the bird with a gentle, yet firm, grip and to keep it in his mouth until the handler takes the bird from him. On the other hand, a hard-mouthed dog will damage or crush the game, or perhaps shake it, puncture it or even spoil it for table use.

Spaniels are also expected to be able to retrieve game from water. Most upland bird hunters use their spaniels occasionally or even regularly for waterfowl. Also, the planning committees of field trials have the right to require some retrieves in the water after a good swim. Therefore, the best flushing dogs should be expected to retrieve waterfowl, especially in moderate temperature and cover conditions. Spaniels usually do not have the coat to work in the coldest icewater, nor the size and drive to swim long distances or to work the heaviest rushes, but they are expected to perform reasonable tasks in the water and ought to be trained to do so.

OBEDIENCE TRAINING

Before beginning any training of your flushing dog be sure to read Chapters 11, 12 and 13. The obedience commands used for spaniels are almost identical to those used for other breeds, and include the following: No, Hup (used for sit), Stay, Come, Kennel, Charge, Down, Heel, Hie on and Stop that noise. You can begin training your spaniel puppy on these commands anytime after he is seven weeks of age according to the directions given in the chapters previously cited. Your obedience training will actually continue concurrently with your training in quartering, flushing and retrieving.

BEGINNING TRAINING IN QUARTERING

Your first task in training your spaniel as a flushing dog is to develop his enthusiasm for searching out cover to find game. With puppies, this enthusiasm can be developed by taking your dog for daily walks in fields and meadows. In the beginning choose fields with light cover in which your puppy can freely run and play. He will learn to sniff at strange scents, investigate interesting looking cover patches and to develop independence and initiative in his playful searching. At this stage, keep verbal commands to a minimum. Wave him out with a cherry "Hie on" and encourage him to investigate and run on his own. The purpose of this stage of training is to develop the independence, courage and desire to search coverts for game. Let him freely flush any birds (songbirds included) or animals he can find. Call him to you only when he gets out of gun range.

As he becomes bolder and more aggressive in his searching, and grows larger physically, you need to start encouraging him to quarter back and forth in front of you. The best way to do this is to walk briskly forward, waving your puppy to go out ahead of you, and then to traverse a zig-zag pattern yourself. This will encourage your dog to do likewise. Call him to come only when he ranges out ahead too far. If he travels too far to one side, blow a sharp blast on your whistle, and then start going in the opposite direction, waving him with your arm to go in that same direction. If you move to your left, wave him "Over" in this direction with your left arm. If you move to your right, wave him "Over" in that direction with your right arm. He will soon begin to move out ahead in a zig-zag pattern. A dog who is full of desire and enthusiasm will like to keep moving and will develop a tendency to quarter if he learns that he should not get beyond range of your gun.

You ought to be very cautious, however, in trying to "handle" your dog at this young age. If you continually blow your whistle and wave to him, he will learn to depend too much on your directions, so at this stage never try to control him unless he is getting out of range. Let him do as much on his own as possible, at least in this stage of training, otherwise you may develop a mechanical worker who depends too much upon you.

From the beginning, however, you should try to teach him to stay within range. If your dog has a lot of enthusiasm and drive, and moves out too far and does not come when called, you may have to let him drag a check cord which you can easily pick up and jerk lightly whenever you blow the come signal (several staccato blasts on the whistle). When he comes back into range, wave him on again with a "Hie on." Or you can hold one end of the long check cord in your hand, pulling it up tight only when the dog ranges too far out after you have blown the signal to come. Some handlers prefer heeling their dog each time he gets out too far, before sending him out again. Either way, your dog will learn to stay within range.

This training in quartering will usually take months to accomplish, especially if you start with a young puppy. Don't expect him to learn how to thoroughly cover the ground ahead of you in several easy lessons. Your dog must develop physically and mentally, as well as be thoroughly obedient to you, before he will be able to hunt cover with both aggressiveness and control.

TRAINING IN FLUSHING

After your dog begins to enjoy your daily walks through the fields, you can give him planned opportunities to flush game. If you are fortunate to live in an area where natural game abounds, then take him to these spots for your training. Or, if you can afford to do so, take him to private game preserves where game abounds. Don't try to shoot the birds at this stage of training since you will want to introduce your dog to the gun very carefully before you do any shooting over him. However, he needs a chance to flush birds to build up his enthusiasm and drive for the sport.

One way of developing bird interest in the young puppy is to tie a bird wing to the end of a string which is attached to a long bamboo pole. Have a friend hold the pole so the bird wing is dragged on the ground 10 or 15 feet ahead of you. If you hunt into the wind your puppy ought to catch the scent of the wing and move forward to catch it. When he starts to pounce upon it, have the friend pull the wing into the air to simulate a bird flushing. Daily sessions of this exercise will develop a real enthusiasm for finding and flushing birds.

Another way to teach flushing is to plant live birds (pigeons) in a field ahead of you. Some trainers put the bird in a trap which can be sprung to release the bird when the dog finds the game. Traps can be purchased which are operated electronically, or which are operated by a simple hand pull. Another device tosses a dead bird aloft when a trip is pulled.

Another system is to use live pigeons which are released in a field just before the dog works the field. Various schemes can be used to keep the pigeons from flying until flushed. One scheme is to tie a long thread to the pigeon's leg. The other end of the thread is held by a helper who releases his grip at the instant the dog flushes the bird. Other trainers whirl the pigeon around to make it dizzy before releasing it. By the time the dog finds the bird the pigeon will have recovered enough to fly away.

TRAINING IN RETRIEVING

The basic principles outlined in Chapter 15 can be followed in training the spaniel to retrieve. A summary of the stages and steps in training follows:

1. Begin with small dummies and work your dog in a small enclosed area.

Wave the dummy in front of the dog's nose until he is interested in catching it, and throw it in front of him a few feet, giving the command to retrieve, which is "Fetch." When he chases the dummy and picks it up, blow the come signal on your whistle, clap your hands and say "Come," and move away from your dog to encourage him to follow you with the dummy. Try to take the dummy from him as he comes near.

2. Gradually increase the distance you throw the dummy until he is retrieving from distances up to 100 yards on bare ground with light cover.

3. Next begin working your dog in heavier cover, throwing the dummy very short distances at first. Gradually increase the distance of the retrieves until he will retrieve in moderate cover for distances up to 100 yards.

4. If your dog frequently drops the dummy on the return because of poor hold, or if he has to readjust his grip on it, or if he starts dropping it at your feet before you take it from him, start working on his holding and releasing the dummy properly according to the directions outlined in Chapter 15. Usually this training does not begin until after your puppy shows real enthusiasm for his work and after six months of age. The command to hold the dummy, or to pick it up, is the same as for retrieving: "Fetch." The command to release the dummy is "leave it."

5. If your dog does not come promptly to you with the dummy, work on the command "Come" without the dummy, and then on "Come" while he is carrying the dummy, according to instructions in Chapter 15.

6. Teach your spaniel to deliver the dummy by sitting in front of you at the command "Hup," or to sit at your heel when you say "Heel" and "Hup." We prefer to have our dogs heel and sit to deliver so they are in position to be "given a line" to a possible second fall.

7. Only after your spaniel is really dashing out to retrieve the dummy and is retrieving and delivering smoothly to hand, should you begin steadying him: i. e., to require him to wait to retrieve until sent. Follow the instructions in Chapter 15. Instructions on teaching your spaniel to "Hup" to flush or to shot are given later in this chapter, but teaching steadiness from a position at your heel is a good prelude to teaching the more advanced lesson.

8. Whenever you send your spaniel from a heeled position, give him a line with your hand to the bird at the same time you give the command "Fetch." This is a good prelude to teaching him to remember and to retrieve marked doubles, or to take a line to a blind fall.

9. Sometime early in his training, and when the water is moderately warm, introduce your puppy to the water according to the directions in Chapter 15. After he enjoys playing and swimming in the water, begin throwing the dummy in the water for him to retrieve. Gradually increase the distance until he will retrieve falls up to 75 or 100 yards. Generally spaniels are not required to retrieve long falls in the water nor are they required to do difficult work in ice water or heavy cover, so don't push your dog too hard on water work. Gradually introduce him to retrieves in light cover, increasing the distance slowly as he develops confidence and ability. Ordinarily, don't ever expect him to reach the level of proficiency of one of the trained retriever breeds. The work these dogs are expected to do is almost impossible for spaniels. One best rule here is to develop your dog's ability in the water as much as he seems willing and capable of doing, but don't push him be-

yond the limit of his physical strength and ability. You may ruin him if you push him too hard in cold water or in extremely heavy cover.

10. After your spaniel is retrieving smoothly, introduce him to feathers according to the directions in Chapter 15. You can begin with bird wings for young dogs, then graduate to dead pigeons, then to live pigeons, and finally to dead pheasants and to shackled ducks. The larger birds should be used only after your spaniel is fully developed physically.

11. Introduce your dog to the gun according to the directions in Chapter 15. We firmly believe it is better to introduce spaniels to the gun in conjunction with their training in retrieving, rather than in relation to flushing birds. A full discussion of teaching the spaniel to retrieve shot birds from a "Hup" position from where the birds were flushed is given later in this chapter.

12. After your spaniel is retrieving birds smoothly from land or water, begin training him on double marked retrieves according to the directions in Chapter 15. Ordinarily, spaniels should not be expected to mark, remember and retrieve doubles at long distances or in as heavy a cover as do the retriever breeds. So try to develop your dog to the limit of his ability, without expecting the impossible of him.

13. If you are going to use your spaniel for retrieving waterfowl, introduce him to working in and through decoys, and from a boat, according to the directions in Chapter 15.

14. The final stage of training in retrieving is to teach your dog to handle (to take directions from your hand and whistle signals) so he can do blind retrieves (birds he has not marked down). Some spaniel owners never try to train their dogs to handle at all, but trust their dog to mark and find the falls. If, however, your dog does not see a bird go down, or cannot find it, you will have to retrieve the bird yourself if your dog has not been taught to handle. Certainly, if you are going to do field-trial work with your spaniel, it is helpful if he develops some proficiency at handling. However, precise handling is considered the postgraduate course for spaniels, so only you can decide whether you want to bother with it or not. Certainly you should never start this kind of training until your dog is one and one-half to two years of age. Some dogs are never able to master it. Others do so easily, so perhaps part of your decision must be based upon your dog's ability as well as your own preference. Full directions for teaching the retriever breeds are given in Chapter 15. These directions apply to spaniels also except spaniels are required to retrieve from a "Hup" position when commanded to do so. They are only handled when they can't find the bird on their own. They are not brought to a heeling position and sent from "the line" to retrieve blinds as are the retriever breeds, except in the instance of the second bird of a double fall. Spaniels are handled from whatever location the handler finds himself in relation to the dog at the time the bird is flushed and shot down.

FLUSHING AND SHOOTING THE BIRDS

After your dog has developed real enthusiasm for seeking game, and has learned to quarter, flush and retrieve, you should start shooting birds over him as often as possible. The multiple pleasure your dog gets in hunting

is to find birds, flush them and then to get to retrieve them. If he is expected
to find and flush birds, but you never shoot them so he can retrieve them, he
may discover there is no real point in his flushing birds at all. Furthermore,
if he only retrieves birds which you have thrown and shot, and never has to
find them in the first place, he is not really doing the task he is expected
to do, which is to find the game for you. Therefore, these three components
of the task—finding, flushing and retrieving—must be brought together as
soon as you feel your dog has developed some proficiency in each element
of the task. Some trainers begin shooting birds over the dog just as soon as he
has learned a little about finding and flushing, and has been introduced
to the gun and to feathers. Many times the dog has really not been taught to
retrieve well at all. We would rather work a little longer on teaching the dog
to quarter properly and to retrieve marked singles carefully to hand, before
doing too much actual hunting with him. Certainly you should never shoot
birds over him before he has been properly introduced to gun and feathers.
To make this mistake is to risk the danger of developing gun shyness and/or
hard-mouth.

If birds are scarce in your area, you can use live pigeons released from
traps according to the directions previously given in this chapter. Eventually,
though, he will have to learn that all birds don't spring from traps, so it is
better, at least half of the time, to plant live uncaged birds which he is expected to find and flush, and which you can shoot, and which he is ordered
to retrieve. Of course you can hunt private game preserves which are well
stocked with birds, but this gets expensive. A good plan is to buy your own
birds and plant them in areas where you have permission to hunt.

The only way you can develop your spaniel into an experienced hunter
is to give him lots of practice, so the more often you work him under actual
hunting conditions the better.

HUPPING AT FLUSH, SHOT OR COMMAND

This is the final stage in training the flushing dog, just as handling is the
final stage in training the retriever. By this time your dog should be steady
in his retriever training; that is, he should not retrieve until ordered to do so.

Your next task is a continuation of this one. That is, you now have to teach
him to hup and to remain steady in the spot where he flushed the bird, or
wherever he is when a bird is shot. When two spaniels are worked on parallel
courses, as in spaniel trials, both dogs are expected to "Hup" at flush or shot,
and to remain steady. Only one dog is ordered to retrieve. The other must
remain where he is sitting. Obviously this kind of control requires perfect
obedience and a lot of training.

To begin with, walk behind your dog as usual while he is quartering
ahead of you, but keep your dog in fairly close. Then have a helper throw
and shoot a bird out ahead of your dog, or slightly off to the side. At this
instant tell your dog to "Hup." If he runs after the bird before you send him,
take him back to the spot where he was when the bird was shot, and tell him
to "Hup." Then try the same thing again. If he persists in going after the
bird before sent, put a long check cord on him and try again. At the instant
the bird is thrown and shot, say "Hup." If the dog breaks, give a sharp, but

firm, jerk on the check cord and say "Hup" again. If he won't hup, go up to him, smack his behind and say "Hup." Continue practicing this (with the check cord attached) until he will "Hup" consistently every time the bird is thrown and shot. Incidentally, you can save on live birds by using dead but fresh ones (we keep ours in the freezer), and having the gunner simply fire into the air when the bird is thrown.

Next try the same procedure with the check cord removed. If your dog breaks, chastise him severely, put him back on his spot and say "Hup." Then try again. If your dog is especially aggressive, or a real hardhead, it may take a number of daily sessions before he will "Hup" at flush and/or shot consistently and with the check cord off.

The final stage is to make him "Hup" each time he flushes the bird himself, or each time a companion dog flushes the bird, or anytime a shot is fired (whether or not the bird is hit). You may have to resort to the check cord again until your dog is steady, particularly in those instances when he flushes the bird. It is a real temptation for the dog flushing the bird to also want to chase it or to retrieve it immediately, but with patience this tendency can be overcome and the dog brought under control.

One last caution: Discipline him only enough to do the job, yet without spoiling his enthusiasm for hunting or retrieving. If he grows hesitant about doing either task, ease up on the pressure and discipline, until he grows eager once more.

HUNTING THE SPANIEL

If you have gone through the training steps and procedures suggested in this chapter, taking your spaniel hunting will not be much different than taking him training. The only possible difference might be that now your purpose is to shoot birds. In training, your first goal has been to train your dog and only secondarily to shoot birds.

Of course there are many lessons your dog has to learn under actual hunting conditions. Flushing a whole covey of birds sometimes causes confusion in a dog's marking. Your dog may be watching a bird other than the one you shoot, and so not mark the fall. However, through practice and experience he will steadily improve.

Another difficult thing for young dogs to learn is to trail wounded birds. If your dog continues to look where a bird fell, but does not pick up the trail, try to put him on the trail and urge him to follow it, assuming you know in which direction the bird ran. Gradually, he will learn how to follow the trail.

Crippled ducks present a different situation, since the dog can only smell a duck in the water when the duck is on the surface. The duck that dives and swims a considerable distance under water may get away from the dog that does not keep a sharp lookout in every direction. Experienced dogs seem to be able almost to anticipate the direction in which a duck is going to move, and are waiting close by for the duck to surface. Other dogs never seem to be able to catch up with cripples no matter what you try to teach them. Such dogs have to depend upon you to handle them to the cripples.

When you take your dog hunting for upland game try to hunt into the wind, if possible, so that the dog can smell the birds farther away and will continue to move in the direction of the scent. If you hunt with the wind at your back, your dog may have to keep doubling back to push the birds out, so it is harder for him to cover the ground efficiently.

Also, you have to learn to watch the actions of your dog to know ahead of time when he is on a hot scent. He will usually begin to wag his tail vigorously and move excitedly on the trail or air currents toward the bird. Once you learn to interpret his actions you can be ready to shoot when the bird is flushed.

Running pheasants present a difficult problem for the young dog and for the hunter. If you allow your dog to move at a fast pace after the pheasant, the bird is sometimes flushed out of range. Some hunters run after their dog when they know he is on scent in order to be there to shoot when the pheasant is flushed. Other hunters make their dog stay within range and move at a more leisurely pace even when the dog is on scent. It does no harm to make your dog stop until you catch up (blow one sharp, short blast on the whistle —the signal to "Hup") and then wave him on with a "Hie on" when you know you are in good shooting range. If your dog is a good trailer he will keep after the bird and eventually flush him, still giving you a good shot. Also, running pheasants are most likely to flush when they come to the end of the cornfield or other cover, so be ready for action when you get to the end of a drive. One way to keep pheasants from escaping is to post one or several hunters at the end of the field to block the escape route of the birds.

Whenever you are hunting with companions, whether or not they also have dogs, always make your dog quarter the area ahead of you. Don't let your dog get in the habit of hunting for someone else when you are along. Also, whenever your dog retrieves a bird which someone else has shot, make him always retrieve to you, then pass the bird along to your hunting companion. Field etiquette requires that only one handler control each dog, so don't let your friends shout at your pet or call him to them while he is flushing or retrieving.

Gradually, with time and experience, you and your dog will learn to work together as a team, each of you knowing what to expect of the other, and both of you enjoying the hunt and this wonderful companionship afield.

17

Training and Hunting the Hound

THE COONHOUND

Probably the most difficult to train to perfection of all hounds is the coonhound. A good coonhound must have the highest degree of intelligence, scenting ability, adaptability to different terrain and a wide variety of hunting skills. The difficulty in finding a coonhound who rates very high in all departments explains the soaring prices of top cooners. Within the past five years, several coonhounds have changed hands in the thousands of dollars bracket. However, if you have chosen your prospect intelligently, and know what you want, you should be able to come up with a reasonable cooner in two or three years at a minimum of expense.

Obedience Training

Many houndsmen have said that obedience training is too restrictive for a hound and tends to make him overly dependent on his handler. We used to subscribe to this belief, until we saw several fine hounds who were highly trained for obedience. Needless to say, the level of obedience required in a retriever is not mandatory in a coonhound, but it certainly adds to the pleasure of the hunt to be able to call your dogs in when you want to quit, and have them fully under control when they get there. Therefore, we recommend beginning obedience training for the following commands, as instructed in Chapter 13.

1. COME—This is the most important of all commands.
2. SIT—This puts your dog under control once he is in, so you can leash him.
3. KENNEL—The command to enter the car, his pen, the house, etc.
4. HEEL—Your dog will walk quietly at your side, instead of towing you all over the woods.
5. CHARGE—To lie down.
6. DOWN—Not to jump up on people or furniture.

These commands are all easily taught. Any fairly intelligent hound will catch on very quickly and he will be a much better hunting companion because of it.

Age to Begin

The age that a young coonhound should be started hunting is widely debated. Those in favor of later starting maintain that too much hunting as a puppy will spoil his desire, as he is not mature enough to cope with the fatigue of a long chase. Those in favor of starting the pup very young feel that more permanent impressions are made at an early age, and that, trained from the start on one kind of game or scent, he will be less likely to run off game. There is merit in both arguments, but to subscribe wholly to one or the other is oversimplification of the problem. We do not like to work with a dog who has been raised to the age of one year like a common piece of livestock. On the other hand, we have seen many good prospects ruined by too much impatient pushing on the part of the handler.

Beginning Training

We are going to propose a method of training which will pay heed to the danger of early overtraining and will utilize the increased educability of the puppy at the same time. This method is more time-consuming than the old "by-guess-and-by-golly" method of just turning the hound loose and hoping for the best, but the time spent will yield commensurately better results. A thoughtful and well-planned training program will not harm the very best prospect and will, in many cases, transform a mediocre prospect into a serviceable cooner.

To begin with, your coonhound puppy should be raised as close to you as possible. We have found that dogs raised in the home develop into bolder, more tractable workers and seem to hunt as much for their masters as for themselves. The more time you spend with your puppy the better. Training sessions should be short and frequent. A few minutes at a time, several times a day, is ideal for the very young puppy. Gradually increase the length of the training periods until they run fifteen minutes or so in length, and are reduced to one training session per day until the dog is fully trained.

Do not take the very young coonhound (under five or six months) hunting. The hunting instinct can be encouraged as soon as the pup is old enough to run around and chase things. An unwashed, preferably fresh, coon tail or a piece of hide is an excellent training aid. You can begin to tease your pup with this as soon as he will pay any attention to it. An excellent method is to obtain a long bamboo fishing pole and tie your tail or hide to the end of the pole with a 6- or 8-foot piece of heavy fish line. With this you can simulate a good chase and get the pup to go all-out in pursuit. This method offers the advantage of keeping the game away from the handler so that the pup begins to develop his independent hunting spirit. In this respect, the longer the bamboo pole the better. Every now and then, when the pup has put on an especially good show of chasing and barking, you should allow him to catch the lure and fool with it, tugging lightly against him with your pole in order to develop his tenacity.

When the pup has developed a real liking for this sport, and this should not take long, begin trying to make him tree-minded. This trait can be developed by terminating the fishing-pole-coon-tail maneuver in a small bush or sapling just out of the pup's reach. After a few repetitions of this your pup should begin to bark under the tree in an effort to catch the lure which he sees up there.

Introduction to Gun

Now introduce your hound to gunfire with nothing louder than a cap pistol. After he has barked up the tree for a minute or so, fire the cap pistol and drop the lure out so that he can wool it. This will teach him to associate gunfire with game, which is the surest way to avoid gunshyness. When the pup really seems to enjoy the excitement of the lure in the tree, and the noise of the cap pistol, you can increase to a .22-caliber blank pistol. Unless you intend to use a shotgun while hunting coon, or if you plan to use your hound on bear or mountain lion for which high-powered rifles must be used, you need break him to nothing louder than the .22 blanks.

Developing Training Ability

If your pup has progressed well up to this point and is showing reasonable promise in all areas, and in his obedience work, which should accompany the hunting training, he is ready to start using his most important faculty, his sense of smell. Puppies vary a great deal, so don't become discouraged if your pup does not exhibit intelligent use of his nose right away. We have had hounds who did swell jobs on a simple trail at three and one-half or four months of age, and others who were much slower but when mature had just as good scenting powers as the more precocious individuals. The only thing we can suggest here is to plan the difficulty of the work by your pup's ability, and realize that he will learning nothing by failure, and a great deal by success.

The job of training the pup to trail by scent can be accomplished with the same equipment used in the earlier training, with the addition of some coon training scent. A small amount of the coon scent should be applied to the lure before each training session until the dog can work it well; then you can begin to skip every other application, making the scent weaker and weaker in order to develop his cold-trailing ability. You will need some help the first few weeks in training your hound to scent, as the pup should be held back until the lure is dragged out of sight and up a tree. Here the fishing pole is useful to keep the coon scent away from the man scent so that the pup does not begin to run the human track. It is still a good idea to have your training partner wear rubber boots, freshly washed in hot water. This will reduce the strength of his trail to a minimum. In the early stages of this training, release your pup as soon as the lure is out of sight, making sure by teasing him with it beforehand that he will be properly motivated to run the trail.

On his first release, after the lure has been dragged out of sight, he will no doubt appear completely confused and lost. At this point you can go in and encourage him to pick up the trail, which after a few tries he will undoubtedly do. The tree at the end of these trails should be close and easy to begin with, and can be made more demanding as your prospect improves. Don't be discouraged if your pup will not give voice on these trails or on the tree. Frequently it takes live game and a fight or two to cause a dog to really open up. As your pup progresses, make the trails longer and tougher. Finally, put the lure up a tree where he cannot see it and try to get him treeing by scent location alone. Plenty of earnest praise should reward any job well done.

Introduction to Water

Your pup should be introduced to water at an early age, as he will encounter plenty of it while coon hunting in most parts of the country. The best way to do this is to incorporate it into the training program from the very beginning, starting with the shallowest riffles, barely enough to get the pup's feet wet, and progressing to water of swimming depth. A good water dog will take any water of reasonable size in an effort to pick up a trail that has been lost along the stream or river bank. Naturally there is a limit to the extent of water that you would expect your hound to swim after a coon. It would ruin an evening's hunt to have your dog cross a quarter-mile of deep river if you could not get across to get his game out to him. Any hound, if started in the water correctly, will eventually set his own limits as to what he is willing to swim. There is little you can do about that. A top water dog is a lot rarer than a poor one, so don't be worried about yours being too good.

Introducing the Live Coon and Fighting Cage

After your dog is working fairly well on the man-laid lure scent (this is known among houndsmen as a "drag"), you are ready to progress to a lead coon and a fighting cage or bag. A small coon can easily be trapped in the early summer using a live trap and canned fish for bait. Before laying a track with the captive coon, it is best to excite your hound by allowing him to fight it through a fighting cage. These offer the advantage of a lot of excitement and action with no injury to the coon or dog. If your young dog will not take to fighting the coon right away, tease him with it a little by holding the cage above his head, then put it on the ground where he can get at it. Both dog and coon will soon get the idea and will put up a good fight. We have seen this done with old trained hounds and a caged coon, which was equally experienced, and the coon would actually come out of his box in the cage and try to get at the dogs. No doubt if they had both been out in the open, the coon would quickly have made for the nearest tree.

If your pup still will not fight, and you have no other hound to put with him, borrow a farmer's Shepherd who is friendly with other dogs. Most Shepherds will fight a coon on sight, and the excitement of the fight will probably draw your pup in. The reason we caution against using a dog that will fight other dogs is that your pup may be ruined if he takes a whipping from another dog while going after game. There is also a chance that an experience of this kind might make him quarrelsome at the tree or around downed game. A hound with this fault is practically worthless as a pack dog.

Almost any hunter will want to hunt his hound with others of his own or his friend's from time to time. Fighting, like other serious faults, can usually be curbed if the offender is reprimanded early enough. A good beating with a broomstick, applied to the haunch where it will do him no permanent damage, will suffice. After the corporal punishment, you should put the offending dog on a lead, and take him in for the night. This adds to the punishment and gives him awhile to think it over. It should be noted, however, that a beating should always be delivered with a cool head. Two or three hard, well-placed blows will do. Anything more becomes sadism. Try to avoid any physical punishment with a hound, but fighting is one place where you must be hard-boiled.

Once you have your dog so interested in fighting the confined coon that the minute you take him out of his pen, and tell him to "Go catch a coon," he will quickly go where the lead coon is kept and begin to fight it, you are well on the way to having a "coon-minded" hound. At this point, you can leave the dog in his pen, take the lead coon out and lay a trail that is not too difficult, and put him in a tree. Now take out your hound and let him range out until he strikes the beginning of the trail, carries it to the tree and barks treed. Don't strain a young dog's patience at the tree, but get to him quickly and praise him lavishly. Then lower the coon in the fighting cage and let them have a good go-around. Your dog may take some time to work in this manner, but persevere and you will be well rewarded.

As your dog becomes more skillful at this phase of the game, increase the difficulty of the tests; run him through water, ploughed fields or any other terrain available. At this time you can begin to leave him for longer periods at the tree. Some dogs are natural tree-stickers and some aren't. The weak ones can be improved by gradually increasing the length of time you let them bark at the tree before going to them. Your dog will quickly learn that you will not fail him, and in time should become a two or three hour tree dog, if he has sufficient game interest.

Hunting the Coonhound

You are now ready to take your young hound coon hunting. It should be noted here that many excellent hounds have been developed without benefit of the above training program. It is suggested for the man who wants the surest way to a coonhound in the shortest time, and who has no other hound with which to train his pup. Most hounds are trained simply by taking the pup out, when he is old enough to follow, with an old hound that is straight on coon. This method frequently works very well, especially with an outstanding prospect, but if your dog is average, he may take more education and encouragement to make a good coonhound. Hunting wild coon is a far cry from the easy sport you have been having training, so don't expect, even if your hound will do everything right on the lead coon, that you will tree wild coon with him the first night out. It is important that you take him to an area where there are lots of coon, preferably one which has been hunted lightly, so that the coon will not give too long a chase. If coon are out, your hound will probably start to trail, opening according to the freshness of the track. You should examine the tracks immediately if you are hunting in soft

Bluetick coonhound barking treed during a night hunt. The coonhound should be trained to stick to the tree until the hunter arrives.

Leonard Lee Rue III

dirt along a river bottom so that you can catch him if he is running deer.

You should know by now what your hound is doing according to the way he uses his voice. When your dog changes to tree-bark, you should make all haste to get to him. Unlike the training situation, where only one track is present leading to the tree, there may be the tracks of several wild coon in the immediate vicinity which would tend to pull him off the tree. A dog who trees a little, then runs off to strike a new track, is of little value as a coonhound.

Do not be hard on your dog if there is no coon up his first few trees. If coon cannot be seen, lead your dog a short distance from the tree and encourage him to pick up the scent on the coon. Coon will frequently "tap" a tree, which means they will climb a tree, crawl to the longest branches and jump out. This is a diversionary tactic on the part of the coon. It will often fool a young hound, but the veteran cooner will bark up the tree, then circle out to check the surrounding area for a track leading away from the tree. If no track is found leading away from the tree, the old hound will settle to hard tree barking. Your young hound should learn this quickly with a little help.

As your dog becomes increasingly coon-wise, you can take him to areas where there are fewer coon and tougher hunting conditions. These are the areas which, if hunted frequently, can make a top cooner out of a so-so hound. Each time your hound trees, leave him a little longer as you did in training him with the lead coon. A good plan is to keep walking toward the treeing hound until you are within a couple hundred yards of him, and you are sure you have not been seen or heard, then sit down on a log and wait. If you have the patience, build up this waiting period to a couple of hours. You will soon have a treehound you can be proud of. A better coonhound will result if you refrain from shouting encouragement to him while hunting. The dog should do the barking not the hunter.

Other Treeing Game

Follow exactly the same training procedures outlined for the coonhound to train for any treeing game. It is not practical, of course, to keep a pet bear, mountain lion or even a bobcat for training purposes, although it has been done, but prepared scents can be used. Most coonhounds will readily take to trailing bear scent as it is very similar to coon scent. It does, however, take a hound of exceptional endurance, speed and fighting instinct to successfully hunt bear. For cat hunting the preliminary training can be done with housecats. After the young hound is working well on domestic cats, it is best to hunt him with trained cat hounds until he is well started.

THE FOXHOUND

Training the Foxhound is far easier than training the coonhound because there is less the dog must know. The Foxhound is bred to trail and the instinct to tree is not considered at all. Practically everything a Foxhound learns will be gained through actual hunting experience. There is very little you can do to teach him the ways of hunting wild fox. However, you can encourage the development of the hunting instinct in young Foxhound pups by using the cane-pole technique, only substituting a fox tail or hide with a little fox scent on it. Allowing the pups to catch the hide occasionally will help, but this is not nearly so important as the chasing. Foxhounds rarely catch their game, and they seem to be happy with just the thrill of the chase.

If you do not have a trained Foxhound to start your pup with, you must be very careful to avoid his running off-game. The best plan is to take him out in some open country during the daytime, and drive until you spot a fox. In some areas this can be easily done, while in others it would be practically impossible because of brush or woods. When you have spotted a fox, take your young hound directly to the place and encourage him to pick up the trail. The rest is up to the hound. He will learn more each time you take him out, so the more often he is hunted the better. A fox will make a wide circle and, in many instances, your hound may run a complete circuit and never go out of hearing. On other occasions he may be out of hearing much of the time, depending on the terrain and the wind.

If the hound shows any reluctance to follow the trail of a fox, to open on trail or to quit a trail, don't be completely discouraged. If you have these problems, you must start hunting your hound with a trained Foxhound. Often the excitement of another hound working a trail and giving voice is all that it takes to get a young dog started. The fox has just as many tricks in his bag as the coon, so don't expect your hound to learn overnight, or even in a season's hunting. Even the best hounds will take two or three years to learn all they are capable of learning about fox.

A young hound should not be pushed into the all-night chases of an experienced pack too soon. Before a year of age, the hound has not developed his full lung capacity or heart growth and probably will not have the stamina to stay in the race. It can be very discouraging to a young hound to drop out of a race because of fatigue. No doubt many potentially good hounds have been ruined and turned into "quitters" because they were hunted with experienced hounds when they were too young to keep up with the older dogs.

THE BEAGLE

The Beagle, in his hunting style and instincts, is very similar to the Foxhound, only on a smaller scale. Beagles are fast, open trailers by birth, and take enough joy in the case so that they hunt as well with or without a kill. Many sportsmen who admire and would like to follow Foxhounds, but have neither the space nor the money to do so, hunt the little Beagle instead.

Of the hounds, the Beagle is perhaps the most easily trained. It is not necessary to have an old trained dog to start your young Beagle. Almost any dog will chase rabbits, and in the very early stages of training this is about all you have to get your hound to do. When the pup has sufficient maturity, and shows an interest in chasing game—usually at eight to ten months of age, sometimes later—take him to some thickets where there are plenty of rabbits and flush some out for him. At first he will run simply by sight, but as the bunnies begin to give him the slip, he will resort to using his nose. Eventually, after sufficient practice, he will begin to strike trails on scent alone, following them up until the rabbit is flushed. The only thing you can do to improve the work of your Beagle from this point on, is to get him out hunting as often as possible. It may be necessary to break the Beagle from running off-game, but owing to his small size, he seems to adjust more naturally to a game animal that he can pursue more or less successfully. In almost every area this is the cottontail rabbit.

TRAINING TO COME TO THE HORN

Many houndsmen like to train their hounds to come to the hunting horn. The horn usually consists of a cow horn cut off at the end, cleaned up and polished. It is blown exactly as you would blow a bugle. It is a good plan, if you wish to call your hounds in with one of these, to blow it to recall your hounds every time you feed them and to call them when they are out running in the yard. They will soon learn to associate your particular style of blowing the horn with pleasant experiences and come quickly to it. The advantage in the hunting horn is that it can be heard for long distances and the hounds seem to have a natural affinity for the sound, coming to it readily.

No matter how well your hounds are trained, there will always be some individuals who, when trailing game, will not come to the horn. This does not indicate that they are any better hounds. It simply suggests that the drive to catch the game is greater than the impulse to return to the sound of the horn. It must also be taken into account that some hounds are more tractable than others. Occasionally the fox and coon hunter will lose several dogs out of the pack during the hunt. This happens when the trail runs out of hearing, and the dogs do not show up during the course of an evening's wait. When this occurs, leave an old shirt, burlap bag or jacket exactly where the car was parked and return to the spot early the next morning and blow your horn. Usually the hounds will either be sleeping near the article left, or they will be roaming around within earshot. Once you have established this practice, and the hound knows you will not desert him, there is little danger that you will lose him unless he is caught in a trap or has been shot.

BREAKING THE HOUND FROM RUNNING TRASH GAME

The major problem of the houndsman, if he has good, gamy dogs, is to keep them running one kind of game exclusively. When a dog is broken so that he will open on only one species, or a selection of desired species such as bear, coon and cat, he is referred to as "straight." Many hounds are so trained that they pay no attention to off-game, or "trash," and they are highly prized. A "check dog" is one which can be sent in when another hound is open-trailing, and if the game is other than the desired species, he will not join in the chase but will return to the hunters. As you will see, these dogs are invaluable in breaking the trash-running hound.

If you have hounds who from the beginning start running off-game, it will be necessary to use some method of force to discourage them from running such game. It must be pointed out that a minimum of breaking should be done. Many hounds do not have the constitution to stand up to a great deal of punishment and still work well. For this reason, punishment should be administered sparingly, according to the offense, and only when you are certain of the game your hound has been chasing.

Perhaps it is best to intentionally expose your young hound to the opportunity to chase off-game during the daytime when you can see what he is doing, and you can take steps to correct him. If you have a coon or foxhound, you can take him out during the day and look for fresh deer prints, or better, sight deer, and take the hound to the place to see if he will take the trail. If the hound shows any interest at all in the trail, he can be called in or caught and reprimanded on the spot. This is far better than taking an unbroken dog to the woods at night, and constantly wondering what he is chasing. This method can be employed to "straighten out" most hounds. All you have to do is locate the fresh trail of the undesired game.

Some hounds, however, will not be so easily discouraged, and they may require more severe methods of force to make them straight. There are a number of methods by which these dogs can be effectively broken, but the problem remains, how much breaking can take place without ruining the hound. One method commonly in use today, although the equipment is very expensive, is to use an electronic remote-control trainer which can inflict a painful shock. The idea is sound, and these devices are very effective in the hands of an expert, yet most of the houndsmen I have known who have trained their dogs with the electronic trainer said that their hounds would not chase anything for some time after the treatment. It seems that the hound may associate the punishment more with the act of hunting and opening on trail, than with running the trash. The electronic trainer can be used either during the daytime, by putting the hound on the trail of trash, or it can be used while night hunting in conjunction with a check dog. When the hound you wish to train is heard to open on trail, the check dog is released. If he opens with your dog, you know your dog is running the correct game. If the check dog does not open, and returns with a sheepish look on his face, a shock is delivered to your hound as he is running trash. Obviously, the success of such a venture depends on the reliability of the check dog. He should also be as cold-nosed as your young hound; if he is not, he may just be returning because he cannot pick up the trail. Do not use an unproven check dog with unbroken hounds. This would mean that you would have to see the dog pass up several known fresh trails of trash without his paying them any attention whatever.

We have had good luck breaking hounds from running trash by using breaking scents. These are scents of the undesired animals in very strong concentrations which, when applied repeatedly to the dog's collar and head, become so repugnant to the hound that he will no longer chase that game. This seems to me to be the most positive way to break hounds as it involves no physical violence or infliction of pain, and refers in the most direct possible way to the off-game. We had a fine young Black and Tan coonhound that gave chase on a couple of deer trails. Two weeks daily application of deer-breaking scent cleared up the problem completely. If a hound should revert to the habit of running trash again, repeat the treatment. It is no great inconvenience to administer it.

No matter what method of breaking you select, be sure that you know exactly what offense your hound has committed before you adminster punishment. Never let circumstantial evidence suffice. If the trail your hound is running simply does not seem like the trail of the game you are after, either due to its length or other qualities, be suspicious, but don't punish the hound until you are sure. You may have a fine young hound who hit an unorthodox-running individual of the species you are after; this happens frequently. Punishment at this time could permanently ruin your hound. It is far better to put up with a little trash running until you are absolutely sure, than to risk the future of a fine hound.

18

Pointing Dog
Field Trials

THERE HAS been a hot debate going for years over the question of the performance of field-trial dogs in the hunting field. A good share of the negative
attitude among hunters concerning field-trial dogs stems from experience
they have had with dogs of trial breeding who have not been properly
trained. These dogs are so highly developed, and have so much natural drive,
that keeping one under control without having done some serious training
is practically impossible. On the other hand, there are probably no hunting
dogs—that is, those not bred and trained for field-trial competition—who can
hold their own in bird finding, pointing and control with the polished field-
trial pointers and setters. It is, in fact, the express purpose of those who support the field-trial sport to promote the breeding and training of better
hunting dogs. The problem of excessive range, which seems to be the major
complaint against field-trial dogs, is not so much a fault of the dog as it is
one of the trainer. Any intelligent bird dog can be taught to fit his range to
the kind of cover he is hunting (see Chapter 14).

There is little doubt, however, that the "class" bird dog of the trial ideal
is a little more dog than is needed for most hunting conditions. Most knowledgeable dog men would subscribe to the idea that it is better to have too
much dog—one you can train down to the kind of performance you want—
than too little; a dog who simply lacks ambition. As a result of this desire
for speed, range, intensity and super bird-finding ability, the field-trial game
has revolved around the Pointer and the English Setter, who are best suited
for it. These breeds have been developed to a high degree of excellence, and
have captured practically all of the placements in field trials since the early
days of the sport, although the Irish Setter enjoyed a flurry of success at the
very beginning of formal trial history.

HOW DOGS ARE JUDGED

The first formal field trial for pointing dogs was held near Memphis, Tennessee, on October 8, 1874. At that time the competitors were judged on a
number system, with the best possible score being 100. Nose was allotted a

maximum of 30 points; pace and style, 20; breaking (steadiness), 20; pointing style and staunchness, 15; backing, 10; roading, 5. The winning dog of this trial scored 88 points.

A large number of field-trial clubs over the country now hold field trials for pointing breeds. The system most widely in use now, however, is the spotting system, rather than the rigid numerical system used in the earlier trials. Using this system, the judges are able to consider the dogs' work more effectively as a whole, and are not burdened with a lot of arithmetic. In the spotting system of judging, each dog is considered to be in competition against every other dog in the trial. The trials are not run off in heats nor is the elimination by paired competition.

The specific characteristics the judges watch most carefully for are:

1. *Pace*—Freedom of movement, speed, vigor and ground-covering ability.

2. *Range and Pace*—The manner in which a dog covers his ground, and how much he covers. A dog who quarters his ground too carefully, in the manner of a spaniel, is considered too methodical and wasteful of motion, while the dog who belts out of sight the minute he is turned loose is graded down for not covering his ground intelligently. Above all, the important thing in range and pace is to take advantage of the wind, the cover and to move efficiently and effectively within a given terrain.

3. *Steadiness*—The dog must not offer to move after birds when they flush from the covey, or when they are shot.

4. *False Pointing*—A dog's point is considered to be false when no game can be produced in front of his point. This is not to say that birds may not have been there, but if the dog has not moved tightly enough on the body scent of the birds, the bird may have slipped away. If this happens, the dog is said to have stuck on foot scent. If the handler walks in to flush the covey in front of the dog and no game is immediately produced, the dog should be allowed an opportunity to relocate his game.

5. *Locating Birds*—To be classed a good locator, a dog must move in on his coveys quickly and with confidence, "pinning them down" so to speak. The dog should be close enough to his quarry so that his point is a reaction to body rather than to foot scent. A dog pointing body scent will move with his birds if they offer to walk away from his point. This is a commendable quality. The dog pointing foot scent, however, will more often false point, since his game can frequently run away from his point, leaving him pointing scent left on the ground. For this reason, a pointing dog who works hound-style—that is, who takes his scent from the ground rather than from the air—is very much at a disadvantage not only because he is apt to point on foot scent frequently, but because he is likely to be slow and pottering, covering insufficient ground.

6. *Blinking*—This is a bad fault, and it pertains to leaving point, or leaving an area where the presence of birds has been clearly established. It is not to be confused, however, with the dog leaving his point momentarily to establish a better position on the covey. The latter maneuver shows bird sense and is commendable. Probably the main cause of blinking is punishing the dog too severely for such faults as breaking or lack of staunchness on point. Ordinarily, a dog with good hunting instincts, that has not been too harshly corrected, will not blink.

7. *Temperament*—This quality in a dog is rather hard to describe. A fine

temperament might be defined as an instinctive correctness in all of a dog's actions. A dog with this characteristic always seems to locate game, if any is to be found, knows how to handle himself in difficult or unusual situations, is honest and true in his work and can easily adapt to a variety of terrain and cover. Tractability comprises a large share of good temperament, and the desire to please the master and work for him is the predominant expression of it.

8. *Pointing*—The quality of a dog's pointing is not always judged by the number of coveys he locates, although this is an important feature of his work. Pointing pertains, rather, to the way he moves in on his birds, and his manner of holding close to them, taking body rather than foot scent. A dog's pointing ability may often be assessed best when game is scarce or difficult to handle. In times like these, a pointing dog is really put to the test. Under circumstances where birds are very numerous, and too easily worked, an inferior dog may make a good showing locating coveys.

Dr. P. R. Bolton, noted for his work in developing the field-trial sport in the United States, categorized pointing-dog work in three main divisions and additional subheadings.

1. Ground Work—a) Intelligence; b) Speed; c) Range; d) Stamina.

2. Bird Work—a) Accurate and quick location; b) Pointing; c) Staunchness; d) Style.

3. Training—a) Hunting to the course; b) Responding to the handler; c) Steadiness.

A dog who conforms to these standards would make a perfect bird-hunting companion. This, of course, is what the authors of these standards had in mind when formulating them. Therefore, if the pointers and setters can be faulted, it is not the idea of field trials that is wrong, but the judgment of a few breeders and judges. Some judges overlook some of the necessities of steadiness, reasonable range and tractability in their search for dogs with a lot of "go."

THE PRINCIPAL STAKES

Pointing-dog trials are divided into three stakes: the Open All-Age, which is for dogs who are fully trained and who are usually over two years of age; the Derby stake, which is restricted to dogs under two years of age, sometimes a few months older, depending on the ruling of the American Field, and the time of year the trial is held; and the Puppy stake, which is for dogs under one year of age or up to fifteen months, again dependent on special ruling.

The Open All-Age is generally where the fully trained dogs will be seen at work, and if you want to observe bird dogs in action for your first time, this stake will give you the best idea of what they are capable of doing. If you intend to watch the open stake, however, you must be mounted on horseback or you will not be able to follow the action. Entry fees are often steep in the Open stake, and rarely does a handler risk entry unless he feels he has a reasonable chance of doing well. The competition is very stiff in this stake, and anything but a creditable job will usually mean that the offending dog will not be called back for the second series.

The Derby is for young dogs, and it is not generally expected, nor hoped, that they will be fully trained. Allowances for wildness, lack of bird sense, unsteadiness, etc. are made, although a finely finished dog in this class does occur, and is to be rewarded proportionately with the quality of his work. More important, however, is the opportunity to look for dogs with great potential in this stake. It is conceivable, especially in this or the puppy stake, that minor faults would not be seriously considered if the overall performance was breathtaking. It could easily happen that an outstanding young dog with such minor faults could beat a more completely trained dog who was lacklustre with respect to intensity, style and birdiness.

The Puppy stake is for really green dogs, under one year of age, and no great performance is expected of them, although many dogs of this age can produce birds in respectable style. Here the judges are definitely trying to locate potential. There are qualities about the young dog's running, the way he reacts to game, his spirit and style, that would indicate what kind of performer he might become.

TRIAL PROCEDURES

A pointing dog field trial is run in the following manner: First, the entries are taken, usually a week or better in advance, so the club will know how many dogs will be run and what kind of terrain should be set aside. Then, just before dogs are run, they are chosen by lot and paired with a brace-mate according to the order in which they were chosen. The location of the first series is then announced, and the trial moves to that location. If there are many dogs entered in the stake, the first series must be rather limited as to the time each brace is allowed in the field. In the Open and Derby stakes, a minimum of thirty minutes is required for any series, while the Puppy stake is cut to a minimum of twenty. The judges and gallery follow the dogs on horseback and the gallery is kept a respectable distance from the working brace of dogs by marshals. Following the dogs on horseback greatly speeds up the field trial because less time is consumed walking to the dogs, and the mounts and riders lend considerable color to the event, but it is erroneous to conclude that the only way field-trial dogs can be followed is by horse. Certainly, most polished field-trial performers could be controlled nicely and hunted by foot.

When the dogs locate their game and point, they are called "point" by their handler, and the birds are flushed. It should be borne in mind, however, that the dogs are under judgment during their entire stay in the field, and may not be taken up until the O.K. is given by the judges. In the event a dog has such great range that he gets lost, the judges allow twenty minutes for the dog to return. If he does not show up within the allotted time, he is removed from the competition.

The second and subsequent series consist of those dogs who the judges wish to see in further action. Their decision is based on their own assessment of the competitor's work, and is final. Any open disagreement or flagrant arguing with the judges' decision may result in the participant being barred from that and future events, and in his removal from the trial grounds. This protection is necessary for the judges as it gives them the authority they need and makes their job a good deal simpler.

It is a distinct honor to be asked to judge a dog trial of any kind. Particularly in the pointing dog and retriever trials, it indicates a faith that your honesty is above reproach, and that you are thoroughly versed in the area of dog work at its best. Generally, those selected for judges are dog men themselves who have campaigned actively for years in trials and who know what goes into the making of a top-flight performer.

19

Retriever Field Trials

RETRIEVER TRIALS have grown tremendously in popularity since the Second World War. In 1944 there were only 14 AKC licensed trials in the United States. By 1951 the total had grown to 53 trials with 1,950 dogs starting in the 4 principal stakes. By 1965 the number of trials had increased to 131, with 12,225 retrievers entered. The following table for 1965 and 1976 (exclusive of National trials) reflects the sizeable increase in the number of licensed trials, which may include from 2 to 4 stakes. The number of participating dogs in 1976 was more than double that of 1965. Average numbers for dogs per stake also increased markedly.

	Stakes		Dogs Starting		Avg. No. Dogs	
	1965	1976	1965	1976	1965	1976
Open All-Age	126	161	4281	8283	33.4	51.4
Amateur All-Age	118	160	3029	7178	25.6	44.9
Derby	123	170	2647	6915	21.5	40.7
Qualifying	108	158	2268	5213	21.0	33.0
Totals	475	649	12,225	27,589		

As a general rule, participation by breeds includes about 90 percent Black Labs with the remaining 10 percent made up mainly of Goldens, Chesapeakes, and yellow Labs.

If you are interested in getting notices of trials scheduled each year and in following the results of those trials, write to: Retriever Field Trial News, 4213 South Howell Avenue, Milwaukee, WI 53207. This helpful newspaper is published by the National Retriever Field Trial Club and the National Amateur Retriever Club.

TRIAL PROCEDURES

At the present time any one of the six retriever breeds recognized by the American Kennel Club is eligible to run in field trials, subject to age and other restrictions discussed in this chapter under the principal stakes. A recent rule requires that all entrants either be AKC registered or a part of an AKC registered litter. Without special permission from the AKC the latter may be run only three times before being registered.

Each dog registered in a particular field trial is given a number and the dogs are called up in the first series of tests by number. Each dog called is expected to follow at the heel of his handler to the area from which he will be run. Derby dogs may wear collars and may be brought to line on a lead. The judges designate a "line" on the ground behind which each dog must be worked. The handler orders his dog to "Sit" and "Stay" and then signals the judges when he is ready.

Meanwhile the bird throwers and the gunners are in position out on the field or water, ready to provide shot birds for the dogs to retrieve. At a signal from the judges, the first bird thrower tosses his bird. It is shot by one or both of his gunners. If the test is a double, a second bird thrower throws his bird, which is shot. On triples, a third bird thrower and pair of gunners are provided. Birds may be live shot or thrown dead and a blank shot fired at the discretion of the judges. Meanwhile, the dog must remain steady behind the line. Only after a judge calls the dog's number is the handler permitted to send his dog. Usually, dogs are trained to retrieve the birds in reverse order from that in which they are shot. Some trainers prefer to give the dog the choice of which bird to retrieve next, unless ordered to do otherwise by the judges. Others choose to have the dog retrieve the birds in exact reverse order, giving a careful line to each bird. The order in which birds are retrieved in a multiple mark is generally arrived at in accordance with what is easiest for the dog to remember.

Once the handler has given a line to a particular bird, the dog should hunt for that bird. If he hunts the area and doesn't find it, and switches to another bird, the dog is dropped from the trial.

Usually, live shackled or dead ducks are used in all water work for marked retrieves in licensed trials, and shot pheasants are used for all marking and retrieving on land. The shackled ducks are never actually shot; the gunner fires into the air to attract the dog's attention, and then the duck is thrown high into the air and as far away from the thrower as possible to land in the water. The pheasants are occasionally shot live, but usually a shot is fired and a dead bird thrown.

In Sanctioned trials, which are informal trials sponsored by a local club for fun and practice with no championship points awarded, pigeons are often used for land work and shackled ducks for water work.

For blind retrieves on land or water, dead birds are used at all times so that the bird will not call or flap around, thus attracting the dog's attention and giving him a clue to its whereabouts.

In every trial the bird throwers and gunners must operate with exactness and precision. When dead birds are thrown, they must land in the same place each time to give each dog an equal chance. The gunners have to shoot each live bird over the same location and at the same distance to make the series equally challenging to all dogs. A bird that is crippled and runs away puts one dog at a disadvantage, yet the judges can't give the dog who retrieves a cripple more points than the dog who retrieves dead birds, since

Lab retrieving a bird to his handler during a field trial while judges observe dog's form and record their scores.

there is no way of determining how the other dogs might have done on the cripple. Dogs who get a cripple or other unfair fall are given the courtesy of a re-run.

The judges score each dog in each series, usually on a sliding scale between one and ten points. Some judges put down a score for each retrieve and take an average for the series. Also, the judges usually draw a diagram of each dog's travels in finding a bird and then make notes of his actions. When all dogs called have run a particular series, the points are added up; some of the dogs with lower score are eliminated, and the remainder are called up for the next series. As many series are run as needed to determine a clear winner. An All-Age stake must have land marks, water marks, land and water blinds, a test with decoys, and an honoring test. This usually takes four or five series.

Dogs are scored on line behavior, steadiness, marking, memory, the efficiency with which they go about finding each bird, bird handling (dogs must be soft-mouthed), water work (entry, style and aggressiveness as well as marking), ability to take a line, obedience to whistle, commands and directions, handling ability (for advanced stakes only) and general style, enthusiasm, keenness of nose and aggressiveness. Space does not permit a complete discussion of all major and minor faults for which judges can deduct points, or even eliminate a dog from a trial, but these can be found in the book of rules and standard procedures which has the approval of the American Kennel Club.

RULES REGULATING FIELD TRIALS

If you want to know what is expected of a good retriever in field trials, write to the American Kennel Club, 51 Madison Avenue, New York, New York 10010, and ask for a free copy of the latest edition of "Registration and Field Trial Rules and Standard Procedures for Retrievers," and for the latest copy of the recommendations (with amendments) of the Retriever Advisory committee. The recommendations cover such subjects as trial procedure, evaluation of dog work, natural abilities, abilities acquired through training and the classification of faults.

THE PRINCIPAL STAKES

The Derby stake at a retriever trial is for dogs who are over six months of age and not yet two years of age on the first day of the trial at which they are being run. Usually, a dog is about eighteen months old before he can compete successfully in the Derby stake. Because this stake is for the youngest dogs, the tests are the easiest of any which are required in official stakes, and a polished performance is not always necessary. However, in recent years competition has been so tough that winners often have to perform almost perfectly to deserve a place. This means that the dogs must mark well, find the birds with a minimum of searching, handle birds with tenderness, yet with sureness, and show a lot of speed, style, keenness of nose and enthusiasm in their work. Steadiness while on the line is also required.

The Qualifying stake at a retriever trial is for dogs over six months of age who have never won first, second, third or fourth place, or a Judges' Award of Merit in an Open All-Age, Limited All-Age, or won first, second, third or fourth place in an Amateur All-Age stake, or two first places in Qualifying stakes at licensed or member club trials. This stake is the only intermediate stake between the Derby and the Amateur or Open-Point stakes, so it often serves as a means of getting experience for a dog who is too old for the Derby and not good enough for the advanced stakes. The tests vary depending upon the particular judges, but usually include about four series with opportunities to test the marking of the dogs in fairly good cover on both land and water. The tests usually include doubles on land or water with falls out to 150 yards, and usually at least one triple fall on land or water, but at shorter distances. One or two blind retrieves will be included to test the dog's handling ability, although usually these blinds are short retrieves. The dogs will also get a severe steadiness test, with birds shot off the line directly in front of each one. An honoring test is usually required, where a dog who has just worked is required to sit at heel and be completely steady while the next dog works.

The Amateur All-Age stake is for any dog over six months of age, if handled in that stake by persons who are amateurs (as determined by the Field Trial Committee of the trial-giving club). An Amateur handler is defined as one who does not make all or part of his living training and handling dogs. Just because this stake is for amateur handlers, don't be fooled into thinking that it is easy to win. Competing in any licensed Amateur All-Age stake are dogs who are Field Trial Champions, or even National Champions, and which may have been trained by the finest professionals in the country. In other words, the handlers must be amateurs, but the dogs are the finest in the country. Also, some of the amateur handlers know their business as well as the professionals. The tests are often as difficult as any in the Open or Limited stakes and will be described under these stakes.

The Open All-Age and Limited All-Age stakes are identical except for qualification. The tests are the same and the computation of points is the same. Limited All-Age stakes are run by clubs which anticipate a greater number of entries than they might handle in an Open All-Age stake. The Limited All-Age stake is for dogs over six months of age who have previously been placed, or awarded a Judges' Award of Merit in an Open All-Age stake; or who have been placed first or second in a Qualifying; or who have been placed or awarded a Judge's Award of Merit in an Amateur All-Age stake carrying championship points.

Obviously these are the most difficult stakes of all and only the best dogs can hope to place. Furthermore, the number of entries is usually large. There may be twenty-five to fifty dogs in the trial, many of whom are Field Trial Champions, and many who are handled by the finest professional trainers in the country. All of the tests are usually fairly difficult. Dogs are expected to mark triples, and occasionally even four birds, on land or water, and in the heaviest cover. Falls are usually planned at varying distances: from right in front of a dog, to distances of several hundred yards. The handling tests on blind retrieves provide opportunities to determine how well a dog takes a line to each bird. Sometimes a diversion shot is fired (with or without a bird off to one side), and then a dog is required to take a line in another direction after a bird that has been hidden. Sometimes dogs are placed on the line at a considerable distance from water and then required to take a line between two posts on shore and directly across the water to a planted bird on the far shore. At other times, two birds are planted on a direct line, one at a short distance and the other at a greater distance, and a dog is required to pick up the farther bird first. Obviously, the handler has to give his dog a line upwind of the short bird, direct him out to the far bird, and then after the far bird is retrieved to hand, send his dog to the short bird.

One difficult handling test in the water is to require a dog to swim a long, narrow channel to a planted bird without setting foot on either shore before reaching the vicinity of the bird. This is made especially tough if the swim is against the wind (most dogs hate to swim against a heavy chop and strong wind) or if the dog has previously been required to retrieve a marked fall on one of the shores which are on the way to the planted bird. Any dog has a tendency to want to return to a spot from which he previously retrieved a bird. These kinds of tests therefore require complete obedience and the finest kind of control, especially at great distances. Some dogs respond well to a whistle at short distances, but begin to ignore their handler as they get farther away.

The marking tests are also tough. Dogs may have to cross streams, large sloughs or deep gullies, or go through heavy cover on their way to the marked falls. Any one of these impediments helps to throw a dog off line or to make it difficult to remember the last birds retrieved. Some of the hardest marking tests are conducted in flat fields of clover, alfalfa or prairie flowers, which tend to hide the scent of the birds. Also, many dogs have difficulty in remembering the location of falls in flat fields since there aren't any significant landmarks to help in pinpointing where birds fell.

Dogs must be absolutely steady on the line and are not permitted to creep out ahead of the handler before being sent. Honoring tests are always required to test a dog's steadiness on the line.

FIELD TRIAL CHAMPIONSHIPS

At present, to acquire an Amateur Field Trial Championship a retriever must be registered with the American Kennel Club Stud Book and must win: 1) a National Amateur Championship stake; or 2) a total of 10 points in Open All-Age or Limited All-Age stakes or a total of 15 points which may be acquired as follows: In each Open All-Age, Limited All-Age or Amateur All-Age stake, there must be at least twelve starters, each of which is eligible for entry in a Limited All-Age stake, and the handler must be an Amateur (as determined by the Field Trial Committee of the trial-giving club), and the winner of first place shall be credited with 5 points, second place 3 points, third place 1 point and fourth place ½ point. But before acquiring a championship, a dog must win a first place and acquire 5 points in at least one Open All-Age, Limited All-Age or Amateur All-Age stake open to all breeds of retrievers, and not more than 5 points shall be acquired in trials not open to all breeds of retrievers.

To acquire a Field Trial Championship a retriever must be registered with the American Kennel Club Stud Book and must win: 1) a National Championship stake; or 2) a total of 10 points which may be acquired as follows: In each Open All-Age or Limited All-Age stake there must be twelve starters, each of which is eligible for entry in a Limited All-Age stake, and the winner of first place shall be credited with 5 points, second place 3 points, third place 1 point and fourth place ½ point. But, before acquiring a championship, a dog must win first place and acquire 5 points in at least one Open All-Age or Limited All-Age stake open to all breeds of retrievers, and not more than 5 points of the required 10 shall be acquired in trials not open to all breeds of retrievers.

THE NATIONAL CHAMPIONSHIPS

Each year, three National Retriever Field Trial Championships are determined: the National Derby Field Trial Champion, the National Amateur Field Trial Champion and the National Open All-Age Field Trial Champion. The National Derby Championship is awarded automatically, without a national trial, to the Derby dog who has won the most Derby points in licensed field trials during the year.

To be eligible for entering the National Amateur Championship Field Trial a Retriever must: 1) win one 5-point first place and 2 additional points in Amateur trials during the preceding fiscal year; or 2) win the previous National Open Championship under an amateur handler; or 3) have won the National Amateur Championship the previous fiscal year.

To be eligible for entering the National Open Championship Field Trial a Retriever must: 1) be the winner of the preceding National Championship stake; 2) be the winner of the preceding National Amateur Championship stake; or 3) win a first place and a total of seven championship points in Open All-Age stakes during the preceding fiscal year.

The above entry requirements apply at present, although they may be changed by the Board of Directors of the American Kennel Club. Over the years, the number of qualified retrievers has grown until now usually one hundred or more retrievers compete in any yearly trial. The trials usually last over a period of five days, during which time ten difficult series are run. Since only the finest dogs in the country are run each year, you can be sure that any dog who wins is a very exceptional retriever.

TRAINING FOR FIELD TRIALS

If you are preparing your retriever for running in field trials, there are a number of things you will have to work on very intensively.

The most important task is to develop your dog's ability to mark and remember falls. You have to have a dog with a good memory in the first place, but nothing improves memory and marking ability like daily practice for months at a time. Work your dog in many different locations, in every conceivable type of cover, over varied terrain (flat, hilly, rolling, etc.), at a variety of distances, under various weather and temperature conditions, at various angles to the wind, on land and on water, with dummies, pigeons, ducks and pheasants, with birds thrown and shot at different angles from the bird thrower and from you, and under different light conditions. If he does consistently well for his age, he might have a chance in a field trial.

Your dog has to be absolutely steady, so never let him get into the habit of breaking to shot, or creeping forward on his rear end ahead of the line. Some dogs require a lot of discipline, even repeated severe but reasonable punishment, before they can be trusted to be absolutely steady. Even then some of the finest dogs lose trials by breaking. So resolve that this is one lesson you must teach well, yet without destroying your dog's enthusiasm and spirit.

Work also on developing your dog's bird-handling ability. He should learn to hold every bird firmly in the center of its body, yet tenderly enough to prevent puncturing the skin of the bird. Don't let him get in the habit of dropping his birds or readjusting his hold on the way in. Furthermore, he should always deliver it to your hand, holding the bird firmly until you take it from him.

Work on your dog's speed and style. If he is hitting the water slowly, wade or row out into the water, leaving him sitting on shore. Call him to you, encouraging him to hit the water hard and to swim fast. Or repeatedly throw a bird or dummy into the water from where you stand until your dog goes into the water with a real splash. If your dog starts slowing upon his returns on land after he has found the bird, start calling him to you, urging him to speed up. Incidentally, some dogs begin to slow up in returning if they are disciplined after the return, so always praise your dog every time he returns with a bird. Never call him to you to discipline him.

Work on your dog's line. He should "barrel out" on the line you send him, even on blind retrieves. If he goes out in the wrong direction, call him in and send him again, being careful to indicate with your hand the line along which you want him to go. If he comes to the edge of the water and runs alongshore before entering, give him the "Sit" signal. Go to him, discipline him and send him again, but from a shorter distance to the water, gradually increasing the distance from the shore until he takes a perfect line across both the land and water. If he has any tendency to run along the shore in returning with a bird, blow the "Sit" signal, then wave him in directly toward you as you blow the "Come" signal. If he starts to run the shore again, say "No," make him go back to the original spot and call him to you. Of course, only after your dog learns to handle can you direct him to the original spot. If he hasn't learned to handle, you or a helper will have to go to him to lead him back to the spot, and then you go back to your original position to call him. Keep practicing until he will come back on a direct line.

Work on your dog's obedience, especially on "Heel," "Sit," "Stay," "Come," "Kennel," "Stop that noise" or other commands he may be weak on. Work especially on the "Sit" and "Come" signals with the whistle, and at long distances from your dog, as good preparation for improving his handling.

Work on handling, one of the hardest lessons to teach well. Continue to use the baseball diamond method of teaching which direction you want your dog to go. Practice long casts "over" to the right and to the left. Practice "Get back" and "Come." Practice at varying distances on both land and water, until your dog will handle well at distances over 200 yards (not an easy feat to accomplish). Don't let him ignore any whistle. Make him stop and look at you before you give him the next direction. Practice sending your dog at any angle into the wind (which is the hardest to do) or at any angle cross-wind or with the wind. Remember, not only does your dog have to learn how to handle, but you have to learn how to handle him. Many trials have been lost by good dogs because the handler blew the whistle at a wrong time, gave poor directions, forgot where a bird fell or otherwise distracted or confused the dog. Incidentally, your dog can see your arm movements easier if you wear a white jacket or shirt.

There are other fine points of the game you can work on too. Try to break him of the habit of urinating while going after or bringing in a bird. If he does this regularly, he will be penalized. Never let him get in the habit of switching birds. Work him on diversion shots, channel swims and on birds shot from the line. Only by trying to anticipate all of the possible things your dog will have to know and do under field-trial conditions, and by regularly practicing, can you hope to have him at his best when the day of the field trial arrives.

Finally, don't expect him to win every time; the finest dogs in the country lose more trials than they win, or even place in, so don't expect your dog to be perfect.

20

Spaniel Field Trials

THERE ARE several important reasons why field trials for spaniels should be encouraged. First, field trials are really the only way to sort out the best hunting strains of spaniels for breeding purposes. Unless spaniels are run against one another in competition, dog owners and buyers who are interested in good hunting stock only never really know which dogs they want to buy or breed. Too many spaniels these days are unfit for hunting. This is especially true of Cocker Spaniels, who became so popular as pets and show dogs. Without field trials the breed would continue to deteriorate as hunters. But if field trials continue and flourish, there may be some hope that the hunting qualities of the breed can be perpetuated.

As far as we are concerned, bench shows, while they have their place, do nothing to encourage the proper development of sporting dogs. Bench champions are developed by breeding dogs for particular physical characteristics without regard for intelligence, physical stamina, keenness of scent or bird retrieving instinct. Field-trial champions, however, are developed only by breeding and training the best in hunting stock.

Second, field trials benefit both the dog and his owner because trials provide a stimulus for the owner to train his dog regularly and properly to prepare him for competition. Bird seasons are so short that many dogs would never get trained regularly at all if field trials did not exist to provide opportunities to run dogs at other periods of the year. Running dogs in field trials is an exciting sport, and gives us all a chance to work our dogs year-round.

Third, field trials provide an opportunity for the novice trainer to watch good dogs work and to learn how to train his own dog. Therefore, if you want to really learn how to be a better trainer and to discover what a good spaniel should be expected to do in the field, attend spaniel trials in your area. Or, better still, join a spaniel club in your state and become a participant in trials. Field trials seek to duplicate as closely as possible actual hunting conditions, so you can be certain that if you learn how to train your dog to compete effectively in field trials, he will also be a delightful and effective hunting companion.

TYPES OF TRIALS

There are three types of field trials which are held. A licensed field trial is a field trial at which championship points may be awarded and which is given by a club or association which is not a member of the American Kennel Club, but which has been specially licensed by the American Kennel Club to give the specific field trial designated in the license.

A member field trial is a field trial at which championship points may be awarded, and which is given by a club or association which is a member of the American Kennel Club.

A sanctioned field trial is an informal field trial at which dogs may compete but not for championship points, held by a club or association, whether or not a member of the American Kennel Club, by obtaining the sanction of the American Kennel Club. Such trials are usually for practice and for fun and give the dogs a chance to compete.

Separate trials are now held for the various breeds of spaniels, since it is against the rules of the American Kennel Club for two or more breeds of spaniels to compete together in trials where championship points are awarded. (English Cocker Spaniels and American Cocker Spaniels may compete.)

PRINCIPAL STAKES

The official stakes at spaniel field trials are: Puppy, Novice, Limit, Open All-Age, Qualified Open All-Age and Amateur All-Age.

A Puppy stake is for dogs who have not reached their second birthday on the first day of the trial in which the Puppy stake is included, but who are over six months of age.

A Novice stake is for dogs (over six months of age) who have never won first, second, third or fourth in an Open All-Age stake, a Qualified Open All-Age, or an Amateur All-Age stake or first in any other regular stake (Puppy stake excepted) in a licensed or member spaniel trial. A Novice Handler stake is for novice handlers only and only for dogs who qualify for a Novice stake. A novice handler is one who has never handled a dog placed first, second, third or fourth in an Open All-Age stake, a Qualified Open All-Age stake or an Amateur All-Age stake, or a dog placed first in any other regular stake (Puppy stake excepted) in a licensed or member spaniel trial.

A Limit stake is for dogs who have never won first place in an Open All-Age, or two firsts in any regular official stake (Puppy stake excepted), at a licensed or member club spaniel trial in the United States or at any spaniel trial in any other country.

An Open All-Age or Qualified Open All-Age stake is for all dogs over six months of age. A Qualified Open All-Age stake is for dogs who have placed first, second, third or fourth in any stake (except Puppy stake) at a licensed or member club Spaniel field trial. A dog imported from Canada or the United Kingdom may be admitted to such stake on presentation of evidence of such dog having placed in an equivalent stake in either of those countries.

An Amateur All-Age stake shall be for dogs over six months of age who are handled by amateurs. The status of the handler is determined by the field-trial committee of the club holding the trial.

NATIONAL CHAMPIONSHIPS

At the present time there are two different National Championships awarded annually to Springer Spaniels and one to Cocker Spaniels. Thus, each year there is chosen a National Springer Spaniel Field Champion and a National Amateur Springer Spaniel Field Champion. Also, each year there is chosen the National Cocker Field Champion or the National English Cocker Field Champion. These winners are determined at the National Championship field trials which are run each year. These trials are for all dogs over six months of age and who by reason of previous wins are qualified under the special rules approved by the Board of Directors of the AKC.

FIELD CHAMPIONSHIP

The number of Open All-Age or Qualified Open All-Age stakes to be won in order to become a Field Champion, and the number of starters necessary in each Open All-Age or Qualified Open All-Age stake, is fixed and determined by the Board of Directors of the American Kennel Club.

At present, to acquire a Field Championship an English Springer Spaniel must win: 1) a National Championship stake; or 2) two Open All-Age stakes or two Qualified Open All-Age stakes or one Open All-Age stake and one Qualified Open All-Age stake at different trials with at least ten starters in each stake.

To acquire an Amateur Field Championship an English Springer Spaniel must win: 1) a National Amateur Championship stake; or 2) two Amateur All-Age stakes at different trials with at least ten starters in each stake.

To acquire a Field Championship a Cocker Spaniel or English Cocker Spaniel must win: 1) a National Championship stake; or 2) two Open All-Age stakes or two Qualified Open All-Age stakes or one Open All-Age stake and one Qualified Open All-Age stake at different trials with at least six starters in either stake.

In addition to the above requirements, a dog must show his ability to retrieve game from water, after a swim, before he can be awarded his field championship. The holding of water tests during a field trial is left to the discretion of the Field Trial Committee of the club conducting the trial. Dogs competing must, if required by the judges to do so, take such a water test.

FIELD TRIAL PROCEDURES

The standard procedure is for two dogs to be run simultaneously and for the order of running in pairs to be decided by draw. Dogs worked by the same person or belonging to the same owner are separated when possible. The judges carry on the trial of two dogs simultaneously, working parallel beats as far as possible and not requiring any cooperation in quartering. At the end of the first series the judges call up any dogs they require further to be run in additional series. In championship stakes dogs must be run in pairs for at least one of the first two series, both if possible. After the second series the judges, at their discretion, may elect to run additional series with the dogs running singly under both judges. At National Championship trials, and at the National Amateur Championship trial for English Springer Spaniels, the dogs must be paired with another dog for at least two series on land and for four land series if possible.

Each dog called up is asked to walk at heel until bidden to seek game. When so ordered, he should seek game in a brisk, quiet manner, thoroughly quartering the designated cover within gunshot, without unnecessarily covering the ground twice. He should leave no game in his territory, show courage in facing cover and flush game boldly and without urging. Handlers may control their dogs by hand, voice or whistle, but only in a quiet manner. If a dog gets too far out in following the line of a bird, he should be called off the line and later be cast back on it.

When game is flushed a dog should "hup" to flush, shot and command. After the game is shot, the dog should fetch but only when ordered to do so, and then to retrieve quickly, briskly and tenderly to hand. Dogs who mark the fall, use the wind, follow a strong runner and take directions are of great value. Water tests may be included in one or more series, depending upon the desires of the judges. Usually the dogs are worked in cover adjacent to the water, and the shooting planned so that falls are in the water.

Spaniels who bark and give tongue while questing are considered objectionable and are severely penalized. A dog who causes his handler and gun to run after him while line running, is considered out of control. A dog given a certain line to follow when questing game should not interfere with the other contestant running parallel to him.

In awarding points for the work of each dog in a series the judges give attention to the following:

Control at all times, and under all conditions.

Scenting ability and use of wind.

Manner of covering ground and briskness of questing.

Perseverance and courage in facing cover.

Steadiness to flush, shot and command.

Aptitude in marking fall of game, and ability in finding it.

Ability and willingness to take hand signals.

Promptness of style of retrieve and delivery.

Proof of tender mouth.

The work of the gunners is an important part of the total procedure in trials. Gunners have to keep up with the handler, try to cleanly and consistently kill the game at a uniform distance and not too close to each dog, and then stand quietly after each shot so as not to interfere with the dog and handler. Ordinarily, when a dog makes a retrieve no other birds are shot unless ordered by the judge for special reasons.

Dogs are expected to be able to work up and downwind, are shot over in the ordinary sporting manner, and are worked on land and water. Live, full-winged game birds are always used on land in stakes in which championship points are awarded. The use of traps or contrivances from which game can be released is prohibited in any Open All-Age stake carrying championship points. Judges are empowered to turn out of the stake any dog who does not obey his handler, or any handler who willfully interferes with another competitor, or with his dog.

Any dog considered unfit to compete, or bitches in season, are not eligible for competition, and bitches in season are not allowed on the field-trial grounds.

The winner and placements are determined by adding up the number of points received by each dog in the combined series. The four dogs with the highest points place first, second, third and fourth, respectively, although special prizes may be awarded as well, with any special awards accurately described.

SPECIAL STAKES

Brace or Team stakes are sometimes run with the dogs composing a brace or team belonging to the same owner. In these stakes no dogs shall form part of more than one brace or team at the same meeting and each brace or team shall have but one handler. A brace consists of two dogs and a team consists of three or more dogs. Dogs are expected to work their ground harmoniously together, performing as in a single stake.

A Shooting Dog stake is for dogs over six months of age and is a stake in which the owner or handler of the dog also does the shooting. This stake is judged both on dog work and on gun handling and shooting, emphasizing the manner in which the gun and the dog work together. Dogs are run singly and their work and that of the gunner observed by both judges.

21

Hound Dog Trials

MANY EXPERIENCED hunters scoff at the mere mention of any kind of field trial or formal competition for hunting hounds. Certainly, some of their complaints have been based on valid objections to the conditions of running and the scoring systems of these trials. Still, in these competitive days when everyone wants the best, the trials have survived, and, in fact, thrived. This stems from the fact that hunters are no longer satisfied with a breeder's claims about his dogs but insist on seeing the dogs in action against top competition. There can be little doubt that, on the terms these trials are run and judged, the best hounds generally win. To say that they always do would be as false as to assert that there is no relationship between winning and quality. There is an element of luck in any sporting competition, but in hound trials it is minimal.

COONHOUND TRIALS

The coon-dog field trial of a few years ago, in which a drag was laid (a coon-scented bag was pulled along the ground, laying a track), and the dogs ran a foot race to a tree surrounded by a herd of human spectators, has given way to a new and more exacting kind of coon-dog trial, the registered night hunt. These events are licensed by the United Kennel Club and are run to determine which hound is the most efficient coon dog in the hunt. We say most efficient, instead of best, since many hunters disagree with the idea that winners of night hunts are always good coonhounds. Quality of voice is not considered, or is it an advantage to have an extremely cold-trailing, comparatively slow hound, which many hunters prefer. The night hunt does test the ability of the hound to tree a coon though, and he must prove that he will stay at the tree.

In general, the hunt tests a hound's ability to strike and run a coon track without giving up or coming back to the hunters, to open frequently on trail and to be a solid tree dog. Further, the competing coonhound must not: fight another dog under any circumstances, bother bitches, loaf around the

186

hunting party rather than hunting out, open falsely, bother stock or run any form of trash. When applied rigorously, this is a pretty stiff set of rules. Only a decent coonhound can survive one of these competitions without cancelling out on minus points.

The night hunts are often preceded by a day of activity such as: water races, in which coonhounds are allowed to swim after a coon towed on a raft, to determine the fastest swimmer; bench shows, in which the hounds entered are judged for looks; and barbecues. These are generally quite lively affairs, and one can make a full day's outing of most registered night hunts by adding other events to the hunting competition.

At about eight o'clock the night of the hunt, names of dogs and handlers are drawn out of a hat and put into casts (groups) of four hunters and four dogs. By this means you never know who you and your dog will be hunting with. This is a good test of a coonhound: that he must work in any company. Each group of four hunters is attended by a judge, who also acts as the score keeper. Actually, keeping the scorecard is primarily a mechanical procedure, if the hunters' hounds are called honestly when they open. Each cast then drives to a likely area to hunt coon, and the hunters turn their dogs loose for three or four hours of hunting, depending on previous agreement.

The hounds are judged in the woods largely by sound. The first hound to strike (open, or bark) a track is given 100 points plus; the second, 75; third, 50; fourth, 25. These points are good as long as the hound barks every 10 minutes, does not chase stock or off-game, and does not come back in to the hunters. If a hound does any of the above things, his strike points are subtracted. This means that if the first strike dog is wrong, he is penalized more heavily than the second, third or fourth. By the same measure, he is rewarded more highly if he is right, and if the coon is treed.

Coonhounds have a distinctive bark when they tree. This change in tone or rhythm is known as a "changeover" among hunters. When a dog changes to his tree bark, the handler is expected to call him treed. The same scale of points is used here as was employed on the strike: 100 for first; 75 for second; 50 for third; and 25 for fourth. The party must wait five minutes from the time the first dog trees, and then begin walking to the tree. This gives all of the dogs in the cast ample opportunity to get in on the tree. When the hunters reach the tree, they put the dogs on a leash to avoid the possibility of a fight, and begin to shine highpowered flashlights on the tree. If a coon is seen, the dogs are given all of their points (strike and tree) for that coon, and the party goes on, leaving the coon unharmed, to hunt another coon. If no coon is seen, and it is certain that there is not a coon in the tree, or if off-game is seen in the tree, such as cat, gray fox or opossum, the hounds are given minus points instead of plus points in the amount of plus points they had accrued on that coon. If there is some doubt about the tree such as too much foliage to see the coon, or if it is a den tree (a tree with a hole in it large enough to accommodate a coon) all of the points will be circled, and they count neither for nor against the competitors in tallying the final score.

There is a good deal more to scoring a wild coon hunt than this, but this summarizes the essentials well enough so that a general picture can be obtained. A complete set of the night hunt rules may be obtained by writing to The United Kennel Club, 321 West Cedar Street, Kalamazoo, MI 49006.

Those wishing to compete in formal night hunts, must also have a knowledge of what the handler must know, and what kind of hound he must have to compete successfully. The important items are discussed below.

First, we do not believe in the practice of entering a half-trained hound in a hunt, hoping that he will ride along on the weight of another dog's good work, or that he will learn something from them about coon hunting. Enter nothing but a reliable coonhound, as there are already too many people following the previous line of thought. If your hound is not a solid tree dog, you don't have a chance of getting any points, because there will almost surely be at least one hound in the cast that is weak at the tree and will trail away from it, pulling the other hounds with him.

Second, make sure your dog is well enough trained so that pulling him from the tree without getting the coon out to him will not spoil him. Don't hunt a hound that is not a thoroughly trained tree dog. If you put the game out to him every time he trees, and then, before he has full confidence, pull him away from three or four trees in one evening without making a kill, you will see that such practices don't make a good hound. Even the top hounds will lose ground under heavy night hunt competition, and it takes some fur in their teeth to put them back in their best form.

It should be taken into account that not all good coonhounds can do well in a night hunt. As I suggested in the beginning of this chapter, the night hunt competition measures efficiency. If you have a wonderful, cold-nosed hound who can work out the hard trails and check out his tree carefully, you might as well not bother entering him in a night hunt where the competition is stiff, as you will undoubtedly run into some Walker or English Hounds that move a track like lightning, range wide and tree hard the minute they hit the good tree. These dogs may not be what you want in a coonhound, but they pose the toughest competition in a night hunt, and you'll have to beat them if you are to win.

You will find occasional exceptions to this rule, however. A few years ago at a night hunt in southern South Dakota the weather had been extremely dry, and it was a very cold, windy spring night, anything but the ideal for coon hunting. Very few dogs came in at the end of the night with anything but minus points. Still, a fourteen-year-old long-eared Black and Tan, who was famous for his cold nose and his positive working qualities, came in with 750 plus points, no minus points, and he won the hunt hands down. It would pay you well to consider this when selecting a hound for the very cold, dry or mountainous country. If your dog is not cold-nosed in that climate and terrain, he is useless; whereas a hotter-nosed hound may work admirably in the mild, damp central and southern states.

The real benefit of the night hunts is not the personal aggrandizement of the winning handler, or proving which breed of coonhound is best, but putting the hounds before the public, and allowing them to be seen in action. When this is done, the buyer can have a better idea of what he is buying and may choose his breed accordingly. Very few of the better coonhound breeders have passed up the opportunity to prove their hounds in this kind of competition. Many of them maintain, however, that winning in the hunts has little significance. This indicates that the type of hound they most enjoy hunting is not the type who will consistently win in competition, and it is an expression of the feeling that by breeding faster, hotter-nosed, short-eared hounds, we are getting away from the old hound type. Without question this development has become fact. Whether it is good or bad is a matter of opinion.

FOXHOUND TRIALS

The foxhound field trial sport is far bigger than many people recognize. The annual National Championship lists from 300 to 400 entries, and is certainly the biggest event in the sport. The national trial is run under the rules of the National Foxhunter's Association, which has its headquarters in Lexington, Kentucky. An excerpt from the bylaws of the National Foxhunter's Association, Inc. describes the purpose of foxhound field trials.

"To conduct, enter into or engage in field trials, a trial of foxhounds in actual performance in the hunting fields; to hunt, chase, run under pursuit with hounds, fox or other quarry on foot or on horse or mount, which are considered worthy of pursuit by sportsmen, and to do any and all things pertaining to the act or practice of hunting with hound and horse.

"To hold and conduct, enter into or engage in field trials for the purpose of testing the qualities of foxhounds in hunting, trailing, endurance, speed, gameness, skill and ability to hunt, find and drive a fox, having in view the development and improvement of the foxhound, and to encourage judicious breeding.

"To enter hounds in contest, to test their physical or mental ability to hunt, find and drive a fox, according to set rules, and undertaken for amusement or recreation or for winning a stake."

It can be seen from the above quotation that foxhound field trials are not set up artificially, but represent an effort on the part of the people heading this sport to improve the actual hunting capabilities of their breed. This is what most field trials for all breeds have tended toward in recent years, largely as a result of general reaction among sportsmen to artificial tests which are no true gauge of a hunting dog.

Without going into a full account of foxhound field trial rules, a summary of the procedure should give a good idea of one of these contests. The big trials are run over a three-day period, and every hound competes all three days. It sounds as though it would be very confusing since better than 300 hounds are released each day at daybreak from the same point to hunt, but there are twenty-five to thirty official mounted judges on hand all of the time, and the dogs are marked with large numerals on their sides so they can be scored accurately. The hounds are expected to hunt constantly for every five-hour hunting period for three days.

Foxhounds are judged for four qualities in competition: hunting, trailing, speed and drive, and endurance. Points for these various attributes are awarded in the following manner.

Hunting: A hound may receive points for hunting only once per hour, no matter how many judges observe him at work. He must demonstrate here that he is actually out looking for game. A hound receives 10 points for the first hour; 15 for the second; 20 for the third; 25 for the fourth; and 30 for the fifth. These points are accumulative.

Trailing: This pertains to the hound's moving a track with open voice. Points may be tallied every twenty minutes, and are accumulative, ranging from 10 points for a cold, slow trail, to 30 pounds when a fox is seen ahead of the hound. Points in between are awarded according to how well the hound is moving the track.

Speed and Drive: Here a hound is judged on his ability to drive a fox at a fast pace, according to his position in the pack of hounds. He may accumulate points every ten minutes for this attribute. If he is running first in the pack, 35 points are given; second, 30; third, 25; fourth, 20; and fifth, or anywhere else in the pack, 15.

Endurance: A hound may be awarded points for endurance only after the first day, and he must have acquired points for speed and drive first. These points are given only on the judge's recommendation and may total no more than one-quarter of the points accumulated in the other three categories.

There are a number of faults for which a hound will be removed from the competition. Among these, the most prevalent are: running-off game or livestock, except deer, for which the hound cannot be scratched or receive points; cunning running, running silent and getting ahead of the pack; running another dog's or man's track; babbling or barking where there is no track, or on a track already run; loafing, not hunting; failure to hark to another dog's strike; running silent; and failing to answer the roll call on the first or the last day of the hunt.

It can be seen, then, that foxhound field-trial competition is extremely demanding, and in order for a hound to win, the breaks must be working in his favor. Mr. Henry Gibson, one of the country's leading foxhound hunters and authorities, said, in assessing the element of luck in a foxhound field trial: "In order for a foxhound to win in the competitions today, he must be lucky, but he also has to be a good foxhound." We could conclude from this that, while there is no question of the very high quality of the winners in foxhound competition, there are many unsung champions, who because of chance, have not been fortunate enough to have been observed while doing their best work. Much the same thing is true, incidentally, of other forms of sporting-dog competition. Occasionally, great dogs stand out because they consistently are able to finish near or at the top in the most demanding competition. These are the top dogs who are so sought after for breeding purposes, and when we consider that only through organized field trials can these dogs be surely known, we can see the true value of this form of sport for the improvement of the sporting breeds.

BEAGLE HOUND TRIALS

Beagle trials are conducted in much the same manner as foxhound trials except instead of being run in huge packs, the hounds are run in pairs in the manner of bird-dog trials. Like the foxhounds, the Beagles are expected to cast out well to strike a track, and, once they have struck, are graded on their ability to work the track out, give good voice, figure out loses in the track, take heavy cover and not give up on a track. As might be expected, a Beagle who can turn in a creditable performance in the workaday hunting field, and produce a reasonable amount of game before the gun, may not be much good as a field-trial dog. In today's competition, where breeding practices have been carried to a very high degree of perfection, professional trainers are employed extensively, only the very best hounds are run in competition, so the old plug hunting dog does not stand a chance. As has been demonstrated, this is true of the field-trial game in the other breeds as well.

After each brace of hounds has had a chance to perform, the judges may call back any hounds which have, in their opinion, demonstrated sufficient hunting ability to compete in further series. The trial may be carried on for three or more series until the best performers come to the top. This will, of course, vary from event to event; a winner one day may well go out in the first series under different conditions than on another day.

With respect to running order and elimination, it can be seen that the Beagle trial is very much like a bird-dog event. There the resemblance ends, however. Like the foxhound trial, it is not expected that a Beagle will ever catch, or even make close contact with, his game. He has the innate ability and desire to chase and trail game without ever catching it. Any hound which does not have this ability will give up after a short time on a trail, and so will not make a field-trial contender of any consequence.

The Beagle field trials are almost always run on cottontail rabbits, although various kinds of hares have been run in trials in the past. A good field-trial Beagle is expected to use his voice in much the same manner as a top foxhound, or a good coonhound. He should open only occasionally and with discretion on an old, cold trail, and should increase the frequency and excitedness of his barking until the game is jumped, at which time the barking becomes frantic. A hound who uses his voice too freely, or barks when there is no game scent present, can be accused of being a babbler, and is of little use as a field-trial performer or hunter. It must be allowed, however, that some very cold-nosed Beagles may open on a track that no other hounds in the area can smell. One should use a great deal of patience in judging, therefore, before a hound is condemned for babbling. We have known many beaglers to argue that the best working Beagles use a short chop voice on trail, since they can tongue more freely while running a hot track. Conversely, they claim a bawl-voiced Beagle will be slowed down by his voice. The same argument has been used against bawl-voiced coonhounds and foxhounds. We have never noticed that the quality of mouth on a hound had anything to do with speed. We have seen some very fast Beagles that had beautiful bawl mouths. In fact, the best we have known have been bawl-mouthed. We have watched hounds of all breeds open trailing and they seem to be able to roll that bawl voice out at a dead run as easily as a chop-mouthed hound. It must be pointed out here that in hunting, as in field trials, the bawl-mouthed dog has a little more appeal in terms of excitement and beauty of voice than the chop-mouthed individuals.

The sport of Beagle field trialing has many very attractive advantages. Like the sport of hunting Beagles, it is comparatively inexpensive, although no field-trial sport can be considered economical when the traveling, training and time required to campaign a really good specimen is considered. Further, a Beagle field trial is a true test of the hound's hunting ability. Those who maintain that all field-trial competitions are artificial, and have nothing to do with real "hunting dogs," are clearly off base when they level this criticism at the beagling world. Training for trials and running your Beagle in organized field trials will insure top performance from your hound during the hunting season.

Index